Indonesia's Foreign Policy

THE ROYAL INSTITUTE OF INTERNATIONAL AFFAIRS is an unofficial body which promotes the scientific study of international questions and does not express opinions of its own. The opinions expressed in this publication are the responsibility of the author.

The Institute and its Research Committee are grateful for the comments and suggestions made by Ruth McVey and Anthony Short, who were asked to review the manuscript of this book.

Indonesia's Foreign Policy

MICHAEL LEIFER

Published for
The Royal Institute of International Affairs
by GEORGE ALLEN & UNWIN
London   Boston   Sydney

9133040
DLC

3-27-84 JH

George Allen & Unwin (Publishers) Ltd,
40 Museum Street, London WC1A 1LU, UK

George Allen & Unwin (Publishers) Ltd,
Park Lane, Hemel Hempstead, Herts HP2 4TE, UK

Allen & Unwin Inc.,
9 Winchester Terrace, Winchester, Mass. 01890, USA

George Allen & Unwin Australia Pty Ltd,
8 Napier Street, North Sydney, NSW 2060, Australia

First published in 1983
for the Royal Institute of International Affairs,
Chatham House, 10 St James's Square, London SW1Y 4LE

British Library Cataloguing in Publication Data

Leifer, Michael
    Indonesia's foreign policy.
1. Indonesia – Foreign relations
I. Title
327. 598   DS638
ISBN 0-04-327069-7

Library of Congress Cataloging in Publication Data

Leifer, Michael
    Indonesia's foreign policy.
Bibliography: p.
Includes index.
1. Indonesia – Foreign relations. I. Title.
DS644.L364 1983   327.598   82-24420
ISBN 0-04-327069-7

Set in 10 on 11 point Plantin by Fotographics (Bedford) Ltd,
and printed in Great Britain
by Biddles Ltd, Guildford, Surrey

Contents

To the memory of
Nathan Leifer and Philip Shwartz

Acknowledgements

In the course of writing this book, I have enjoyed the forbearance of successive Directors of Studies at Chatham House and financial support from the Nuffield Foundation and the Staff Research Fund of the London School of Economics and Political Science.

Many Indonesians have been generous in sharing their views with me. In London, Sudjati Djiwandono and Juwono Sudarsono did so while conducting their own research. In Jakarta, I was helped, in particular, by General Rais Abin, Alex Alatas, Des Alwi, Rosihan Anwar, Suryono Darusman, Idrus Nasir Djajadiningrat, General Hasnan Habib, the late Mohammad Hatta, Professor Fuad Hassan, General Sudjono Humardani, General Sutopo Juwono, Professor Mochtar Kusumaatmadja, A. B. Lubis, Mochtar Lubis, vice-President Adam Malik, General L. B. Murdani, General Ali Murtopo, General Abdul Haris Nusution, Mohammad Natsir, Umarjadi Njotowijono, Mohammad Rum, Anwar Sani, the late Ali Sastroamijoyo, General Satari, General Sajidiman, Sabam Siagian, Munawir Sjadzali, the late Achmad Subarjo, the late Admiral Sudarsono, Sudjatmoko, Suli Suleiman, the late Sumarjo, Sunario, General Sumitro, Harry Tjan, the late Sudjarwo Tjondronegoro, Jakob Utama, Yusuf Wanandi and the late Wilopo. They are, of course, not in any way responsible for the content or conclusions of this volume for which only I can be called to account.

My wife played an invaluable part in helping me to complete the manuscript. Margaret Cornell was a meticulous and sympathic editor for Chatham House.

London, October 1982   *Michael Leifer*

Introduction

The Republic of Indonesia is a post-colonial new state without historical antecedent within its contemporary territorial bounds. It was given political form through the ability of the Dutch to impose administrative unity on a distended archipelago and a social diversity. This imposed colonial unity provided the frame for nationalist ambition and state succession.

Indonesia attained independence on 27 December 1949, as the outcome of an international conference at The Hague at which the government of the Netherlands agreed to transfer sovereignty. Independence had been proclaimed over four years previously on 17 August 1945, just two days after the surrender of Japan, the wartime occupying power. From the moment of this claim to independent statehood, the embryo Republic was confronted by a Dutch challenge to its very existence. Foreign policy took the initial form of attempts to secure international recognition in order to deny the restoration of the colonial power.

Underlying the conduct of foreign policy was a distinctive approach to the attainment of independence which was the result of an early calculation by the nationalist leadership that armed struggle against the Dutch could not prevail. Armed resistance was not ruled out but independence was sought and obtained primarily through a diplomatic process involving third-party mediation. Such a process was made possible from the outset by a British military presence in Indonesia charged with taking Japan's surrender. When other external interests were engaged during 1947 through the medium of the United Nations, the international identity of Indonesia was strengthened. Indeed, President Sukarno pointed out the following year on the third anniversary of the proclamation of independence:

> The Indonesians have entered the international arena. If not instantly, the world gradually will undoubtedly participate in the settlement of the Indonesia-Dutch conflict. This is what has become the basis of the foreign policy of the Republic.

The experience of attaining independence in this manner demonstrated the utility of a diplomatic technique which was employed subsequently in prosecuting other international disputes, if with mixed success. In addition, the bitter encounter with the Dutch, and an evident ambivalence towards Indonesia's claim to independence on the part of the major powers, had a formative influence on the international outlook of political leaders after the transfer of sovereignty. The use of the term 'international outlook' is intended to suggest a common, rather than a strictly uniform, set of attitudes towards the outside world by those Indonesians involved in the making of foreign policy. Indeed, the conflict with the Dutch served also to reinforce political cleavages within a less than homogeneous nationalist movement.

During the period of national revolution, distinctly divergent and competing modes of foreign policy practice were advocated. One such mode was *diplomasi* (negotiation) which was the instrument used, in the main, to secure the eventual transfer of sovereignty. The alternative mode, that of *perjuangan* (struggle), or the display of fighting spirit, arose from a conviction that an authentic independence could be secured only through an uncompromising confrontation with the Dutch. This view played an important part in sustaining the early momentum of national revolution and, ultimately, in denying Dutch attempts to impose a military solution. Despite the divergent nature of these modes, their protagonists had a meeting point in shared experience which carried over into independence.

The struggle for independence exposed the weakness and vulnerability of the Indonesian state arising from its fragmented social and physical condition. In addition, an awareness of the attraction of Indonesia's bountiful natural resources and the importance of its strategic location between the Indian and Pacific Oceans reinforced an apprehension of external powers. By contrast, that common international outlook encompassed also a proprietary attitude towards the regional environment. Pride in revolutionary achievement, a consciousness of vast territorial scale, an immense population, extensive natural resources, as well as a strategic location, produced the conviction that Indonesia was entitled to play a leading role in the management of regional order within South-East Asia.

The presence of such disparate elements in international outlook has been displayed in corresponding differences in the conduct of foreign policy which have been stimulated by the degree of competitiveness within successive political systems. These differences have found expression in the contrasting styles and goals of the administrations of President Sukarno and President Suharto. The foreign policy of the latter has been characterized by a cautious pragmatism, but it has also exhibited regional ambition. President Sukarno prosecuted international disputes in a forceful and flamboyant manner but did not forgo the use of diplomacy and third-party mediation. Despite striking differences between them, Sukarno and Suharto have also displayed common priorities and a continuity of some interests. A shared strategic perspective has straddled their contrasting governances. The enunciation and restatement of a maritime archipelagic doctrine has indicated a common determination to reconcile national vulnerability with a sense of regional entitlement. That shared perspective has reflected the outlook of a metropolitan political elite who contemplate the Indonesian archipelago from the vantage point of Jakarta, the capital city on the pivotal island of Java.

Although a professional service charged with responsibility for the conduct of foreign relations was established early on, it was afflicted during the immediate post-independence period by inter-party contests for patronage. Changes in the balance of political advantage within fragile parliamentary governments were reflected in changes of personnel and hierarchy within the foreign service. In the succeeding period of Guided Democracy, in which President Sukarno became the political voice of Indonesia, the foreign service was demoralized, as professional standards were subordinated by considerations of ideology as well as patronage. Under the authoritarian and more stable military-based rule of President Suharto, there has been a revival of professional standards. Although the Foreign Ministry enjoys a measure of political latitude, ultimate sanction for the conduct of foreign policy, especially where matters of security impinge, comes from a military establishment. Its dominance is indicated by recurrent bypassing of the Foreign Ministry and in the filling of senior official and ambassadorial posts which has given rise to intra-bureaucratic tensions.

In the decade of Parliamentary Democracy, the making of foreign policy was greatly influenced by the open clash of domestic political forces. When more free from party constraints during the period of Guided Democracy, it became increasingly the preserve of a privileged few. From the late 1950s, with Sukarno politically pre-eminent, the foreign-policy process resembled decision-making in a royal court in which the king is the ultimate authority, subject to a variety of competing influences from courtiers. Such a context has been sustained in essential respects from the transfer of power in March 1966 to Lt. General Suharto, who later assumed presidential office. However, an important measure of influence has been exercised by ministers responsible for foreign relations. Dr Subandrio, Foreign Minister from April 1957 until March 1966, and Adam Malik, his successor until September 1977, were able to temper the practice of foreign policy, with the latter the more influential. Professor Mochtar Kusumaatmadja, the present incumbent, has been the most proficient public exponent of Indonesia's interests, but as a technocrat and not as a political figure.

If the making of foreign policy has been a prerogative political process in the main, it has been affected also by Indonesia's social diversity. As mentioned above, there is no historical precedent for the Indonesian state within its contemporary territorial bounds; nor does there exist a pre-colonial basis for national unity in any single great cultural tradition. Indeed, the absence of such a tradition and the presence of competing ones, indicated by political party and regional divisions in the first decade of independence, exposed the integrity of the Indonesian state to challenge. Although that challenge was overcome and state integrity has been maintained, opposing conceptions of the identity of the Republic have not been fully reconciled. One notable source of internal political tensions with implications for foreign policy has been Islam.

Islam is acknowledged as the religion of over 90 per cent of a population of approximately 150 million. Devotion to orthodoxy, however, is another matter. Imported via India from the fourteenth century on, Islam has made an uneven impact. In the eastern and central parts of the most heavily populated island of Java, it was only superimposed on entrenched animist and Hindu-Buddhist values. To-day Islam enjoys a numerical superiority in Indonesia only in a statistical sense. Its devout followers are in a minority and subordinate position to nominal Muslims, primarily adherents of pre-Islamic values. Islam was denied a place in the constitutional structure and symbols of state at independence. Moreover, its political champions have long resented the syncretic formula enunciated by President Sukarno in June 1945 in which endorsement of belief in a single deity was qualified by affording every Indonesian the right to believe 'in *his own* particular God'. The unwillingness, over time, of the orthodox Islamic community to approve with conviction this fundamental principle of *Pancasila* – the officially sanctioned five philosophical precepts of the state* – has generated government suspicion that they would prefer to establish a theocratic polity.

With a limited exception during the period of national revolution, successive Indonesian governments have taken care not to allow foreign policy to be dictated by Islamic considerations. They have sought to avoid incautious engagement in international issues which might be exploited either to advance claims presented by Muslim groups or to enhance the political standing of Islam in the Republic. The example of Islam highlights a characteristic inter-relationship between foreign policy and domestic politics in Indonesia. That inter-relationship has also been exemplified by the use of foreign policy to serve domestic political purposes and by domestic responses to alleged deviations from an ideal course.

* The four other principles are: Nationalism, Internationalism, Popular Sovereignty and Social Justice.

That ideal course in foreign policy has been expounded within the country as 'independent and active'. It was articulated originally in September 1948 by the late Mohammad Hatta, the first vice-President and then, concurrently, Prime Minister. The maxim 'independent and active' was inspired by a concern to fend off left-wing demands for the Republic to align itself with the Soviet Union and, correspondingly, to avoid provoking the Dutch and also alienating the United States. In addition, it was a considered attempt to define the appropriate role for Indonesia in a bipolar world. That role has fluctuated over the decades since independence and has rarely conformed with precision to the ideal formula advocated by Hatta. None the less, the maxim of an independent and active foreign policy has exercised an abiding influence on successive Indonesian governments. It has done so because of an experience of state-making which demonstrated that an independent integral Indonesia could not be taken for granted and that outside powers would readily compromise its interests. Moreover, the divisive domestic impact of any foreign policy which has aroused partisan passions has confirmed the political utility of such an ideal formulation.

Indonesia's national apophthegm of 'Unity in Diversity' may have been conceived in an attempt to attract American sympathy. It indicates, none the less, the predicament of a state which comprises a brittle combination of people and territory. Its foreign policy has sought logically to overcome that intrinsic brittleness in order to transform it into an aggregation of common strength. The chapters which follow will attempt to investigate and illuminate the course and nature of that foreign policy since the proclamation of independence.

Indonesia's Foreign Policy

1 National Revolution and the Seeds of Foreign Policy

The experience of attaining independence has left a distinctive imprint on the foreign policy of Indonesia. The period from August 1945 until December 1949 engendered a view of the international environment which has not been eroded by the passage of time. Any initial political innocence was superseded by a realistic and even cynical appreciation of the interests and conduct of those external powers which became engaged in the bitter and protracted struggle for liberation from Dutch rule.

The demand for an independent Indonesia had assumed coherent form from the late 1920s.[1] It was voiced most vigorously by a small group of secular nationalists drawn, primarily, from the lesser nobility and the Dutch-trained professional class. Sukarno and Hatta, respectively the first President and vice-President of the Republic, were preeminent members of this cadre. Following the Japanese occupation of the Netherlands East Indies in March 1942, they led an Indonesian elite in accommodation to the Nipponese New Order in the hope that the nationalist cause might be advanced. After a year of harsh rule, the Japanese began to foster political and para-military organizations on Java in order to assist their fading war aims. This initiative provided the nationalist leadership with its first opportunity to gain access to a mass constituency.

In September 1944, with the fortunes of war turning strongly against Japan, Prime Minister Kuniaki Koiso announced his government's intention to sanction the independence of the East Indies 'in the future'.[2] In May 1945, influenced by the pace of the Allies' military success and mutinies by local militia, an investigating committee of collaborating Indonesians was convened in Jakarta to discuss the terms of independence. Their deliberations dealt, in part, with the boundaries of the state. At a second session in July, a majority resolved that these boundaries should encompass Malaya (including Singapore), British Northern Borneo, Portuguese Timor and the eastern Australian half of the island of New Guinea, as well as the full territorial extent of the Netherlands East Indies.[3] This claim to a Greater Indonesia was denied by Japan's veto and the circumstances of the termination of hostilities.

It was not until 11 August, after atomic bombs had been dropped

1

over Hiroshima and Nagasaki, that Field Marshal Terauchi, the Supreme Commander of Japan's Southern Army received Sukarno and Hatta at Dalat in Southern Vietnam. Only then were they authorised to proceed with the establishment of an independent Indonesia within the bounds of the Netherlands East Indies. Sukarno and Hatta returned to Jakarta on the very eve of Japan's surrender. Knowledge of its imminence posed a cruel dilemma. The prospect of achieving some form of independence had been contingent on Japan's benefaction. The certainty of Allied victory meant that the Japanese military authorities in the Netherlands East Indies would be prohibited from countenancing any change in the political *status quo*. Moreover, given the known attitude of the Allies to Japanese-inspired polities, any Indonesian initiative to complete a process of independence begun under Japan's auspices would give the embryo state an objectionable taint.[4] In the circumstances, the nationalist leadership was confronted by the bleak alternatives of either any unilateral action being frustrated by the Japanese authorities under the terms of surrender, or a condoned violation of such terms damning the Indonesian state from the outset. Abhorrence of a tainted independence influenced the attitudes of the *pemuda* or militant nationalist youth who had been inculcated and infused with Japanese martial ideals. These young men who sought both national and personal liberation wished to assert Indonesia's independence immediately. They succeeded in stamping their culture on the early period of national revolution.[5]

Sukarno and Hatta were aware of the views of the Allies but they were more immediately apprehensive of approving any action which might provoke the Japanese military authorities whose residual exercise of power was regarded as the critical consideration. Decisive in the resolution of the quarrel within the nationalist movement over how to proceed was the recognition that only Sukarno and, to an extent, Hatta enjoyed sufficient standing to issue a proclamation of independence with a substantive claim to popular acceptance. Their abduction by a group of *pemuda* in an abortive attempt to precipitate such a proclamation served to demonstrate the political indispensability of the nationalist leaders. Sukarno and Hatta refused to act without some form of approval from the Japanese because of a fear that otherwise an independent Indonesia would be short-lived and crumble in the wake of anticipated disorder. Fear of such disorder, as well as a judgement that the nationalist movement could not match the physical resources of its adversaries, was responsible for the manner in which the claim to independence was in the main advanced.

In the event, the proclamation of independence took place with tacit Japanese acquiescence influenced by a desire to contain *pemuda* passions. The military authorities gave an implicit indication that a proclamation would not be obstructed so long as it was not identified with Japan and did not pose a challenge to public order.[6] Its singular form, drafted in the house of a sympathetic Japanese Admiral, revealed some of the problems which confronted the nationalist leadership. At ten a.m. on Friday 17 August 1945 Sukarno read out a laconic text signed by himself and Hatta:[7]

> We the people of Indonesia hereby declare Indonesia's independence. Matters concerning the transfer of power and other matters will be executed in an orderly manner and in the shortest possible time.

This innocuous statement was beamed throughout the archipelago and to the outside world through the short-wave transmitter of *Domei*, the Japanese newsagency, by its Indonesian staff who included Adam Malik, a future Foreign Minister. The following day, a republican constitution was promulgated and Sukarno and Hatta were elected respectively President and vice-President of the new state by a pre-independence preparatory committee.

The proclamation was made in a political vacuum. Japan had capitulated to the Allies on 15 August but its forces remained in place committed to upholding the *status quo* until formally relieved of administrative responsibility. However, apart from an Australian investment of Borneo and New Guinea, the Allies' South-East Asia Command (SEAC) was not in a position to begin its official task of dispossession. Moreover, its early intelligence on Indonesia was meagre and misleading. When news of the proclamation of independence became known outside the archipelago, it was construed as Japanese-inspired, especially by the Dutch. In consequence, the embryo Republic began the task of securing international recognition with the taint of Japanese militarism on it after all – an impression confirmed by the collaborationist record of its first President whose wartime radio speeches on behalf of Japan had aroused the ire of the Allies. The first Indonesian cabinet – of collaborationist composition because of the need to ensure Japanese toleration and also administrative continuity – was faced with the intractable problem of how to overcome the consequences of a proclamation which had been made possible only by deferring to Japanese priorities.

In order to mitigate the anticipated hostility of the Allies and to frustrate an early restoration of Dutch colonial power, the nationalist leadership sought to demonstrate the administrative viability of the new state and its government's sense of responsibility. Concurrent with appeals for international recognition, they solicited the approval of the Allied Powers by attempting to display a capacity to ensure public order. President Sukarno indicated such a priority at the beginning of September:[8]

> The policy now adopted by the Indonesian Republic must be oriented to the international world. For this, the prime condition is diplomacy. Yet no nation can enter the international arena by diplomacy alone. Behind that diplomacy, indeed the very basis of that diplomacy, must be a power force.

By 'a power force' Sukarno did not mean a military organization which was not formally constituted until early October. He was alluding to a functioning administration which could command authority and so prevent the outbreak of anarchy and terror, which were, in effect, to characterize the early months of the revolution.

An initial advantage accruing to the nationalist leadership in their attempt to consolidate an identifiable Indonesian administration was the extensive delay which transpired before Japanese control was superseded. The jurisdiction of SEAC had been extended from Sumatra to include the entire Netherlands East Indies with the exception of West Timor at exceedingly short notice on the very day of Japan's capitulation. Forces and naval transports available were inadequate 'to secure the speedy, orderly re-establishment of civil governments' as well as to evacuate Allied prisoners of war and civilian internees and round up three-quarters of a million Japanese within the enlarged area of command.[9] Apart from preliminary reconnaissances, a limited landing on Java by a British-Indian battalion began only on 29 September six weeks after the proclamation of independence. It took place in the knowledge that SEAC would require the cooperation of the administration which had been assumed by the Republic. Evident recognition of the problems involved and also a desire not to become embroiled in the restoration of Dutch rule were conveyed in a broadcast from Singapore on the day of the landings, which reported the views of the British Military Commander, Lieut. General Sir Philip Christison, who had been instructed personally by the Minister for War. The need to safeguard prisoners of war and civilian internees located vulnerably in camps throughout Indonesia governed his attitude. The content of the broadcast indicated that Christison had 'no intention of meddling in Indonesian internal politics' but was concerned to maintain law and order to fulfil his primary tasks. It was his declared intention to call together representatives of the Dutch authorities and the leaders of all Indonesian parties with any substantial following in order to prepare the way for the promulgation by the Dutch of an authoritative statement on the future of the Netherlands East Indies. Pending an agreement between the Dutch and representative Indonesians, he would ask party leaders 'to treat him and his troops as guests and tell them that they must support temporary British administration' whose purpose appeared to be to hold the ring.[10] A conspicuous omission from the broadcast was any mention of penal redress against those Indonesians who had collaborated with the Japanese. It had been a constant theme of earlier broadcasts by the Allies. Such omission at that juncture served to modify the political context within which Indonesian independence was being asserted.

Versions of this broadcast, as well as of a statement by Christison in Jakarta, revised the expectations of the Indonesian nationalist leadership.[11] Although Britain had entered into a civil affairs agreement with the Netherlands in August and Christison openly acknowledged Dutch sovereignty, the substance of his reported views suggested an alternative policy. Indeed, Admiral Lord Mountbatten, the Supreme Allied Commander in South-East Asia, had advised that negotiations be opened with the Indonesians as soon as possible 'as a matter of military expediency'.[12] The Republic's leadership derived assurance from the unwillingness (and inability) of the British to suppress the independence movement on behalf of the Dutch. None the less, two companies of Dutch troops were landed and the Netherlands Indies Civil Administration headed by Lt. Governor Dr H. J. Van Mook returned from Australia. In addition, several companies of the Dutch colonial army were reconstituted from released internees. The provocative conduct of these ill-disciplined units served to reinforce the militant outlook of the *pemuda* who had secured ready access to Japanese arms.

The challenge to public order posed by the armed *pemuda* was utilized by the Republic's leaders in an attempt to persuade the British to exclude Dutch forces in return for cooperation in the civil administration. It was argued that, until the Indonesian question had been reviewed by a competent world body, the incumbent administration should be recognized explicitly as a *de facto* government. The British military authorities were unwilling to make this concession but the course of *pemuda* violence culminated in a convergence of British interests with those of the nationalist leadership. This prospect had been implied in a communication from Sukarno to Mountbatten at the end of September. He wrote:[13]

> We do not ask the Allied military forces to recognise the Republic of Indonesia. We only ask you to acknowledge facts, namely that to the feelings of the people there exists a Republic of Indonesia with a Government. All Government officials and the entire population are ready to help the Allied Forces to retain public order, if only they are not hurt in their national feelings.

He went on to warn with specific reference to the landing of Dutch troops:

It would be preferable in these days of tension not to irritate the popular sentiment as the outbreak of mob rage will have far reaching consequences.

The demand for *de facto* recognition and the exclusion of Dutch forces constituted the initial negotiating position of the aspirant Republic. The alternative of disorder was presented to the British as the likely consequence of a failure to respond in an acceptable manner. Corresponding demands were put to Christison with an indication of the prospect of left-wing and radical elements wrenching leadership from Sukarno and his moderate colleagues.[14] One might wish to discount the measure of special pleading in this approach to those seen to have it in their power to advance the Republic's cause. Yet there can be little doubt that the authority of the newly established government was tenuous. It was at this time that a willingness was indicated to engage in negotiations with the Dutch, provided they were based on the right of self-determination and held in the presence of 'a third intermediating party'.[15] This initiative (or concession) marked the introduction of a distinctive characteristic in the practice of Indonesia's foreign policy which would be sustained over the following two decades. Indeed, in late October, Sukarno called on the American Consul-General in Jakarta with a specific request that his government arbitrate in the dispute between Indonesia and the Netherlands.

A readiness to contemplate a political solution was encouraged by the violent course of events in the east Javanese port of Surabaya in late October and early November. Objections by Indonesian irregulars to a demand for arms surrender, perceived as a preliminary to the landing of Dutch troops, gave rise to a confrontation in which an entire British-Indian brigade came close to being overrun. The refusal of the Indonesian forces to heed an ultimatum to withdraw after the killing of a British brigadier provoked an onslaught at divisional strength from 10 November which was met by three weeks of courageous and fanatical resistance.[16] The battle of Surabaya represented a turning point both for the British military authorities and the Republic's leadership. For the former, subject to growing domestic and international criticism for deploying Indian and also Japanese soldiers against the independence movement, the ferocity and scale of the military conflict at Surabaya demonstrated the likely costs which would be incurred in any further attempt to fulfil SEAC's task by resort to force. Given the attendant risks to prisoners of war and civilian internees, the need to proceed by political means was self-evident. Accordingly, the British became even more determined to encourage bilateral negotiations which had been obstructed by the adamant refusal of the Dutch government to countenance even exploratory talks between its representatives in Jakarta and

Sukarno and his colleagues whom they regarded as Quislings. Preliminary discussion at the end of October between Dr Van Mook and Sukarno, Hatta and Foreign Minister Achmad Subarjo, had been repudiated publicly by The Hague.

Just prior to this display of Dutch obduracy, Admiral Mountbatten's political adviser Esler Dening had already made it clear to Sukarno that his cabinet was tainted in the eyes of the Allies and that an alternative leadership, more acceptable for the conduct of negotiations with the Dutch, would serve the Indonesian cause to better advantage. The ensuing violence in Surabaya played its part in encouraging Sukarno and his colleagues to move in the direction suggested by Dening because of a concern not to alienate the great power support Indonesia required to achieve independence. They had already rejected a policy of armed struggle in favour of negotiations within the framework of good offices proffered by the British. For this course to become fully operative, the Republic would be obliged to present a more acceptable international face. In other words, a change of leadership was required in order that the representatives of Indonesia would be seen to be free from Japanese associations.[17]

New Leadership and Negotiations

Such a leadership was readily available in the person of Sutan Sjahrir, an outstanding intellectual of democratic socialist convictions who had been imprisoned by the Dutch and who had refused to cooperate with the Japanese.[18] Sjahrir's record and that of his chosen cabinet made him acceptable not only to the British and Dutch governments but also to the militant *pemuda*. However, Sjahrir's administration did not represent a break in continuity; it was committed to the policy determined by Sukarno and Hatta of seeking international recognition by projecting 'an external stance of peaceful moderation'. This approach had been exemplified by the publication on 1 November of a *Political Manifesto* promulgated by Hatta on behalf of the Republic. This statement justified the nationalist cause by citing Holland's abdication of responsibility in surrendering Indonesia to the cruelty of Japanese militarism. A commitment to democratic ideals was coupled with a qualified willingness to protect the rights and property of foreign private enterprise and to honour the debts of the Netherlands East Indies government. In addition, an invitation was extended to 'the peoples of all nations – most of all the United States, Australia and the Philippines' to participate in exploiting the country's great latent wealth. The political rise of Sjahrir represented continuity in terms of these commitments and in his

7

willingness to enter into negotiations with the Dutch on the basis of Indonesia's right to self-determination.

Sutan Sjahrir became Prime Minister and concurrently Foreign Minister on 14 November 1945; Sukarno and Hatta retained their offices but relinquished executive authority. Only four days before assuming office, Sjahrir had published a pamphlet which strengthened his credentials as a vigorous opponent of the legacy of Japanese occupation. For example, he argued that 'the revolutionary-democratic struggle must begin by purifying itself of all Japanese fascist stain'. He also expressed his considered appreciation of the international environment in which the aspirant Indonesian state was placed and his view of the appropriate foreign policy which it ought to follow. In an analysis influenced by Marxist ideas, Sjahrir pointed out:[19]

Indonesia is geographically situated within the sphere of influence of Anglo-Saxon capitalism and imperialism. Accordingly Indonesia's fate ultimately depends on the fate of Anglo-Saxon capitalism and imperialism.

He continued:

The most significant change that has taken place with regard to our own country has been the expulsion of Dutch power from Indonesia by the Japanese military. However, Japan's subsequent defeat has meant that for the time being she has been eliminated from Southeast Asian politics, and her entire pre-war position has been assumed by the United States which is now far and away the greatest power in the Pacific. Vis-à-vis Britain's century-old politique in the Far East, the Americans feel themselves everywhere (also, of course, in Indonesia) as reformers and innovators. If the British cannot adapt themselves to this American politique dominated as it is by the laws of capitalist development, it is clear that they will eventually be overwhelmed by the superior force at the United States' disposal. It is clear that till now Dutch power has simply been a pawn in a political chess game that the British have been playing. But we must recognise that Dutch power here has by no means the same significance for American as it does for British foreign policy. In this fact lie possibilities for us to win a new position for ourselves in harmony with the political ambitions of the Giant of the pacific, the United States.

This line of reasoning foreshadowed the practice of foreign policy of the embryo Republic up to the attainment of independence, though its premises did not provide for the advent of the Cold War and the interest of the United States in encouraging a strong Dutch ally in Europe. Deference to its priorities displayed both in international orientation and in the nature of domestic political order was contemplated as most likely to advance the nationalist cause. Indeed, further on in the text, Sjahrir urged:[20]

> The building up of our government in a democratic manner and increasing world confidence that we are capable of a disciplined ordering of our state and nation, without undermining our economic, political and cultural relations with the world outside. So long as the world we live in is dominated by capital, we are forced to make sure that we do not earn the enmity of capitalism.

After publishing this political credo and on assuming executive office, Sjahrir embarked on a policy of *diplomasi* under the mediating aegis of the British military authorities. Exploratory conversations took place with Van Mook in mid-November and in December. A major stumbling block was Van Mook's insistence on the return of Dutch troops which Sjahrir would not countenance in the absence of a recognition of the Republic. In December, however, Anglo-Dutch talks at the country residence of the British Prime Minister, Clement Attlee, elicited an official Dutch commitment to negotiations. Against this background, discussions were resumed between Sjahrir and Van Mook in February 1946 in the presence of Sir Archibald Clark Kerr, Britain's ambassador-designate to the United States.

The Dutch negotiating position was based on a speech delivered by Queen Wilhelmina in December 1942.[21] It provided for little more than a cosmetic advance on the political situation prior to the Japanese occupation. The proposal contemplated a federal commonwealth of Indonesia in political union with the Netherlands within the ambit of the Dutch Crown. It did not contain any recognition of the political reality of the Republic but merely provision for internal autonomy following an unspecified preparatory period during which a Dutch Governor-General would exercise sovereign powers.[22] This proposal fell far short of Sjahrir's pre-condition for negotiations but, given the refusal of any government to respond to recurrent appeals for recognition, there was no alternative to negotiations; armed struggle had been ruled out.

Revelation of the content of the Dutch proposals provoked political reaction within the Republic. A group of *pemuda* and alienated politicians from the first cabinet attempted to remove Sjahrir from office. They were led by veteran nationalist-communist Tan Malaka, the principal exponent of the strategy of *perjuangan* (struggle). They espoused a much more militant policy towards the Dutch, expressed in a demand for negotiations on the basis of full independence and only after all foreign troops had left Indonesia.[23] This show of opposition prompted Sjahrir to resign at the end of February. He was reinstated

9

soon after when the loosely bound *Persatuan Perjuangan* (Struggle Front) failed to secure sufficient support to form an alternative coalition government. With strong backing from Sukarno, who supported the strategy of negotiations if using the language of struggle[24], Sjahrir secured a renewed mandate from the Central Indonesian National Committee or provisional parliament, meeting in Yogyakarta which had become the Republic's capital. He returned to Jakarta in the middle of March to resume talks with the Dutch. The abortive challenge from the Struggle Front served as a salutary reminder that the militant alternative to negotiations could readily manifest itself again should Sjahrir appear to make concessions over the central issue of the recognition of the Republic.

Sjahrir agreed to the proposal that a political relationship be established between Indonesia and the Netherlands, but only on condition that the former would be represented solely by the Republic recognized as the sovereign authority over the territory of the Netherlands East Indies. Van Mook countered with an offer which constituted the first real basis for negotiations since the proclamation of the Republic. Taking as a model the recently concluded Franco-Vietnamese Accord (which used the formulation 'a free state within the Indochinese federation', itself within the French Union), he put forward the notion of an independent federal Indonesia in political union with Holland, within which the Republic would represent the island of Java. Although far removed from the Indonesian position, Van Mook's initiative marked the first occasion on which the Dutch had indicated a willingness to accord any form of recognition to the Republic. As a basis for substantive negotiations, it was an offer that Sjahrir could ill afford to ignore. The position of the Republic had begun to weaken as increasing numbers of Dutch troops arrived under SEAC auspices. Moreover, the British presence had become a declining asset as a growing determination to withdraw forces was reflected in pressure on the Indonesians to make concessions. In such circumstances, without any prospect of international recognition from any significant source and with the Dutch attracting a favourable international response to their initiative, it would have been impolitic to have presented an uncompromising face to the outside world.

At the end of March 1946 Sjahrir replied to Van Mook's proposal in a way which marked a substantive retreat from the Republic's original negotiating position. He indicated that he was prepared to demand no more than the *de facto* recognition by the Dutch of the Republic on the islands of Java, Madura and Sumatra as the nexus for its participation in a federal state, itself within a political union with the Netherlands. This positive response kept up the momentum of negotiations whose venue moved to Holland in April. But the policy of *diplomasi* was sustained only at the risk of arousing political opposition within Indonesia because of the willingness to concede Dutch authority east of Java. In order to contain this opposition, Tan Malaka and other leaders of the Struggle Front were arrested.[25]

Indonesian-Dutch negotiations began at a hunting lodge near Arnhem in the middle of April and concluded at The Hague later the same month.[26] There was, however, no meeting of minds because neither delegation was in a position to make concessions. The caretaker cabinet led by Willem Schermerhorn, the Dutch Prime Minister, was only weeks away from the first post-war elections. He virtually confessed that he did not possess a mandate to arrive at a conclusive agreement, while the Indonesian delegation was bound by strict instructions. Indeed, a leakage of information about Sjahrir's apparent willingness to compromise over full recognition of the Republic had prompted charges of betrayal in the Indonesian press. The progress of the talks was obstructed from the outset when the Dutch presented a draft document in the form of a protocol and not a treaty as had been the case in the Franco-Vietnamese negotiations. In addition to the issue of legal status, the document excluded Sumatra from the jurisidiction of the Republic. The Dutch government gave the strong impression that it was not prepared to accept the Republic as anything more than a province limited to Java within a federal Indonesia.

The inconclusive outcome of the negotiations in Holland served to highlight once more the sensitive inter-relationship between the search for some practical measure of international recognition for the Republic and the temper of domestic politics in Indonesia during the period of national revolution. An immediate consequence of the failure of the negotiations, which the Republican side had entered on the basis of a major concession, was to test the very credibility of the policy of *diplomasi* and to lend support to the charges of Sjahrir's political opponents. They argued persuasively that the Dutch were guilty of bad faith and were intent solely on buying time until they were in a position to impose a settlement by *force majeure*. This charge appeared to enjoy substance when the Dutch elections in May gave rise to a coalition government dominated by the Catholic Party which indicated a hardening of opinion on the Indonesian question.

Sjahrir's retreat from the Republic's initial negotiating position was made public by vice-President Hatta towards the end of June. The news provoked his abduction by a radical military grouping identified with Tan Malaka. The prevailing course of foreign policy was sustained only as a consequence of a decisive intervention by Sukarno who, backed by Hatta and with the reluctant support of the Army Commander General Sudirman, secured Sjahrir's release and endorsement for the continuation of a policy of *diplomasi*. But the policy was maintained against a

11

background of decreasing expectations for the Republic and decreasing unity among its leadership.

Initially, an attempt had been made to confront the British and the Dutch with established political facts. From the middle of 1946, however, the Dutch set out to create their own political facts and to undermine the claim of the Republic to represent all the inhabitants of the East Indies. By July, all the islands east of Java had been transferred by SEAC to Dutch control. The same month, Van Mook convened a conference of delegates from the eastern archipelago at the hill station of Malino in South Sulawesi at which approval was secured for the creation of a federal United States of Indonesia comprising four autonomous territories – Java, Sumatra, Borneo and the Great East. In the course of this conference, Van Mook encountered explicit demands for an independent Indonesian state separate from the Netherlands[27], but the Malino resolution lent authority to the idea of a federal state within which the Republic – cut down in size –would be only one part.

In the face of physical and political encroachments by the Dutch and with the impending departure of SEAC forces from Java and Sumatra, the Sjahrir government had no practical recourse but to continue with negotiations, if outside a strictly bilateral context. After the failure of the talks in Holland, the Republic had renewed appeals for international support for its cause; for example, by indicating a willingness to supply rice to famine-stricken India. An exchange of rice for textiles, however valued, was not the same as effective recognition. Conscious of the weakness of their international position, the Republic's leaders accepted the good offices of Britain's Special Commissioner for South-East Asia, Lord Killearn, who was determined to obtain a political settlement before November 1946 when SEAC forces were to withdraw completely from Indonesia.

Renewed negotiations began in Jakarta in October and, after an initial agreement on a truce to halt sporadic fighting, continued in November in the resort of Linggajati near the Javanese port of Ceribon. Both sides concentrated on the status and the territorial extent of the Republic and its likely relationship with the projected United States of Indonesia. The outcome of these discussions was a concession on the part of the Dutch, who agreed to recognise the government of the Republic 'as exercising *de facto* authority over Java, Madura and Sumatra'. In addition, the parts of those islands occupied by Allied or Dutch forces were to be 'included gradually through mutual cooperation in the Republican territory'. In return, the Republican delegation agreed to cooperate with the Dutch 'in the rapid formation of a sovereign democratic state on a federal basis to be called the United States of Indonesia', comprising the Republic, Borneo and the Great East, which they would endeavour to establish within a Netherlands-

Indonesian Union under the Dutch Crown before 1 January 1949. A draft accord, which dealt also with the joint interests of the Union, was initialled by the principal negotiators on 15 November 1946 in the presence of Sukarno and Hatta. It remained subject to ratification by the Netherlands Estates General in The Hague and the Central Indonesian National Committee in Yogyakarta.

On the surface at least, the policy of *diplomasi* had achieved its first major success, given the apparent measure of Dutch recognition. Although this recognition did not match the original claims of the Republic, it did not seem that it would be possible to turn the clock back to the point when the new Indonesian state had been depicted by the Dutch as the product of a Japanese-inspired *coup de théâtre*. In other words, if the Republicans had been obliged to face up to political reality in moderating their claims to sovereignty, the Dutch had acknowledged the fact of that sovereignty in the most heavily populated parts of the archipelago and also appeared to have conceded a co-equal status to the government of the Republic in the formation of the United States of Indonesia. However, what had been initialled was subject to ratification. This process and prospect were clouded by an atmosphere of mistrust between the Republicans and the Dutch, aggravated by political contention within the Netherlands and by the growing strength of the Dutch military position in Indonesia.

At the end of November, Britain withdrew the SEAC military presence from Java and Sumatra. By then, the Dutch had deployed 55,000 trained men who were being augmented by a steady flow of reinforcements. At this juncture, the draft accord became the subject of conflicting clarifications which turned, in great part, on the status of the Republic as indicated in Article 15. From the Indonesian point of view, this Article was intended 'to ensure that the *de facto* recognition of the Republic during the interim period was not nullified by the perpetuation of Dutch sovereignty over the Netherlands East Indies and by the Republic committing itself to the United States of Indonesia'.[28]

Article 15 of the Linggajati Agreement stipulated that:

> In order to reform the Government of the Indies in such a way that its composition and functioning shall conform as closely as possible to the recognition of the Republic and to the projected constitutional structure, the Netherlands Government pending the realisation of the United States of Indonesia and of the Netherlands-Indonesian Union shall forthwith initiate the necessary legal measures to adjust the constitutional and international position of the Kingdom of the Netherlands to the new situation.

The political significance of this tangled prescription became apparent

13

in the course of correspondence between the two parties.[29] The immediate practical matter in hand was whether or not Indonesians admitted into the Foreign Service of the Netherlands prior to the formation of the United States of Indonesia could act as representatives of the Republic, as Sjahrir maintained, or solely for the Kingdom of the Netherlands. Van Mook insisted that 'representation in a strictly international sense will only become possible after the United States of Indonesia has been constituted'. At issue was the international status of the Republic. The correspondence, together with shrill demands emanating from Yogyakarta, indicated that, for the Republicans, the Linggajati Agreement did not represent a final compromise but was contemplated as a stage on the way to full independence. As Sukarno later confirmed:[30]

> we desperately needed breathing space and thus I accepted the United States of Indonesia as a temporary tactic. I knew some day future bargaining sessions would demolish this and return us to our basic concept of one sovereign independent unitary state.

Despite the climate of mutual suspicion, the Linggajati Agreement was signed by the leaders of the two delegations on 25 March 1947, much to the surprise of some observers, given the absence of a common interpretation of all its articles. One such observer pointed out 'Linggajati whatever its craftsmanly statesmanship, really represented only a somewhat premature agreement to agree". [31] The fragility of the accommodation achieved was exposed by a Dutch note in May which amounted to a virtual ultimatum. It demanded that the Republic proceed with the immediate formation of an interim federal government. Central to the Dutch demand was an insistence that the sovereignty of the Netherlands be maintained *de jure* over the whole of Indonesia during the transition period to a federal state and that 'the foreign relations of Indonesia be taken care of by the respective services of the Kingdom under the ultimate guidance of the Crown'.[32] The note made explicit the objection to the Republic conducting itself as an independent state as had been its practice from the outset. From the advent of Sjahrir's Administration in 1945, representatives had been despatched overseas to plead the Republic's cause, if without securing substantive recognition. However, virtually concurrent with the signing of the Linggajati Agreement, the Indian Prime Minister, Jawaharlal Nehru, had sent an aircraft to transport Sjahrir to New Delhi where he attended the non-governmental Asian Relations Conference as the representative of the Republic of Indonesia. Deputy Foreign Minister Haji Agus Salim also travelled to New Delhi and then went on to Cairo where he set up an office to promote relations with Arab-

Islamic states. Ultimately, he concluded treaties of friendship with Egypt and Syria. The Dutch regarded such activities as politically presumptuous. But they were, in fact, unable to prevent *de facto* recognition being accorded to the Republic in the wake of Linggajati by the United States, Britain, Australia and China, but not by the Soviet Union.

In order to avoid military confrontation, Sjahrir indicated a willingness to make concessions over the terms of the interim government, including separate foreign representation. This further retreat from the Republic's initial negotiating position undermined his domestic political support and he was obliged to resign towards the end of June. He was succeeded on 3 July by his more radical Minister for Defence, Amir Sjarifuddin, who was equally acceptable outside Indonesia because of his wartime anti-fascist record. Haji Agus Salim was appointed Foreign Minister. In response to American pressure to come to terms with the Dutch, Amir went even further than Sjahrir in offering concessions. However, he refused to accept the establishment of a joint gendarmerie which would operate in Republic-controlled territory. At issue was not only the status of the Republic as a co-equal partner in the formation of a federal Indonesia but also its very survival. Dutch determination to dictate the terms of that formation was demonstrated when they embarked on a military offensive in Java and Sumatra on 21 July in violation of the mandatory provision of Linggajati to settle disputes by arbitration.

UN Intervention

The resignation of Sjahrir, his replacement by Amir and the resort to force by the Dutch, marked the end of the first phase of the policy of *diplomasi*. It had secured tangible, if limited, gains. Above all, the international standing of the Republic had been enhanced as a result of the degree of *de facto* recognition conferred after the signing of the Linggajati Agreement. That recognition, however, could not provide a physical defence for the Republic, which appeared to crumble before the Dutch military onslaught. In the circumstances, its political leadership could only persevere with *diplomasi*, seeking, ideally, the interposition of a third party which would uphold Indonesia's claim to independence. What transpired was less than ideal but, at this juncture, the international associations of the Republic began to pay dividends. A direct consequence of the Dutch resort to force was a heated international response which involved the United Nations in the problem of Indonesian independence and, therefore, transformed the political context within which the struggle was taking place.[33]

At the end of July, the government of India, followed by that of Australia, brought the matter of the Dutch military action before the UN Security Council. Australia's submission took precedence because its delegation cited Chapter VII of the UN Charter which dealt *inter alia* with breaches of the peace. Dutch arguments about domestic jurisdiction were set aside and an additional measure of international status was conferred on the Republic when, in the middle of August, Sutan Sjahrir was invited to participate on its behalf in the Security Council's deliberations. A Dutch attempt to secure corresponding invitations for representatives of other states in the projected Indonesian federation was denied. Accordingly, the conflict assumed the character of one between two parties, each with international status. In the Security Council, Sjahrir advocated the despatch of a UN supervisory commission to enforce the ceasefire which had been called for at the beginning of the month, and also to arbitrate in the dispute. He was obliged to settle for much less and was unable to attract sufficient support for an Australian proposal for the restoration of the *status quo ante bellum*. Moreover, the United States and its Western associates were not prepared to contemplate a justiciable approach to a settlement. They proposed instead a consular commission to supervise the ceasefire and subsequently the despatch of a good offices committee of three to engage in conciliation. Within the Republic, this outcome was received with dismay. Support for its position from the Soviet Union and Poland contrasted with what some regarded as an act of betrayal on the part of the United States. This sobering experience influenced the international outlook of the Republic's political elite.[34] They could interpret the turn of events only as a culpable refusal to deny the restoration of Dutch colonialism on the part of a great power whose public values were, ostensibly, anti-colonial.

Irrespective of the bitterness felt by the Republic's leaders at the failure of the United Nations to adopt any positive measures, they were obliged to cope with the reality of their vulnerable position. The embryo Indonesian state had been reduced to a physical rump subject to a crippling economic blockade. The Good Offices Committee (consisting of representatives from the United States, Australia and Belgium) which arrived in late October, did not possess any formal powers. None the less, it constituted a protective device of a kind against further unilateral annexation of Republican territory by the Dutch. In consequence, the government in Yogyakarta responded to its endeavour to sponsor renewed negotiations. Talks with the Dutch were resumed on 8 December on board the US naval transport *Renville*, anchored off Jakarta.

This round of negotiations bore fruit. A compromise agreement was eventually reached; it resulted from the Good Offices Committee, with

16

American backing, being able to persuade the Dutch to accept six principles appended to an initial draft accord conceived as a basis for a final settlement. The practical significance of this cumbersome diplomatic device was that a place for the Republic within a United States of Indonesia in the original spirit of the Linggajati Agreement was explicitly reaffirmed, even though Dutch territorial gains had to be tolerated. The principal terms of the Renville Agreements signed on 17 and 19 January 1948 were as follows. Sovereignty throughout the Netherlands East Indies was to reside with Holland until the establishment of a United States of Indonesia, which would be a sovereign and independent state in equal partnership with the Netherlands in a Union headed by the Dutch Crown. The status of the Republic (in an undefined area) was to be that of a constituent state of the United States of Indonesia; provision was made for internationally supervised plebiscites in Java, Madura and Sumatra to establish whether or not their populations wished to form part of the Republic or of another state within the federal structure. Finally, all the federal states were to be offered 'fair representation' in any provisional government created before the ratification of the constitution of the projected United States of Indonesia.[35]

The Renville Agreements confirmed the *de facto* truncation of the bounds of the Republic. None the less, its leaders felt obliged to accept their terms, above all because of implicit assurances from the American representative on the Good Offices Committee, Dr Frank Graham. At a meeting between representatives of the Republic and the Committee a few days before the Agreements were signed, Dr Graham had pointed out 'You may note that the Netherlands say one thing about your status and you say another. We don't have powers of arbitration as between the two claims. Whatever you are now, you are. Whatever it is, is regardless of these points'.[36] Graham's remarks were believed to convey the attitude of the US Government which encouraged the nationalist leadership to come to terms with the Dutch. One participant in these talks, and a future Prime Minister of Indonesia, pointed out 'We interpreted this to mean that before we became part of a federal state, the Republic would continue to hold the same status as before, that is, as an independent nation holding sovereignty over the territory of Indonesia even though it had diminished considerably in size'.[37] Central to the Indonesian calculations were expectations of the United States. It was believed that its opposition to any Dutch propensity to resort to force and its support for UN supervised plebiscites in all the constituents of the projected federal state were dependent on the Republic's acquiescence in the Renville package. The logic of the policy of *diplomasi* demanded such acquiescence. The alternative of armed confrontation was not contemplated as a practical proposition because of the conventional military superiority of the Dutch. The sustained identity and existence of the Republic were believed to depend on benevolent third-party mediation and support and this, in effect, meant cultivating the goodwill of the United States which, itself, encouraged short-term concessions in return for the expectation of long-term political gains. Such a policy was not without its risks, given the obligation assumed by the government of the Republic to put the terms of the Renville Agreements into operation. One scholar commented later that 'the Republic would be entering into political discussions with its position materially weakened and confronted with the prospect of progressive deterioration of power'.[38]

If perseverance with *diplomasi* seemed the most practical option for those Indonesians charged with dealing with the Good Offices Committee, the acceptance of the Renville terms provoked a characteristic political response within the reduced perimeter of the Republic on Java. A cabinet crisis ensued similar to that which had forced the resignation of Sjahrir the previous year. In consequence, Prime Minister Amir Sjarifuddin resigned; his internal political support had crumbled. In these critical circumstances, Sukarno skilfully interposed the authority of the presidency between the policy of *diplomasi* and domestic squabbling. Amir was succeeded in office on 29 January 1948 by vice-President Mohammad Hatta, who retained Haji Agus Salim as Foreign Minister. He persisted with the Renville commitment despite cleavages within Republican ranks expressed in opposition to his foreign policy. It should be understood, however, that much of the opposition to the policy and practice of *diplomasi* by politicians in Yogyakarta represented an attempt to secure party and factional advantage. As one historian of the revolution has explained, 'Almost all of these [small number of politicians] accepted the necessity of *diplomasi* when faced with the alternative: a guerrilla war in which they themselves would be the first losers'.[39] By this juncture, *perjuangan* or struggle had ceased to be a practical first option, even if the ideal was still cherished within the Republican army and among local irregular forces.

Hatta resumed negotiations with the Dutch. In February he indicated the Republic's willingness to participate in an interim government. Underlying this step was an abiding apprehension that the Dutch would seek to eliminate the Republic before the transfer of sovereignty and the establishment of a federal state. Indeed, they seemed intent on promoting political change unilaterally within the archipelago, and this had the dual effect of increasing Hatta's own sense of apprehension and of weakening his position within the nationalist movement. They continued to set up new federal units carved out of territory seized the previous July and also kept up their economic blockade of the

Republican zone. Of major significance was an announcement by Van Mook in March 1948 of the formation of a provisional federal government to function until the establishment of the United States of Indonesia, in which the Republic would be permitted to participate only after it had come to terms with the Netherlands. An evident precondition was that it should give up that semblance of international status which its leadership had deemed essential to preserve up to the transfer of sovereignty.

At this time of renewed drift in relations with Holland, the polarization of domestic forces led to a physical confrontation whose ultimate outcome served the interests of the champions of *diplomasi*. Challenge to Hatta's government was posed by the forces of the radical left resentful of their exclusion from office. They were strengthened by a split within the Socialist Party and the adherence to their ranks of Amir Sjarifuddin. They sought to exploit the pressing economic difficulties in the Republican zone and the limited success of *diplomasi*. The catalyst for this intramural confrontation was a foreign policy issue.

Seeds of Foreign Policy

In February 1948, in the wake of the formation of Hatta's government, former Prime Minister Sjahrir had made a statement before the Central Indonesian National Committee which contained the seeds of postindependence foreign policy, namely, a commitment to non-alignment. Its initial practical expression was the rejection by Sjahrir of any alignment with the Soviet Union whose support for the Republic within the United Nations stood in contrast to the ambivalent attitude displayed by the United States. It was the issue of the Republic's relationship with the Soviet Union, in particular the refusal by Hatta to ratify a consular treaty with Moscow, which provided the opportunity for domestic challenge to the government.

The treaty in question had been negotiated in January 1948 in Prague by Suripno, a member of the Indonesian Communist Party (PKI), who had been sent to Eastern Europe by Amir Sjarifuddin at the end of 1947 in an attempt to expand the Republic's international associations. This initiative had been taken before the prospect of a settlement concluded on the *Renville* which precluded such an accord. The revelation in May by the *Tass* News agency that the Soviet Union had ratified the treaty came as an acute embarrassment to Hatta. He was concerned neither to offer provocation to the Dutch nor to affront the United States. He was also obliged to take account of opinion in Yogyakarta which viewed the Soviet Union as a welcome source of countervailing power. In the circumstances, he delayed a formal decision on ratification, gave a

19

private assurance to the Good Offices Committee that a consular exchange with the Soviet Union would not take place as long as he was Prime Minister, and then recalled Suripno for consultations. The response to the Soviet move together with its offer of a trade agreement was depicted by left-wing opponents of the government as a failure to serve the best interests of the Republic.[40]

At the beginning of August, Suripno returned to Java accompanied by an Indonesian described, at first, as his secretary but who was none other than Musso, the former leader of the PKI. Whether or not he had been in exile in Moscow since before the Second World War, Musso's return encouraged dissidence by the radical left. They attracted support from military units including irregular forces apprehensive at the effects of a government rationalization programme designed to ensure central control over the armed forces as well as compliance with the terms of the Renville Agreements. Hatta stood his ground in the face of demands for their abrogation, termination of negotiations with the Dutch, and an alignment with the Soviet Union. On 2 September he defended his position before the Central Indonesian National Committee, during which he expounded his view of the appropriate course for Indonesia's foreign policy. He argued:[41]

Have the Indonesian people fighting for their freedom no other course of action open to them than to choose between being pro Russian or pro American? Is there no other position that can be taken in the pursuit of our national ideals? The government is of the opinion that the position to be taken is that Indonesia should not be a passive party in the arena of international politics but that it should be an active agent entitled to determine its own standpoint with the right to fight for its own goal – the goal of a fully independent Indonesia.

Although this statement in full constitutes the seminal expression of the ideal foreign policy for Indonesia, it was no more than an ostensible declaration of non-alignment, given the continuing expectation on the part of Hatta and his colleagues of ultimate American support for their political goals. Hatta's refusal to revise either the practice or the emphasis of *diplomasi*, as well as an unwillingness to accept the radical left in his government, served to intensify conflict within the nationalist movement. In the middle of September armed clashes took place between dissident military units and forces loyal to the government in Yogyakarta. These clashes marked the beginning of an uprising centring on the east Javanese town of Madiun in which the leadership of the PKI was committed by junior elements. Musso, who had resumed his former party position, was drawn into a physical challenge to the government of the Republic at a time and a place not of his own choosing. The uprising subsequently endorsed by Moscow Radio, was crushed by the end of September. The radical left was consequently discredited for appearing to stab the Republic in the back at a time when it was subject to acute menace from the Dutch. Hatta's government strengthened its domestic position and, of paramount importance, secured a sympathetic response from Washington where the enveloping climate of the Cold War ensured that the crushing of a communist rebellion would be viewed with considerable approval. Accordingly, restraint was urged on the Dutch who would have liked to have used the opportunity provided by the Madiun affair to apply the *coup de grâce* to the stricken Republic.

In the wake of Madiun, external circumstances in favour of persisting with *diplomasi* improved perceptibly. Hatta made renewed efforts to convince the United States that its interests were congruent with those of the Republic. For example, in October, he pointed out to Merle Cochran, the American replacement for Dr Graham on the Good Offices Committee, that 'In the global war which is about to break out, it is imperative that in Indonesia there will be a strong and living democracy to ward off the totalitarian trend that aims to subjugate the world'.[42] He went on to argue that a weak and undemocratic Indonesia would form a serious threat to the wellbeing of the world and that the only side to gain would be the communists. Without needing to be prompted, the US government began to view the problem of Indonesia increasingly in terms of the exigencies of the Cold War. For example, when the Dutch Foreign Minister, Dr D. V. Stikker, visited Washington with the expectation of attracting support, he was left in no doubt by Secretary of State George Marshall that the United States not only favoured a negotiated settlement between the Netherlands and the Republic but also disapproved of any further attempt at a military solution.

Despite changing diplomatic circumstances, the Dutch pressed ahead with demands on the Republic which foreshadowed either its practical liquidation or a second military confrontation. At this juncture, Hatta indicated his government's willingness to compromise further. In negotiations with the Dutch Foreign Minister, major concessions were offered: on the incorporation of the Republic's armed forces within a federal body and on Dutch authority over foreign relations during the interim period before the establishment of the United States of Indonesia. None the less, a fundamental obstacle to an overall accord was Dutch insistence that, during that interim period, the Crown's representative should have the right to deploy Dutch troops within the Republican zone should he decide that a condition of internal disturbance obtained. Hatta's refusal to abdicate completely the governmental status of the Republic, based on a deep suspicion of

Dutch intentions, elicited an ultimatum just before midnight on 17 December 1948. The timing of the demand did not allow for any deliberations. And in the early hours of 19 December Dutch airborne forces launched an attack on Yogyakarta which was captured together with the principal leaders of the Republic. The Netherlands government transported the detained leaders to internal exile, where they were informed that the Republic was no longer recognized as a political entity with a territory of its own and, consequently, that they were no longer recognized as holding governmental positions.

The Dutch military action initially foreshadowed the complete failure of the Republic's political aspirations. Despite concern at the prospect of communist advantage, the US government did not appear inclined to undertake a decisive initiative which would deny the Dutch their political prize, while the Soviet Union and its allies seemed more concerned to embarrass a Cold War rival than to assist Republican Indonesia. Moreover, a cease-fire resolution passed by the UN Security Council made no provision for Dutch withdrawal from the territory seized. Yet, despite the apparent success of the Dutch, a government of a kind survived. Hatta had given a mandate to Minister of Finance Sjafruddin Prawiranegara to assume the functions and responsibilities of government should he and Sukarno be captured by the Dutch. Sjafruddin had left for Bukit Tinggi, the Republic's capital in Sumatra, shortly before the Dutch offensive. From there, he instructed the Republic's delegation at the United Nations that a cease-fire and renewed negotiations with the Dutch could be entertained only on the release of the Republic's leaders and their return to Yogyakarta, a withdrawal of Dutch troops to their positions of 18 December, and the *de jure* recognition of the Republic's sovereignty over the islands of Java, Sumatra and Madura.

Sjafruddin's demand, which also included the formation of an all-Indonesian government on a democratic basis, assumed a practical reality as Dutch attempts to impose a fait accompli by force failed with their inability to overcome the guerrilla resistance of the Indonesian army. At this juncture, the sublimated tradition of *perjuangan* was effectively revived to facilitate the practice of *diplomasi*. The Dutch failed also to secure the cooperation of the Republic's leaders whom they still held in detention. In addition, the resignation of two governments from among the Dutch-inspired federal states, together with growing international opposition, transformed the balance of advantage in the conflict.

That opposition was expressed at an international conference convened by Nehru in New Delhi in January 1949 and by the tone of debate in the Security Council. Of critical importance was a surge of opposition to the Dutch from within the United States, indicated, initially, by a suspension of Marshall Plan aid credits allocated to Holland for expenditure in the Netherlands East Indies and, subsequently, in strong resistance within the Senate to economic provision for Holland itself under the terms of the European Recovery Bill. The strength of this opposition, and concern over its possible impact on the European Recovery Programme in its entirety, strengthened the resolve of the US State Department. The inability of the Dutch to impose a political solution by military means, and the attendant fear that radical left-wing forces might fill the political vacuum within Indonesia, encouraged the Americans to apply pressure on the Dutch to restore the moderate leadership of the Republic identified with the policy of *diplomasi*.[43] The application of that pressure confirmed the original assessment of the appropriate orientation of Indonesia's foreign policy as expounded by Sjahrir in 1945 and demonstrated the practical virtues of being able to solicit the intervention of an appropriate third party to serve the interests of the Republic. Such a practice, which bore fruit during the course of the struggle for independence, became an object lesson for those who came to have charge of the foreign policy of the Republic after its attainment.

Transfer of Sovereignty

The combination of an inability to impose a solution within Indonesia and growing international pressure for the restoration of the government of the Republic to Yogyakarta obliged the Dutch, in February 1949, to propose an early conference at The Hague at which all parties to the conflict would make provision for an accelerated transfer of sovereignty. This initiative set in train a resumption of protracted negotiations which culminated on 7 May in Republican compromise, under American pressure. An agreement was concluded to attend a conference in advance of the restoration of the Republic's leadership to Yogyakarta. The Dutch undertook to return to Republican control only the residency of Yogyakarta and conceded that the Republic would assume one-third of the total membership of the federal parliament. Although this preliminary accord paved the way for the eventual transfer of sovereignty and for the ultimate establishment of the political supremacy of the Republic within the archipelago, it was regarded within Indonesia at the time as a form of capitulation. Especially within the army whose role had become much more relevant to the survival of the Republic, there was a tendency to interpret it as a surrender of interests. None the less, progress to independence of a kind was now unobstructed. On 6 July Sukarno and Hatta and their cabinet colleagues returned to Yogyakarta amidst scenes of great

23

jubilation. Two weeks later, an inter-Indonesian conference of representatives of the Republic and the Dutch-sponsored states agreed on the constitutional form of the federal system. When the respective Indonesian delegations travelled to The Hague in August for the final stage of negotiations, it was the representatives of the Dutch-inspired federal units who went out of their way to display their nationalist credentials, especially over the contentious issue of the disposition of the western half of the island of New Guinea whose separate status had been first intimated by the Dutch towards the end of 1946.

At the Hague, the conviction of the US State Department that it would be necessary for the Republic's leadership to return to Indonesia with the prize of independence in order to contain internal communist challenge governed the outcome of the negotiations. On the other hand, the American role in the conference served also to forfeit goodwill, in particular over the issue of debt payments by the new state to its former colonial master. The negotiations were acrimonious and protracted and agreement was not reached until the beginning of November. In the event, the Dutch consented to an unconditional transfer of sovereignty to a federal state in which the Republic was to be the largest unit and which was to become part of a loose consultative Netherlands-Indonesian Union headed by the Dutch Queen. In return, and in the light of the balance of opinion within the Netherlands Parliament, which would have to ratify any treaty, the Indonesian delegations agreed to tolerate continued Dutch control of the western half of the island of New Guinea, subject to further negotiations within one year. In addition, apart from conceding the restoration of Dutch and other foreign economic enterprises and assets, they accepted a burden of debt amounting to 4,300 m. Dutch Guilders (equivalent then to US$1,130 m.), which was greatly in excess of any figure contemplated and which incorporated the entire internal debt of the Netherlands Indies Government including the cost of Dutch military intervention. This aspect of the Round Table Agreements and the impasse over West New Guinea, as well as provision for a symbolic role for the Dutch Queen as head of the Netherlands-Indonesian Union diminished an independence which, in form, adhered to the Dutch and not the Republican model. It has been observed 'One may well doubt, albeit with hindsight, the wisdom of compelling a Government, about to receive its sovereignty, to accept a debt which it considered had been incurred in the attempt at its own destruction'.[44] When the Central Indonesian National Committee met to ratify the Hague Agreements on 14 December 1949, their deliberations concentrated on the issues of debt assumed by the new state and the unresolved matter of West New Guinea which, as *terra irredenta*, became known as *Irian Barat* (West Irian). Resentment over the terms of transfer did not impede its execution. On 27 December Queen

Juliana's signature gave legal basis to the establishment of the Republic of the United States of Indonesia.

The transfer of sovereignty was accomplished by negotiations. These negotiations were conducted by the advocates and exponents of *diplomasi*, in company with federal partners acceptable to the Dutch. Men of this disposition, whose outlook had been influenced by Western education and values, succeeded initially to the political heights of the new state and assumed responsibility for the conduct of its foreign relations. Their strategy during the course of the nationalist struggle had been based on a pessimistic view of the balance of contending forces and attendant concern at the consequences for Indonesia and their own peer group of the adoption of any alternative radical mode for the attainment of independence. *Diplomasi*, in the words of A. M. Taylor, represented an attempt to make 'virtue out of a necessity', especially given the degree of physical weakness of the Republic displayed openly after the first Dutch military action. The logic of such a policy demanded a special reliance on engaging the intervening influence of outside powers, in particular the United States, which was perceived correctly as being in a position to exercise leverage on the Dutch. To the extent that such a policy was pursued *faute de mieux*, even when it appeared to threaten the residual integrity of the Republic, it constituted a deviation from an independent foreign policy as expounded by Prime Minister Hatta. Moreover, although a policy of *diplomasi* was pursued in a relentless manner, a strong measure of disappointment was engendered by the response of the US government to the Republic's predicament until after the second military action by the Dutch. US ambivalence, arising from a preoccupation with European concerns, encouraged the belief that the Republic might have been left to founder politically had not guerrilla resistance denied the Dutch victory by force of arms and had not Cold War considerations interposed. Mixed feelings towards the United States were matched by a strong suspicion of the Soviet Union, whose initial support for the Republic was interpreted as opportunistic, especially in the light of recurrent criticisms of the Republic's leadership during 1949 which had their origins in the outcome of the Madiun uprising.[45] After the Round Table Agreements, the Soviet Union vetoed a Security Council resolution commending the transfer of sovereignty and the role of the Good Offices Committee in the course of the negotiations.

It was mentioned at the beginning of this chapter that the experience of acquiring independence led to a total loss of any political innocence on the part of the nationalist leadership. Early statements had been to the effect that the world would be obliged to recognize the justice of Indonesia's cause because of its moral strength. In the event, independence was achieved after a bitter and costly struggle in which the critical role of external powers was governed, evidently, by self-interest and not by deference to the ideal of self-determination. This experience strengthened accordingly an attachment to the concept of an independent foreign policy. It was reaffirmed in the light of domestic political dissension which was sustained after the transfer of sovereignty, in part because of a belief that the Round Table Conference Agreements had marked an inglorious beginning. One decisive reaction to these agreements was the unitarian movement which speedily dismantled the Dutch-inspired federal structure and reinstated the unitary Republic by the fifth anniversary of the proclamation of independence.[46] In a sense, the actual acquisition and the initial form of independence represented an anti-climax instead of the culminating stage in a process of liberation. Indeed, after the Hague Conference, Sutan Sjahrir, with whom the policy of *diplomasi* had been closely identified, stated that, while Hatta had achieved more than he had believed possible, he felt that it would be impossible to carry out a really free foreign policy. The victory of the Republic had been 'at the expense of economic and diplomatic liberty'.[47] Whether or not construed as a grudging personal acknowledgement of an ultimate diplomatic achievement in which he had not played a principal role, Sjahrir's comment expressed a widespread feeling. It constituted a recognition of the constraints on the new state and, at the same time, implied an urge to overcome them. Indonesia's foreign policy has reflected these conflicting strains over more than three decades.[48]

On the morrow of independence, such considerations were evident but did not bulk large for those charged with the conduct of foreign policy. The constraints to which Sjahrir had alluded were tolerated by those who first succeeded to high office in the post-independence capital, Jakarta. For this select group, foreign policy enjoyed a limited priority and a subordinate place among competing domestic claims on time and resources.

2 Foreign Policy and Domestic Requirements

The newly independent government of Indonesia was confronted by major problems of economic rehabilitation and public order. These problems were aggravated by an abortive attempt at separatism in the South Moluccan islands and by the disruptive reversion from a federal to a unitary state. In the circumstances, foreign policy had to be tailored to domestic requirements – above all, an alien structure of economic interests which confounded the reality of political independence. The resumption of alien, especially Dutch and resident Chinese, dominance in the economy and the attendant colonial pattern of Indonesia's international economic relationships was endured in order to promote national recovery. This condition of dependence meant that coalition parliamentary governments, cobbled together from unstable political elements could not afford compromising external alignments. Foreign policy was conducted accordingly with a strong sense of constraint; it reflected the strain imposed on domestic consensus by the controversial terms of the transfer of the sovereignty.[1]

Vice-President Hatta retained office as Prime Minister with the formation of the Republic of the United States of Indonesia. Although he was well disposed towards the Western constellation in international politics, he refused to indentify his government with it, preferring to reaffirm the commitment to an independent course which he had enunciated initially in September 1948. Within the new state, the sense of recent liberation from colonialism together with the impact of Cold War rivalries conjured up fears of a new foreign domination which had to be resisted. One response in foreign policy was the rejection of a proposal by the Philippine government for an anti-communist Pacific Pact advanced at a regional conference at Baguio in May 1950. With the outbreak of the Korean War, the Indonesian government refused to adopt a position of either approval or disapproval towards the belligerents and correspondingly resisted pressures from the United States to become a party to its global policy of containment. This non-aligned position had been encouraged by India's Prime Minister, Jawaharlal Nehru, who had strongly espoused Indonesia's national cause. Hatta was extremely sensitive to the domestic political atmosphere which gave rise to such a position. For example, he kept secret a

27

request to the United States for military equipment for the police and was willing only to give a private oral undertaking that his government would observe an embargo on the export of strategic materials to any of America's enemies.

With the establishment of the unitary state in August 1950, Hatta was succeeded as Prime Minister by Mohammad Natsir from the Muslim Masjumi Party. He appointed, as Foreign Minister, Mohammad Rum, who had played a central role in the negotiations with the Dutch and had served as the first High Commissioner to The Hague. In virtually every respect, Natsir's priorities were identical to those of Hatta. In a policy statement to the provisional parliament in late September 1950, he identified eight objectives, the first six of which were concerned with internal order and economic reconstruction. His seventh objective was the settlement of the outstanding issue of West Irian and his eighth the pursuit of an independent foreign policy in the 'ominous conjuncture' of Cold War rivalry. In the course of his remarks, he stressed: 'It is not our intention to pursue a neutrality policy to the effect that we pursue a negative policy'.[2] This statement, which was intended to give positive emphasis to a commitment to treat issues on their merits, none the less accorded foreign policy a subordinate place. An affirmation of an independent position was reconciled with upholding obligations to the Dutch under the Round Table Conference Agreements and with a refusal to make West Irian a matter of urgency.

In a sense, the issue of relations with the Dutch, including West Irian, was excluded from the formal ambit of foreign policy, which was represented as being concerned with matters of balance between the Great Power blocs. Reports of progress in establishing diplomatic relations with the People's Republic of China and the Soviet Union and of trading ties with Eastern Europe were presented to demonstrate the absence of alignment. The government refused to recognize the Bao Dai regime in Vietnam which was perceived as an agency of French colonial interests and, correspondingly, refused to acknowledge the insurgent Democratic Republic of Vietnam led by Ho Chi Minh. Natsir also announced that Indonesia had delayed its application to join the United Nations during the absence of the Soviet delegate from the Security Council, in order not to prejudice its prospects for membership. It became the sixtieth member of the organisation on 28 September 1950. A US intervention was required to fend off a Nationalist Chinese veto in the Security council as a riposte to Indonesia's establishment of diplomatic relations with the government in Peking in June. Within the United Nations, Indonesia's delegation identified itself with measures for a peaceful settlement in Korea and with support for anti-colonial movements.[3]

Natsir's Administration represented a continuity in the principles and practice of foreign policy which was sustained by his immediate successors. If practice involved tolerance of an evident alignment in international economic relationships which inhibited assertion over West Irian, principle was expressed through a recurrent affirmation of independence. An authoritative exposition of Indonesia's foreign policy was provided by vice-President Hatta in the American journal *Foreign Affairs* in 1953. Rejecting the view that there could not be a middle position in the Cold War, he maintained that Indonesia's geopolitical situation did not entail a 'pressing need to make a choice between the two big blocs'. He continued:[4]

Indonesia plays no favourites between the two opposed blocs and follows its own path through the various international problems. It terms this policy 'independent' and further characterises it by describing it as independent and 'active'. By active is meant the effort to work energetically for the preservation of peace, through endeavours supported if possible by the majority of the members of the United Nations.

Matching this mild rhetoric was an appreciation of the need to keep foreign policy in its place. Hatta explained:

Internal consolidation is the primary task. The government must show evidence of economic and social betterment if it is to offset the influence of agitation by radical circles. A foreign policy that aligned the country with either of the Great Powers would render this internal task infinitely more difficult.

The concept of an independent and active foreign policy served as a way of sustaining domestic priorities designed to overcome economic, social and administrative shortcomings. It catered also for a national mood coloured by the recent experience of national revolution and, as such, was regarded as a strict standard of conduct by which governments could be judged. Accordingly, intense competition between political parties of divergent views and constituencies encompassed foreign policy issues which were drawn into the domestic process. West Irian was paramount among such issues. In the course of the first decade of independence, it had a decisive impact on the political system and the conduct of Indonesia's foreign policy.

West Irian

West Irian had been an integral part of the Netherlands East Indies. The refusal of the Dutch to include the territory in the transfer of sovereignty had jeopardised the outcome of the Round Table Conference. In order to avoid deadlock, a compromise formula had been accepted which provided that:[5]

the status quo of the residency of New Guinea shall be maintained with the stipulation that within a year from the date of transfer of sovereignty to the Republic of the United States of Indonesia, the question of the political status of New Guinea shall be determined through negotiations between the Republic of the United States of Indonesia and the Kingdom of the Netherlands.

The claim to West Irian was not in itself divisive within Indonesia. It attracted wide support as a practical test of Holland's acceptance of the legitimacy of the successor state. In addition, the incomplete transfer of sovereignty aroused concern because it derogated from the *raison d'être* for the territorial basis of the republic, namely, that it should incorporate all of the former Netherlands East Indies.[6] Despite a common view of Dutch duplicity, West Irian became a matter of internal contention because of differences in approach to the resolution of the dispute, which echoed differing approaches to the attainment of independence. For the early governments of post-colonial Indonesia, an assertive campaign to recover the least hospitable part of the archipelago was not worth the anticipated economic and political opportunity costs. Indeed, a desire to demonstrate a sense of moderation and responsibility, deemed necessary to attract and retain foreign economic resources and technical skills, had influenced Hatta to circumvent the impasse over West Irian at the Round Table Conference. Hatta and his immediate successors were obliged to pursue the territorial claim but did so in a conciliatory spirit according to the terms of the Round Table Conference formula.

Initial, but inconclusive, discussions with the Netherlands began in Jakarta in March 1950. A ministerial meeting in April agreed to set up a joint commission to visit the territory and report back to a full conference by the end of the year. In the intervening period, increasing strain set in between the two states over the breakdown of federal Indonesia, which had been precipitated by the involvement of Dutch nationals in an abortive coup and a separatist movement. With the advent of the unitary Republic, a militant edge was given to the claim to West Irian by president Sukarno. In an address in August commemorating the fifth anniversary of the proclamation of independence, he announced: 'If a settlement by negotiation cannot be arrived at within this year, a major conflict will arise over the issue of who will be in power in that island from then onward.' He warned that Indonesia would fight until the end of time 'so long as one part of our country is not free'. This defiant expression of nationalist feeling had domestic political significance. It was an attempt to use the West Irian issue as a way of overcoming the constitutional limitations of a ceremonial presidency: Sukarno's initiative indicated a propensity for assertiveness. Up to the acquisition of independence, he had been identified with the champions of negotiation, even if he had found it politic to employ the language of struggle. Now, without ever giving up the option of negotiation, the Indonesian President began to identify himself with the mode of struggle in his utterances on West Irian. In so doing, he set himself apart from the Masjumi-dominated cabinet and drew support from the ranks of the parliamentary opposition. West Irian was an issue of symbolic and emotive significance which governments neglected at their peril. It was not only an objective in foreign policy but also an instrument which could be used to disable political opponents.[7]

Foreign Minister Mohammad Rum led an Indonesian delegation to a conference on West Irian held in The Hague in December 1950. A successful negotiation seemed unlikely from the outset because the joint commission set up earlier had failed to agree and had produced two separate contending reports. Despite efforts by the Indonesian side to provide assurances for the protection of Dutch interests in West Irian, there was no willingness whatsoever on the part of the Netherlands government to contemplate the transfer of the territory. The limit of Dutch concessions was a proposal to transfer sovereignty to the Netherlands-Indonesian Union with no change in administrative control. The context of the negotiations was different from that which obtained at the Round Table Conference. For example, the ostensible neutrality of the United States barely concealed the view 'that the interests of the inhabitants of Dutch New Guinea would be best served by the continuation of Dutch control in some form'.[8] In addition, the advent of a conservative government in Australia had given the Dutch an ally, from a sense of fear that Indonesia would extend its claim to the eastern half of the island of New Guinea. In the event, the negotiations were deadlocked; the two parties failed to produce a joint statement.

The response of the Natsir government was a renewed commitment to a policy of reasoned negotiations without conceding the principle of Indonesia's claim. Such a show of moderation exposed it to domestic political pressure. President Sukarno made it known that he wanted to seize the opportunity presented by the failure of negotiations to challenge Dutch economic interests within Indonesia and also to dissolve the Netherlands-Indonesian Union, which he regarded as the provocative symbol of a limited independence. Sukarno wished to proclaim its dissolution in a public speech, but was denied this course by Natsir who insisted that the cabinet should decide whether or not the President pronounced publicly on important issues of foreign policy.

The immediate constitutional battle was won by Natsir but, in the process, West Irian became a greater test of nationalist rectitude. Sukarno threatened to resign and lent his influence to opposition parliamentary forces intent on unseating Natsir's government, which was accordingly obliged to adopt a tougher position towards the Dutch. In a statement to Parliament in January 1951 Natsir indicated his government's intention to revise the Round Table Conference Agreements, including the Union statutes. However, instead of taking immediate measures, he appointed a commission headed by a distinguished jurist to review their provisions. Natsir's position was firm but restrained. He had no desire to take relations with Holland, with whom a loan worth over US$70 m. had been negotiated, to a turning point. Such restraint served to undermine his domestic standing. His government was obliged to resign in March 1951, ostensibly over the composition of regional legislative councils. The criticism generated over his handling of the West Irian issue was a contributory factor in its political demise.[9]

The experience encountered by Natsir's government over West Irian was shared by its successors in the early 1950s, which had to cope with continuing domestic challenge over foreign policy. The next government was headed by Dr Sukiman Wirjosanjoyo from another Masjumi faction. It was more diverse in political composition and included members from the secular Indonesian Nationalist Party (PNI). It was bound by a commitment to an independent foreign policy which reflected the true outlook of many ministers. Yet, under Sukiman's leadership, the government displayed a conservative Western bias. Repressive measures were taken against the Indonesian Communist Party (PKI) as well as other political enemies. The role of the Chinese Embassy was restricted in an attempt to contain its influence among the overseas Chinese community.[10] However, a public threat to 'trade with the devil' by Foreign Minister Achmad Subarjo in May, intended to appease a critical press, precipitated American diplomatic pressure to prevent the sale of rubber to the People's Republic. The government succumbed to this pressure. Indonesia abstained on a General Assembly resolution recommending a UN embargo on the supply of strategic raw materials to China and also discontinued negotiations over a barter offer from Peking of rice and tungsten in return for rubber. Nevertheless, it complied with the UN embargo and justified this position on the ground of not wishing to change its historic pattern of exports, despite resentment at a loss of foreign exchange earnings because of an attendant fall in the price of rubber.

Further evidence of the weight of American influence had been indicated by the government's decision to send its Foreign Minister to attend the conference on a peace treaty with Japan in San Francisco. Indonesia's participation was controversial. India and Burma, both prominent non-aligned states, had announced that they would boycott the occasion because the draft treaty was of American making and was intended as the cornerstone of US Cold War policy in Asia. The Indonesian cabinet had been divided over the issue. On balance, the Masjumi members had favoured participation, whereas the PNI complement were opposed. In the event, a compromise of a kind was reached, whereby participation was endorsed but signature of the treaty made conditional on securing an undertaking from Japan that reparations would be paid for suffering incurred during the wartime occupation.[11] Foreign Minister Subarjo signed the peace treaty on behalf of Indonesia on 8 September 1951, but against a background of domestic dissent which prevented its parliamentary ratification.

Of much greater import for the divided Sukiman cabinet was the conclusion on its behalf, in January 1952, of an agreement on economic and military assistance between Foreign Minister Subarjo and the US Ambassador in Jakarta, Merle Cochran. Subarjo has described the offer of military assitance as arriving at 'the right psychological moment', given the measure of internal challenge posed, in particular, by the insurgent *Dar ul-Islam* (literally, the House of Islam) movement in West Java.[12] However, the government was obliged to accept the aid package under the terms of the US Mutual Security Act of October 1951, which required a state receiving military assistance to contribute fully 'to the development and maintenance of its own defensive strength and the defensive strength of the free world'. Such language was contrary to the established precepts of Indonesia's foreign policy. Moreover, in concluding the aid agreement, Subarjo had acted without proper reference to his cabinet colelagues. Prime Minister Sukiman had been informed of the negotiations but had not been consulted on their terms. When news of the treaty became public, the government was both embarrassed and discredited. It was obliged to repudiate it and to accept responsibility for the foolhardy conduct of its Foreign Minister who had violated the central canons of the country's foreign policy by entangling it in a tacit alliance relationship.[13] Its political fortunes had not been helped by an evident inability to overcome Dutch obduracy over West Irian, which had reached new heights with the passage of a constitutional amendment incorporating the territory within the Netherlands Kingdom. The resignation of the Sukiman government took place in February 1952 in an atmosphere of national outrage and political opportunism.

The Sukiman government, like its predecessor, had fallen victim to the engagement of a foreign policy issue in domestic politics. Apart from the special circumstances of the aid agreement with the United

States in which public values were affronted, it had conducted itself generally over foreign policy without sufficient sensitivity to popular feeling. However imprecise the formal expression of foreign policy objectives, they evoked a genuine popular response. The need for Indonesia to be free from the influence of Cold War rivals, in particular, was a strong common sentiment. Because of its neglect of this domestic requirement in foreign policy, the Sukiman government exposed itself to attack motivated, in part, by party and factional advantage.

Dr Sukiman was succeeded as Prime Minister in April 1952 by Mr Wilopo from the PNI. His coalition was again based, in the main, on the PNI and Masjumi, but with a different factional base. At the outset, Wilopo did not indicate any major revision of priorities from those of his immediate predecessors. Foreign policy was placed last on the list of the new cabinet's programme when it was presented to Parliament in May. He made explicit the view that the country's foreign policy was based on internal conditions and indicated a sensitive understanding of the failings of the Sukiman Administration. He pointed out:[14]

An atmosphere of unity and solidarity is most needed, if we are to arrive at satisfactory results in our undertakings in the fields of reconstruction and stabilisation. The commitments or consequences resulting from our foreign relations should not be such as to disturb or even trouble Indonesia's 'internal atmosphere'.

Early in June, however, Wilopo found it necessary to make a further statement on foreign affairs, claiming that a confusion of ideas had arisen as to the meaning of the country's independent policy and that a more detailed elucidation was necessary. His reaffirmation of principles was distinctly ambivalent, however. He restated his government's intention not to take sides in, but also not to keep aloof from, Cold War conflict. His exegesis was characterised, none the less, by a commitment to the conventions of international society. With specific reference to the controversial American aid agreement, the Japanese peace treaty, the issue of West Irian and attendant relations with the Netherlands, Wilopo remarked:[15]

The government hopes we will not forget that there are standards of common decency in international relations which we must observe as a self-respecting state. As in the case with our internal relations, where we have to observe certain rules, we must also submit in our international relations to the rules that have been fixed by international law and usage.

In other words, essentially, it is not allowed to revise or cancel an agreement which we have concluded with another state, high handedly, (unilaterally) – without the consent of the said state – if the implementation of said agreement proves to be disadvantageous to us.

In this statement, although the central principles of Indonesia's foreign policy were reiterated, they were expressed within a framework of moderation and international responsibility. Wilopo espoused values which his generation of Indonesians had assimilated in the law schools of Amsterdam and Leiden.

For Wilopo's cabinet foreign policy was primarily a matter of unfinished business. An undertaking was given to replace the Subarjo-Cochran agreement by one whose terms of reference would include economic and technical assistance only and whose conditions would 'not deviate from the framework of international co-operation in general and from the spirit of the United Nations Charter in particular'. Such an agreement was eventually concluded without undue difficulty in January 1953. On West Irian and the related matter of the Netherlands-Indonesian Union, Wilopo committed his government to a resumption of the negotiations which had been broken off in February 1952. Although deference was paid to the urgency of the claim, the general inclination of the cabinet was towards moderation in the light of pressing domestic problems, especially the adverse economic circumstances which followed the end of the Korean War boom in raw material prices.[16] Parliamentary pressure over the issue revived with the Dutch announcement in June 1952 that they saw no value in a resumption of discussions with Indonesia about the status of West New Guinea. Apart from negotiations which led to the termination of the Dutch military mission in Indonesia, the Wilopo government could record nothing more substantial than a protest before the Fourth Committee of the UN General Assembly in October when Holland reported on the administration of West Irian, whose status was depicted as non-self-governing.

The government was also subject to parliamentary pressure over the prospect of diplomatic relations with the Soviet Union which had not followed the latter's recognition of Indonesia in January 1950 and the visit of a delegation to Moscow the following April. In June 1952, Wilopo claimed that the time was not yet ripe to open an embassy. Although the Soviet Union had not greeted Indonesia's advent with any warmth, its initially hostile attitude had been replaced by a friendlier disposition in the year before Stalin's death.[17] The matter of establishing a diplomatic mission in Moscow was raised again in Parliament in February 1953 and drew a generally sympathetic response, because an exchange of ambassadors with the principal communist state was regarded as a way of introducing balance into a self-styled independent foreign policy. The initiative was blocked because of the strong opposition of Masjumi members within the cabinet. By this time, the course of domestic political events was moving against Wilopo's government. A schism within Masjumi had led to the emergence in August of the more conservative Java-based Nahdatul Ulamma (NU – Muslim Scholars) as a major party in its own right. In consequence, the PNI outside the cabinet became more assertive as it no longer felt obliged to tolerate the restraining influence of the Masjumi on Wilopo. Concurrently, the PKI had begun to give Parliamentary support to the PNI and also revised its attitude to President Sukarno in an attempt to overcome the taint of Madiun and to establish its nationalist credentials. Furthermore, Sukarno by his deft defusing in October 1952 of a military display to coerce him into dissolving parliament felt more confident in asserting himself against a cabinet which wished to confine him to a constitutional role.[18]

The domestic position of Wilopo's coalition, beset by economic crisis and regional dissent, was intrinsically weak. It was further undermined by the impact of a number of foreign policy issues. However, what served above all else as the immediate cause for its fall was a crisis occasioned by an attempt to expel peasant squatters from land leased to Dutch-owned tobacco companies in East Sumatra. The government had sought a compromise whereby only part of the estates would be restored but at the same time it would be able to demonstrate an ability to provide security of tenure for overseas economic interests which generated vital foreign exchange. But, in March 1953, police tried forcibly to dislodge some of the squatters. In the ensuing confrontation, five squatters were killed with attendant political repercussions. This emotive episode served the interests of the dominant group within the PNI which wished to undermine the government. A bitter parliamentary attack was launched in May on an already reeling administration, which had appeared to support vestiges of the very colonialism which the recent revolution had been intended to expunge. The government did not seek to defend itself against a motion of no confidence but resigned at the beginning of June.[19]

Those responsible for the conduct of foreign policy in the first three and a half years of Indonesia's independence had been concerned primarily with domestic rehabilitation, which required toleration of Western interests and a tacit international alignment which did not match the rhetoric of an independent and active foreign policy. In the circumstances, a conscious effort was made, with certain exceptions, to subordinate the public profile of foreign policy. This endeavour failed, in the main because of the intensely competitive nature of the domestic political process. Indonesia's political life was a constant battle between and within weak coalition governments and aggressive parliamentary oppositions keen to secure access to the status and patronage which ministerial office provided. The notable feature of the practice of Indonesian foreign policy in the early 1950s was that issues and decisions in this dimension of politics were drawn readily into the domestic arena. In this period, governments which could be shown to have either violated or neglected central tenets of policy were vulnerable to political challenge. Opponents were only too ready to exploit derelictions in foreign policy in order to bring in a new administration motivated by the unstated premise that the political and economic fruits of the revolution should be shared. In this way foreign and domestic politics, never truly separate in any state, became interlocked in symbiotic embrace.

An Active Foreign Policy

After protracted negotiations, Wilopo was succeeded as Prime Minister by Ali Sastroamijoyo, a PNI luminary who had served as ambassador in Washington since independence. His cabinet was notable for the absence of Masjumi participation. During Ali's tenure of office, greater importance was attached to foreign policy but expressed in emphasis rather than in radical innovation. The experience and outlook of the new Prime Minister was a relevant factor in the degree of change. The world of diplomacy was not only familiar but also more exciting than the increasingly intractable domestic economic and social problems which Indonesia faced in mid-1953. In addition, foreign policy was employed to serve the needs of the government of the day rather than the interests of the political opposition. Ali exhibited a strong sense of entitlement on behalf of Indonesia.[20] He was also attracted by new opportunities for an international role which had arisen in the wake of the death of Stalin and the Korean armistice, and were exemplified by the willingness of both major communist powers to accept the political reality of non-alignment. Ali sought to dominate the conduct of foreign policy and chose, as Foreign Minister, a fellow PNI member Sunario who had specialised in international relations within the provisional parliament but who was not a strong personality. In his conduct of foreign policy, Ali did not faithfully reflect the growing influence of Sukarno nor did he foreshadow the fundamental revision of foreign policy with which the President became identified in the early 1960s. None the less, his tenure of office was characterized by a measure of militancy which had been consciously subordinated by his predecessors. It also demonstrated a tendency to indulge in purge and patronage within the recently created Foreign Service whose more senior personnel came to reflect the general disposition of the PNI as well as a political dependence not in keeping with the professed values of the Civil Service.

As Prime Minister, Ali purported to represent the authentic expression of Indonesia's foreign policy and sought validation for this view in differentiating between the outlook of his government and the apparent disposition of its predecessors towards the United States. To this end, an agreement to establish diplomatic relations with the Soviet Union was concluded in December 1953. However, the pursuit of Indonesian interests assumed an initial expression domestically in an attempt to shift the balance of alien control of the economy.[21] Increased foreign exchange allocations were provided for indigenous importers and private Indonesian banks were sponsored. These initiatives did little to change the structure of the economy and increased the opportunity for diverting public funds for private and also political party purposes in anticipation of general elections. The net effect was to aggravate economic decline concurrent with rising inflation dating from the end of the Korean War boom. The feeble condition of the economy and the problems which it presented made foreign policy activity even more attractive for Ali.

Ali's major achievement in this field was the renowned Asian-African Conference in Bandung in April 1955. This historic diplomatic occasion, attended by such international figures as Chou En-lai, Nehru and Nasser, brought distinction to Indonesia and political glory to its Prime Minister. The Bandung Conference was a remarkable piece of political theatre executed with some efficiency, which justified Indonesia's claim to be treated as a country of consequence. It also served the electoral interests of the PNI which dominated the cabinet. It would be wrong, however, to dismiss the occasion as only political theatre. While the diverse group of states represented at the conference were not of one mind on a number of important international issues, their enthusiastic participation reflected a growing spirit of assertiveness on the part of former colonies who were determined not only to underline their independent status but also to let it be known that, as members of a global society, they were entitled to a say in its overall management.

The wider context of the Bandung Conference came from the impact of the Cold War on the new states of Asia arising from the Korean conflict. Following the Korean armistice in July 1953, the conflict had shifted to Indochina. The dominant Asian interpretation of that conflict was that it was not intrinsically a Cold War issue. France with the support of the United States was viewed as seeking to stem the tide of Asian nationalism. In Indonesia, the communist face of that nationalism was considered of limited importance. Moreover, it was suggested that America's policy of containment was dividing the states of Asia who might otherwise work together in harmony.

At the end of April 1954, the Indonesian Prime Minister joined with his counterparts from Ceylon, Burma, India and Pakistan in Colombo, where they called for a halt to the conflict in Indochina with the object of restraining the United States whose policies seemed likely to lead to a major confrontation with the People's Republic of China. On setting out for this meeting, which convened just prior to the Geneva Conference on Indochina, Ali had suggested that he and his colleagues should sponsor a larger gathering of independent Asian and African states with the dual purpose of promoting a relaxation of Cold War tensions and of sustaining the challenge to colonialism. Decisive in the collective decision to proceed with this proposal was the Indian Prime Minister, Jawaharlal Nehru. His initial response was not enthusiastic, but following the historic visit by Chou En-lai to New Delhi in June 1954, at which differences between India and China were reconciled, he recognized the advantage of encouraging the benign international outlook of the new China, and possibly detaching it from the close political embrace of the Soviet Union by promoting an opening to the somewhat apprehensive states of Asia and Africa. Nehru's attitude was strengthened by his anger at America's sponsorship in Manila in September 1954 of the Collective Defence Treaty for South-East Asia to which India's adversary, Pakistan, adhered. This feeling was echoed also by the Indonesian government, which denounced the Manila Pact as an unwarranted intrusion of the Cold War into South-East Asia.

Indonesia and Ali's government became the political beneficiaries of a temporary coalition of Indian and Chinese interests. After a measure of personal diplomacy by Ali and his Foreign Minister Sunario, a preliminary meeting of the original Colombo Powers was held in the Indonesian resort of Bogor in December 1954, where it was decided that invitations to the conference the following April would be extended to some thirty Asian and African governments including those of China and North and South Vietnam. The conference itself, which was attended by over 400 foreign journalists, was a remarkable public event because of its unique character. Ali's satisfaction was evident, for he later recorded that 'It was because of the Bandung Conference that our country very soon acquired a respected place on the map of world politics'.[22] As a diplomatic occasion, its actual accomplishments were less than remarkable. Moreover, the conspicuous paternalism of the Indian Prime Minister contributed to a cooling in relations between Jakarta and New Delhi.

Apart from enhancing its international standing, the composition of the delegates served to demonstrate the government's adherence to an independent and active foreign policy. For example, the presence of a Chinese delegation provided an opportunity to repair an important political relationship which had been soured from the outset. Central to this relationship was a major domestic problem, namely, the status of the resident Chinese community in Indonesia. Their conspicuous and influential economic role under the Dutch and since independence had long been the object of envy and suspicion. Apprehension that they might serve as an alien fifth column had been sustained by China's retention of traditional nationality laws which employed the concept of *jus sanguinis* whereby racial identity defined citizenship. The Indonesians had also been disturbed by the refusal of a significant proportion of the resident Chinese community to take up citizenship after independence, and were keen to deny dual nationality and loyalties. Accordingly, they responded to a general invitation to negotiate on this issue from the Chinese government. Talks began in Peking in November 1954 and continued in Indonesia prior to and during the course of the Bandung Conference. On 22 April 1955 Premier Chou En-lai and Foreign Minister Sunario signed a treaty in which the doctrine of *jus sanguinis* was renounced and Chinese residents of Indonesia who had not acquired citizenship were accorded the right to choose between the two nationalities within two years.[23]

The dual nationality treaty marked a practical step in the development of a new relationship but did not eradicate basic Sino-Indonesian tensions over the resident Chinese community. Ratification of the treaty was delayed until December 1957 because of domestic opposition to the procedure for acquiring citizenship. Moreover, legislation passed in Indonesia in 1958 contravened both the letter and the spirit of the treaty, while attendant measures to exclude 'alien' Chinese from retail trade in rural areas had political repercussions which marred Indonesia's relationship with China. It was only with Sukarno's effective assertion of dominance over foreign policy at the turn of the decade that Sino-Indonesian association progressed in political terms. None the less, at the time of the Bandung Conference, the government of Prime Minister Ali had demonstrated a significant change of emphasis in policy towards China. After its conclusion, Chou En-lai stayed on in Indonesia for two days as an official guest of President Sukarno. Ali paid a visit to China at the end of May where he was received by Chairman Mao Tse-tung. He was flattered by Mao's suggestion that Indonesia act as intermediary in an attempt to overcome problems between China and Thailand and the Philippines. In consequence, he was encouraged to try his hand as mediator between China and the United States, though to no avail because, as he was later to claim, of the unbending attitude of the government in Washington.[24]

If a willingness to despatch small groups of armed infiltrators to West Irian during 1954 indicated a disposition by Ali's government to reject the line of diplomacy, by and large it prosecuted the territorial claim by well-tried means. Negotiations with the Dutch resumed between June and August at The Hague but no progress was made on the issue of West Irian itself. The Indonesian government had to be content with a protocol agreed between the two Foreign Ministers which provided for the dissolution of the Netherlands-Indonesian Union and also annulled cultural and military clauses of the Round Table Conference Agreements.[25] This protocol did not touch on the major role of the Dutch in the Indonesian economy; and its ratification was baulked by the government's inability to command a parliamentary quorum at a time of domestic crisis.

One indication of a difference in emphasis, if not in basic practice, by Ali's government was its request in August 1954 that the West Irian issue be inscribed on the agenda of the ninth session of the UN General Assembly. This decision constituted a logical continuation of the previous government's policy of representing West Irian as an anti-colonial issue and not just a territorial claim. Although a modest resolution submitted by India and other sympathisers attracted a simple majority, it failed to secure the necessary two-thirds majority support required under the Charter for passage of important questions. This wider airing of the issue marked an attempt to solicit international support in order to influence the Dutch. Such support was forthcoming from the Soviet Union, while strong backing was also secured at the Bandung Conference and was incorporated in the final communique.

Despite the popular recognition of its diplomatic achievement at Bandung, Ali's government fell from office in July 1955 over an issue of essentially domestic significance. It proved unable to assert control over the armed forces, in particular over the refusal of a majority of senior officers to accept its nominee for the post of Army Chief of Staff. In this conflict, over the exercise of political power within the country, foreign policy was of subordinate concern. Ali Sastroamijoyo had detached the conduct of foreign policy from the domestic entanglements which had afflicted his predecessors. He had furnished it with a greater sense of national interest but was unable to employ it as a tool with which to dominate the domestic political process. In the event, his international role had no bearing on the fate of his government.

A Change in Style

Ali Sastroamijoyo was succeeded as Prime Minister by Burhanuddin Harahap of the Masjumi Party. Negotiations for his appointment were conducted while President Sukarno was out of the country on a pilgrimage to Mecca. In his absence, vice-President Hatta played a decisive role in selecting Burhanuddin, who assumed office in August. His cabinet did not include PNI members and its composition indicated a slackening in the momentum of militant nationalism and a greater interest in arresting the evident decline in the economy. The imminence of general elections concentrated immediate attention on domestic political interests. In the event, the election results constituted a major failure for Masjumi and its minor party associates which dominated the cabinet. The majority of votes and four-fifths of the parliamentary seats were shared almost equally between the PNI, Masjumi, the NU and the PKI. The results confirmed a regional pattern of political allegiance which indicated an absence of national consensus over the identity and direction of the Indonesian state. They also shifted the balance of representation in favour of the ethnic Javanese.

From a position of underlying political weakness, Burhanuddin's government took an active interest in foreign policy and, in particular, the claim to West Irian which it also took to the United Nations.[26] This initiative reflected the view that a sober approach to the country's deep-seated problems could not be adopted so long as the issue of West Irian could be exploited by radical political opponents. The government confronted the issue by a change in diplomatic style. Its object was to improve relations with Western states, including Australia which had openly opposed Indonesia's claim, in order to influence the international climate for dealing with the Dutch. This conciliatory approach produced a positive response in The Hague and preliminary discussions began in New York during September. Foreign Minister Ide Anak Agung Gde Agung assumed responsibility for negotiations in the face of domestic opposition, including dissension within the cabinet and the open hostility of Sukarno.

Negotiations proper began in The Hague in December 1955 but moved within a week to the more neutral setting of Geneva. They centred on two issues; Indonesia's desire to dissolve the Netherlands-Indonesia Union, so that the Republic would no longer be encumbered by the economic and financial obligations assumed at the Round Table Conference, and also the more controversial matter of West Irian. By January 1956, an interim agreement had been reached over dissolving the Union but no progress was made on West Irian; this served to intensify domestic Indonesian opposition to the negotiations which were represented as demeaning in the light of Holland's persistent refusal to change its stand on jurisdiction. Defections from the cabinet prompted a decision to recall the Indonesian delegation, but this was later reversed. However, this display of political weakness encouraged the Dutch delegation to prevaricate over initialling the agreement on the abrogation of the Union. Negotiations were only resumed in

February after the Indonesian delegation had announced its intended departure. None the less, the Dutch side was unwilling to confirm the limited agreement without provision for third-party arbitration in the event of disputes over its economic and financial clauses. This concession was unacceptable to a caretaker government subject to internal dissension and vociferous political attack. From this point of impasse, events moved rapidly to one of crisis. On 13 February the Indonesian government announced its unilateral withdrawal from the Netherlands-Indonesian Union. The initiative has been described as Indonesia's first breach of legality in defiance of the Dutch since the revolution.[27] It was also an ironic one, given the general political disposition of the government. The assertion of national will did not work to its domestic advantage; its position had become increasingly anomalous in the wake of the general elections. Burhanuddin was able, with some difficulty, to secure the passage through parliament of a Bill abrogating the Union but was obliged to give up office early in March.

The conduct of foreign policy by this short-lived cabinet was paradoxical, even by Indonesia's parliamentary standards, given its initial intent. Burhanuddin and his colleagues had set out to act within the bounds of international convention. His government's political fragility had reinforced a consciousness of its conservative credentials and yet, in the face of Dutch obduracy, it was moved to repudiate a treaty. It thus served to sustain a radical trend in foreign policy and not to arrest it. Paradoxically also, the unilateral repudiation of the treaty with the Netherlands did not secure full domestic endorsement. President Sukarno refused to sign the necessary enabling law, which meant that the act of abrogation lacked constitutional legality. In one respect, however, the diplomacy of the Burhanuddin government bore some political fruit. A cordial visit to Jakarta was undertaken in February by the Australian Foreign Minister, R. G. Casey. A better understanding of Indonesia's interests also appeared to be displayed by the United States. For example, at the beginning of March, an agreement was concluded for the receipt of food aid worth over US$96 m. In the middle of the month, Secretary of State John Foster Dulles enjoyed a brief and uneventful stay in Jakarta, during which he extended an invitation to President Sukarno to visit the United States.

The experience of the Burhanuddin government had demonstrated, once again, the extent to which foreign policy had become the prisoner of an intensely competitive political process. The general elections of September 1955 did nothing to remedy the situation. Indeed, the results exposed the fissile nature of Indonesian politics rooted in conflict over ethno-religious and regional identity. They dashed the expectations of those politicians who had looked to the ballot box as an instrument of national redemption. In the circumstances, the only recourse under the parliamentary system was another coalition government. Ali Sastro-amijoyo was appointed Prime Minister for a second term in March 1956. He presided over a political combination which reflected the decline in national cohesion. Its members could agree only on the exclusion of the PKI from the cabinet, if against the declared wishes of Sukarno. With the confirmation of political polarization and immobilism, a greater readiness was shown to explain the country's malaise in terms of an alien-dominated economic system which functioned as if the revolution had never occurred. In this political climate, the adamant refusal of the Dutch to relinquish control over West Irian highlighted residual colonial dominance.

Foreign policy was a major priority of Ali's second cabinet. It completed the work of its predecessor by securing the passage through parliament of a new Bill which abrogated the Round Table Conference Agreements in their entirety. Presidential assent was readily forthcoming. However, the economic relationship with the Dutch was not severed. Although Ali has claimed that 'the special privileges of the Dutch in Indonesia were abolished'[28], the Bill provided exemption for concession rights and licences and operating permits of enterprises not in conflict with the country's interests and development. In August, the government repudiated that portion of national debt assumed in 1949 which was calculated to represent the cost of Dutch military actions against the Republic. This limited measure was taken in the heady international climate generated by Egypt's nationalization of the Suez Canal the previous month. It had also been delayed until after the International Monetary Fund had agreed to grant a substantial credit to Indonesia. The evidence would suggest that while Ali's government was prepared to engage in a largely symbolic repudiation of colonial links, it was not willing to go much further at that juncture because of the utility of external economic associations. Formal provision had been made for the role of foreign capital in the five-year economic plan promulgated in October 1956. However, any element of inhibition at undertaking initiatives which might undermine international confidence in Indonesia was removed at the end of the following year with an acute revival of antagonism towards the Dutch over West Irian.

The principal shortcoming of Ali's second government was its failure to cope with the domestic challenge to its authority. The major source of this challenge was outer island dissidence arising from deep-seated economic grievance aggravated by conflicts within the armed forces. A corresponding polarization was reflected within the cabinet itself. In the event, the challenge was overcome by the combined powers of an extra-parliamentary coalition between the central command of the armed forces and President Sukarno. This coalition confronted regional rebellion both physically and politically and reasserted the unity of the

Republic which had been called into question. The manner and outcome of the resolution of the internal conflict by the middle of 1958 was of decisive political importance, with collateral consequences for foreign policy. Indeed, a conspicuous link between internal conflict and foreign policy was established as the result of proven Western involvement in regional rebellion on behalf of those interests identified with the crumbling parliamentary system. Regional rejection of the central government's authority in clandestine league with external forces served to justify the eventual overthrow of that system against a background of anti-Western sentiment. Such sentiment, as well as open hostility to the economic position of the resident Chinese, grew progressively during Ali's second term. Cultivated xenophobia had begun during his first term when a number of Dutch residents were arrested and tried on charges of subversive activity, in an attempt to demonstrate their complicity in Islamic rebellion.[29] Anti-Western feeling expressed itself violently in November 1956 after the Anglo-French invasion of Egypt, with mob attacks on the British and French embassies. Official condemnation of Israel, Britain and France contrasted with a statement of regret only at the intervention of the Soviet army in Hungary.

The Rise of Sukarno

Foreign policy took on added significance also because it was a sphere of competence in which President Sukarno had begun to assert himself as part of a broader challenge to the political system which had denied him constitutional power. His personal assertiveness became more manifest from the mid-1950s and was displayed in 1956 when he made extended overseas visits to the United States, Western Europe, the Soviet Union and China. His propensity for personal diplomacy was demonstrated in Moscow in September when he took the initiative in inspiring a joint communique, signed by Foreign Minister Ruslan Abdulgani and Russian deputy-Foreign Minister Andrei Gromyko, which reflected Soviet global priorities.[30] This initiative, taken without reference to Prime Minister Ali, was construed as an arrogation of a constitutional right, while the joint communique which included a controversial reference to military pacts caused additional offence in Jakarta where it aggravated intra-cabinet tensions. None the less, Sukarno's assertiveness in foreign policy was sustained as the parliamentary system began to break down under the strain of unstable coalition governments and the incipient political disintegration of the archipelagic state. In such circumstances, his strident advocacy of the claim to West Irian served both personal and national political needs.

The collapse of the system of parliamentary democracy was heralded in July 1956 when Mohammad Hatta announced his resignation as vice-President. He had been regarded as a representative of non-Javanese interests and his departure from office caused concern in the outer islands. At the end of the year, regional commanders in Sumatra rejected the authority of the central government in protest at the inequity of a foreign exchange rate system which deprived the region of a fair share of the wealth which its exports created. Against a background of political unrest and apparently inspired by his recent visit to China, Sukarno made a portentous public statement on 21 February 1957, which consolidated views which he had expressed over many months. He posed a reasoned philosophical challenge to the system of liberal democracy, which was represented as alien to Indonesian values and as responsible for the country's ills. This *konsepsi* or formula, which recommended the introduction of an alternative political system in harmony with the spirit of the Indonesian people, accelerated the momentum of political change. Sukarno's initiative drew a mixed response from the political parties. In early March, however, the military Territorial Commander in East Indonesia declared a state of war and siege and demanded extensive autonomy for his region and a much greater share of national revenues. On the 14th of the month, Ali Sastroamijoyo submitted the resignation of his government and Sukarno proclaimed a nationwide state of war and siege in an attempt to overcome, by legal means, the challenge from East Indonesia. This act, which served to undermine the status of the political parties, was construed by regional economic interests, and the political parties identified with them and with constitutionalism, as a blatant political affront. However, it brought together the central command of the armed forces and President Sukarno in a relationship which worked successfully to transform the nature of Indonesian politics and which had a major influence on the conduct and course of foreign policy. On 8 April, an extra-parliamentary business cabinet was established by presidential decree with Dr Djuanda Kartawidjaya as Prime Minister and Dr Subandrio, previously Ambassador in London and Moscow and Secretary General of the Foreign Ministry, as Foreign Minister.

The final act which transformed the pattern of Indonesian politics was inspired by a combination of domestic and external factors. West Irian served as the catalyst in this stormy process. The way in which this claim was treated by the UN General Assembly prompted the riposte of a decisive challenge to Dutch economic interests in Indonesia. In turn, this challenge aggravated regional dissent with which the exponents of parliamentary democracy became closely identified. External Western involvement in the regional rebellion made it possible for the issue to be represented as the survival of the Republic in its unitary form and not that of a parliamentary system which protected the interests of the surplus-producing outer islands against those of Javanese centralism.

In November 1957, the issue of West Irian was debated once more by the General Assembly of the United Nations; a third Indonesian initiative had failed the preceding February. This debate had been preceded by weeks of agitation in Indonesia during which Dutch enterprises had been boycotted and Dutch residents subjected to intimidation. The draft resolution before the twelfth session was quite innocuous in its appeal for a negotiated settlement to the dispute. However, the extra-parliamentary cabinet over which President Sukarno exercised political dominance had placed great public store on securing its passage. He had warned that in the event of its defeat 'we will use a new way in our struggle which will surprise the nations of the world'. In the United Nations, Foreign Minister Subandrio, who echoed his President's militant attitude, spoke in similar vein, and held out the prospect of Cold War tensions being invited into South-East Asia if Indonesia were thwarted. In due course, Subandrio's threat became reality as Indonesia played increasingly on America's fear of communism in order to bring indirect pressure on the Dutch.

On 29 November, the resolution failed to secure a two-thirds majority. The next day an unsuccessful attempt was made to assassinate Sukarno during a public visit to his children's school. The close succession of these events generated a fierce expression of anti-Dutch feeling. An official twentyfour-hour strike of all Indonesian workers in Dutch enterprises inaugurated extensive acts of expropriation in which the PKI and its allied trade union organization played a leading role. Prime Minister Djuanda placed all Dutch-owned estates and plantations under government control; this further accelerated the process of expropriation which was arrested only by military intervention. Of even greater international impact was the announcement early in December by the Minister of Justice, G. A. Maengkom, that 50,000 Dutch nationals would be expelled or repatriated in three stages. Subsequent official statements that the services of Dutch experts were still required did nothing to stem the ensuing exodus of more than 30,000, encouraged also by offers from The Hague of immediate repatriation.[31]

Inside Indonesia, the psychological exhilaration at expunging all vestiges of the colonial presence had its immediate costs in widespread economic dislocation and distress. For example, the seizure of the Dutch inter-island shipping line disrupted maritime communications throughout the archipelago. None the less, the Indonesian government persisted with a systematic nationalization of all Dutch-owned enterprises and set out also to revise the pattern of its international trade. International reaction, especially in Holland and Australia where attitudes hardened over West Irian, did not deflect the government from its course. In a report to parliament on West Irian in the second half of December, Subandrio reaffirmed that Indonesia was still prepared to seek a solution through negotiations, but added:[32]

> If, however, no purpose is being served, we shall feel compelled to embark upon a policy of precluding the development of Dutch interests in Indonesia, in the hope that this may be the way of inducing the Netherlands Government to take a wiser attitude.

Allied with bitterness towards the Dutch was growing resentment of the United States and its European associates. Open or tacit support for the Dutch position on West Irian was construed as an indication of a neo-colonial attitude. Subandrio made explicit the view that:

> In essentials, the countries that formerly had dominion over Asia and Africa are solidly united to protect their economic powers there which still constitute the basic foundations of their high standards of living.

This theme was to find recurrent expression and increasing prominence in the exposition of Indonesia's international outlook as President Sukarno assumed personal control of the conduct of foreign policy.

Apart from international reactions to the expropriations and expulsions, the militant pursuit of the claim to West Irian had a major domestic impact because of the link between the challenge to the Dutch economic presence and contention for political and economic advantage between the interests of Java and the outer islands. West Irian served as an instrument of domestic politics. As a national claim, it had the irrefutable objective of physically completing independence. In the process, it became a means of enforcing a centralised unity which had become subject to increasing challenge. The immediate consequence of action against the Dutch, in the light of the suspension of the parliamentary system, was an open expression of regional disunity. The ultimate outcome was the consolidation of Javanese-based interests. Indeed, at this juncture, foreign policy presided over by Sukarno and conducted by Subandrio had as primary reference the vision of a unitary state in which all centrifugal political and economic elements would be contained and overcome.

A maritime expression of that vision was a declaration on 13 December 1957, which extended the breadth of territorial waters to twelve miles and which also maintained:[33]

> All waters, surrounding, between and connecting the islands constituting the Indonesian state, regardless of their extension or breadth, are integral parts of the territory of the Indonesian state and, therefore, parts of the internal or national waters which are under the exclusive sovereignty of the Indonesian state.

This archipelagic declaration constituted a claim to the same quality of jurisdiction over waters surrounding and intersecting the island constituents of Indonesia as the government applied to its fragmented territory. The unique character of that claim had been influenced by the threat to the integrity of the state which had become increasingly manifest since Prime Minister Ali Sastroamijoyo had set up an inter-departmental committee during 1956 to revise the Dutch Territorial Sea Ordinance of 1939 which incorporated only a three-mile breadth of territorial sea. The incentive for revision was the forthcoming first international Conference on the Law of the Sea sponsored by the United Nations. However, conflict over West Irian with the Dutch who engaged in naval deployment close to Indonesia's shores, as well as concurrent regional dissent, made a legal formula which appeared to demonstrate the integral unity of a fragile distended archipelago very attractive. That formula was advanced by a young lawyer, Mochtar Kusumaatmadja, who, twenty years later, was to assume the office of Foreign Minister. His unprecedented legal encapsulation of the maritime interstices and bounds of the archipelagic state caught the mood of a government functioning under martial law which faced the prospect of the country falling apart. The decision of the cabinet was almost certainly influenced by the domestic and international reper-cussions of the failure yet again of the resolution in the UN General Assembly.

It was against the background of formal rejection of the central government's authority in February 1958 by a rebel administration in Sumatra that an Indonesian delegation attended the Law of the Sea Conference in Geneva later that month. At Geneva, Indonesia's archipelagic claim was defended against criticism from the United States, which had deployed a destroyer division through the Straits of Lombok and Makassar in January in order to assert a right of high seas passage. Speaking for Indonesia, former Foreign Minister Subarjo made the underlying purpose of his government explicit. He argued:[34]

If each of Indonesia's component islands were to have its own territorial sea, the exercise of effective control would be extremely difficult. . . . If the interjacent waters were to be regarded as high seas, the Indonesian population might in certain circumstances be left at the mercy of belligerent powers.

Such a worst-case scenario was given credence by the circumstances of regional rebellion which was centred in Sulawesi as well as in Sumatra. The measure of external involvement in these rebellions served to reinforce suspicions of Western intent and to vindicate a continuing commitment to a *Wawasan Nusantara* (Archipelago Outlook), which was reaffirmed by Sukarno by decree in February 1960.

The fortunes of the regional rebellion, which, for practical purposes, were dashed by mid-1958 after direct military intervention in support of the central government, are not a major concern of this study.[35] None the less, the episode was of decisive importance in consolidating a new pattern of politics in Indonesia with a corresponding international dimension. The regional rebels, led politically by Masjumi and Socialist Party notables alienated by the drift of events in Jakarta, had sought external support on the basis of a common anti-communism in advance of proclaiming a Revolutionary Government of the Republic of Indonesia (PRRI) in mid-February. The source of such support had been indicated earlier by the failure of the Jakarta government to secure a positive response from Washington for the purchase of arms, despite the recommendation of the ambassador.[36] This rebuff prompted the despatch of an arms-purchasing mission to Eastern Europe which reinforced American concern about the expansion of communist influence in Indonesia. Open sympathy for the regional rebels became evident four days before the formal rejection of the central government's authority, when the US Secretary of State, John Foster Dulles, declared at a press conference that the political system in Indonesia was not satisfactory to 'large segments of the Indonesian people'[37] American encouragement of the rebels by means of public statements and the clandestine supply of arms through regional partners was not sufficient to enable the Revolutionary Government in Sumatra and Sulawesi to establish the degree of territorial control which might have attracted recognition of even belligerent status. For example, no response was received to the appeal by the PRRI to overseas banks to freeze central government funds accruing from export earnings. American-owned Caltex Oil with wells in central Sumatra continued to pay royalties to Jakarta.

American involvement in the regional uprisings did little to help the rebels but much to fan the flames of anti-Western feeling in Jakarta. A display of US naval power, ostensibly to protect oil installations and to provide for the evacuation of civilians, only reinforced the Indonesian conviction that the United States was engaged in an attempt to undermine the integrity of the Republic. Indeed, Prime Minister Djuanda told the American Ambassador that:[38]

It now looked to the Indonesian Government as if the policy and purpose of the United States was to split Indonesia in two in order to ensure that at least one part of the country would remain non Communist.

Any prospect of more substantial American backing for the rebels was set aside by their rapid collapse and also by the acute embarrassment caused when a former American airforce officer engaged in a bombing raid over Ambon Harbour was shot down in the middle of May.[39] This incident, not announced in Jakarta for ten days, reversed the position of the US government, which had been advised by its embassy in Jakarta that the central army leadership, which had been instrumental in putting down the rebellion, was staunchly anti-communist. Within two days, Dulles had publicly condemned external intervention in the rebellion, and on 21 May the State Department granted export licences for the supply of small arms to Indonesia and announced a shipment of surplus rice. This shift in policy produced an Indonesian response; shortly afterwards, President Sukarno had lunch at the home of the American Ambassador.

The internal effect of the armed forces, success in overcoming, with relative speed, a regional rebellion seen to enjoy external support was to consolidate the position of the extra-parliamentary forces in command in Jakarta. The circumstances and failure of the rebellion discredited not only its active adherents but also notable political figures identified with the parliamentary system, who had refused to condemn the uprising out of hand because of sympathy with its aims. In addition, and importantly, the covert external patrons of the regionalist cause came in for a major share of political odium. Suspicions of nefarious intent were confirmed not only in the case of the United States but also of Taiwan, the Philippines and newly independent Malaya. The British still ensconced in Singapore and Northern Borneo were also regarded with mistrust because of the provision of facilities for the rebels. This legacy of suspicion and mistrust had its sequel in 1963 when Sukarno drew Indonesia into confrontation against the formation of the Federation of Malaysia, which was perceived as a vehicle to serve British neo-colonial interests. The only Western-oriented country with which there was a real improvement in relations was Japan. In the light of an evident need to compensate for a major decline in foreign-exchange earnings attendant on regional dissension, it was more than coincidence that the issue of reparations and a peace treaty was settled by December 1957. Sukarno paid the first of many visits to Tokyo in January 1958, Parliament approved the accord, and diplomatic relations were established in April. Japan proved to be a valuable source of much needed economic support throughout the entire period of Sukarno's effective rule.[40]

Volatility in domestic politics precipitated by impasse over the West Irian issue prompted corresponding changes in foreign policy which were expressed in an alternating alienation from, and accommodation with, the United States, against a background of resort to the Soviet bloc as a source of countervailing power. The return to an amicable relationship with the United States did not endure. The anti-communist emphasis in policy which became apparent once the regional uprising had been thwarted drew its strength from the disposition of the armed forces led by their Commander-in-Chief, Lt. General Abdul Haris Nasution. Support was attracted from the political parties including the PNI, which was disturbed by the electoral showing of the PKI in regional polls in Java in the middle of 1957. The increasing prominence and influence of the armed forces as an extra-parliamentary partner gave Sukarno cause for concern. He had just released himself from the constitutional confines of the parliamentary system; he was in no mood to become dependent, politically, on his physically stronger partner. Consequently, he set out to mobilize a mass constituency on the basis of an emotive nationalist symbolism to which the leadership of the armed forces would be obliged to defer, at least in public.

Sukarno's determination to command the political heights of the country was expressed in a practice of political agitation in which the Communist Party and its allied movements served as a primary vehicle of mass support. Moreover, foreign policy, for whose formulation Sukarno assumed the dominant role, was increasingly utilized as an instrument with which to keep political opponents off balance and to promote internal solidarity. It also took on an expressive and heroic quality as Sukarno, with encouragement from the armed forces, inducted Indonesia into a new political system which he claimed would return the country to the spirit of the revolution. Indeed, foreign policy was conducted as a continuation of a revolutionary struggle with the immediate priority of securing West Irian, which Sukarno described as 'a question of colonialism or independence'. In this respect, it was an expression of the domestic requirements of the political pattern which emerged with the breakdown of the parliamentary system.

A further feature of foreign policy was an attempt to extend the influence of Indonesia beyond regional bounds in order to revise the structure and rules of the international system. Sukarno played the principal role in an exercise designed to free the Republic from all forms of post-colonial bondage. Although this dimension of foreign policy also had a domestic function, Sukarno's standpoint represented continuity in outlook. In April 1955, in his opening address to the Asian-African Conference in Bandung, he had warned the delegates:[41]

And I beg of you, do not think of colonialism only in the classic form which we in Indonesia and our brothers in different parts of Asia and Africa knew. Colonialism has also its modern dress, in the form of economic control, intellectual control, actual physical control by a small but alien community within a nation.

If Sukarno's view suggested continuity, the political experience of Indonesia in the first decade of independence indicated discontinuity. Although foreign policy in that decade had served domestic requirements, it was subject to change in so far as the competitive pattern of politics also changed. In other words, the revised nature of foreign policy reflected a revision of that pattern of politics established on the morrow of independence. At the outset, foreign policy had been the victim of a competitive political system. With the breakdown of parliamentary democracy, it was employed as an instrument with which to control a successor political system which was no less competitive.

3 The Foreign Policy of Guided Democracy

The political system of Guided Democracy was inaugurated by President Sukarno on 5 July 1959 when he revoked the provisional constitution of 1950 and reinstated, by decree, the constitution which had been promulgated immediately after the proclamation of independence in 1945. This system of presidential rule had been in gestation for more than two years. It was justified as an appropriate Indonesian alternative to an imported liberal democracy and as a return to the true spirit of national revolution.[1] As an exercise in political nostalgia, it did not herald revolutionary change. Major economic upheaval had followed the expropriation of Dutch assets and the expulsion of Dutch nationals which permitted, in turn, greater patronage among an established elite, especially the armed forces. Radical change in political form had succeeded the regional uprisings precipitated by the actions against the Dutch. However, if the role of the political parties was undermined and Masjumi and the Socialist Party were actually proscribed, the structure of Indonesian elite society, distinguished by interlocking family-bureaucratic relationships, was altered only at the margins.[2]

The distinctive political features of Guided Democracy were two linked sets of competing coalition arrangements, different in kind yet sharing the common participation of Sukarno. Guided Democracy had been brought into being in the face of parliamentary resistance by the combined efforts of Sukarno and the armed forces. In this coalition, Sukarno represented revolutionary legitimacy, while the armed forces enjoyed the role of physical custodian of the integrity of the state. The latter justified their rising political prominence because of their success in crushing regional rebellion. Moreover, participation in economic management and civil administration in the wake of martial law and the expropriation of Dutch assets had given the armed forces a major stake in the prevailing political system. They had been a party to radical political change in an attempt to cope with a perceived crisis of national authority. As a corporate entity, they constituted a conservative force, expressed, above all, in bitter hostility towards the PKI.

Sukarno was only too conscious of the physical power deployed by his extra-parliamentary partner and also of the fact that he had cast off constitutional shackles without securing access to an assured political

54

power base. In consequence, he found it necessary to promote a countervailing coalition to his physically unequal one with the armed forces. Even before the formal advent of Guided Democracy, he had established a relationship of mutual support with the PKI which had pursued, with evident success, a national united front strategy. The PKI, through effective political appeal and organization, was in a position to deliver the mass support which Sukarno required, in part to compensate for a vulnerability to military pressure. Conscious of its own exposed position and the hostility of the armed forces, the PKI responded enthusiastically to Sukarno's political embrace and protection expressed in his acronym Nasakom. This concept joined together nationalist, religious and communist components as legitimate partners in the political system. In return, the Communists paid for political protection 'by accepting considerable emasculation'.[3] They were obliged to substitute the nationalist rhetoric of Sukarno for their own social goals and to refrain from industrial action.

Sukarno straddled the two sets of competing coalitions, holding them apart and, at the same time, maintaining his own position at the apex of a triangular relationship. One consequence of this triangular relationship between the President, the armed forces and the PKI was an immobilism in domestic policy expressed in a propensity for avoiding or putting off critical decisions. Moreover, as Daniel Lev has explained:[4]

> Soekarno himself never acquired an organisation capable of executing policy over the obstructions of vested political interests. Consequently, only those programs that did not threaten the elite could be attempted seriously and these frequently were in the realm of foreign policy.

The very nature of Guided Democracy, which became increasingly competitive and unstable over time, encouraged a disposition towards external initiatives which would serve as common denominators of political feeling and so sustain the prevailing pattern of power. For example, national revolution against the Dutch was a sacred symbol which had been upheld beyond independence because of the contentious issue of West Irian. In addition, the economic experience of the new Republic had given rise to an underlying belief that Indonesia had been cheated out of its inheritance not only because of residual Dutch entrenchment but also because of a dependent position within a Western-dominated international system. Foreign policy issues which evoked a nationalist response gave Sukarno great freedom of political manoeuvre without arousing internal discord. In this respect, his motives were undoubtedly mixed. Personal vanity and position coexisted with a concern to promote national unity, and there could be no better instrument in the context of Guided Democracy than foreign policy. In his autobiography, he alludes to this priority:[5]

> Indonesia must overcome self-consciousness and inferiority. She needs confidence. That I must give her before I'm taken away. Today Sukarno alone is the cohesive factor in Indonesia. After I'm gone the only cement to hold the islands together will be their national pride.

Sukarno used foreign policy issues to sustain national unity and to underpin a pattern of power of which he was the principal beneficiary. In this undertaking, he employed political skills with which he was richly endowed. He was a magnetic personality and a master of political communication in the Indonesian milieu. His expression of revolutionary ardour was beyond public question and served as ideological orthodoxy. Foreign policy became Sukarno's personal domain. And in his exercise of a prerogative role, he expounded strong convictions about Indonesia's place in the world. In the same way that, at a similar time, President de Gaulle became the personal embodiment of France, Sukarno attained international prominence as the voice of Indonesia. He used his great oratorical powers to express a personal and national sense of frustration, which was reflected only in part in an inability to restore the territory of West Irian to the Republic. That sense of frustration arose also from resentment that a state with the fifth largest population in the world, with rich natural resources and with extensive territory in a strategic location had not been accorded corresponding international standing and respect in the Western world. Sukarno's practice of foreign policy constituted an attempt to transform a limited international role and also to attain a position of eminence and leadership among other post-colonial states. In the event, his dreams were never realized. The Western world was never prepared to accept him on his own terms. He was derided as a sawdust Caesar whose profligate conduct of his country's economic affairs and his own personal extravagances and self-indulgences undermined the credence of any cause he sought to advance. The contrasting adulation which he received in the Soviet Union and China was a contrived and cynical exercise in the pursuit of political interest which, none the less, appealed to his vanity.[6] Afro-Asian governments entertained mixed feelings towards the Indonesian President. They were happy to applaud his fulminations against imperialism but were less impressed with his nostrums or by the extent to which he became a source of division within their ranks.

For a period of just over six years, the aspirations of Indonesian foreign policy were expounded with unprecedented verve and vigour. Sukarno spoke as if it were his historic mission to effect a political reckoning whereby redress against the evils of imperialism would be sought and secured. His condemnation of imperialism in general constituted a development of views which he had expressed before the onset of the Pacific War, drawing in part on the ideas of Marx and Lenin.[7] Such consistent views had been sustained by the experience of the struggle against the Dutch, during which the West's ambivalent stand had almost permitted the Republic to be smothered at birth. They were reinforced by Indonesia's trading dependence on the international capitalist economy and by the course of regional rebellion during which the involvement of the United States and its Asian clients had become manifest. In addition, Sukarno's rhetoric was inspired by a measure of personal animus. Like other leaders of post-colonial states who become the subject of a cult of personality, he was hypersensitive to slights, real or imagined: He held a strong grudge against President Einsenhower for not displaying appropriate courtesy and consideration during his first visit to the United States and also for not taking up a personal invitation to visit Indonesia. He complained in his memoirs that 'Twice Eisenhower publicly humiliated me. When he was in Manila, practically on my doorstep, he refused to visit Indonesia'.[8] A former American Ambassador to Jakarta has recorded the impact on Sukarno of the rejection of his invitation: 'I literally saw Sukarno's jaw drop as he read President Eisenhower's letter. He couldn't believe it.'[9] By contrast, Sukarno was accorded extraordinary deference on visits to the Soviet Union and China which gave him and Indonesia a desired sense of respect.

As a general foreign policy objective, Sukarno set out to challenge the successor to Dutch colonialism described as the forces of *Nekolim*; an acronym for neocolonialism, colonialism and imperialism, coined by Army Commander Lt. General Achmad Yani. One of Sukarno's biographers has explained that Nekolim was the 1960s version of the anti-imperialism of the 1920s, designed to fit a situation where direct colonial rule had been thrown off but where imperialism in the form of economic domination or of Western spheres of influence still existed.[10] In posing this challenge, Sukarno demonstrated that he was a decade ahead of his time. Well before the conventional wisdom of a New International Economic Order was articulated in 1974 by the General Assembly of the United Nations, he had begun to question the structure of the international system. The germ of Sukarno's international outlook was exposed first in a speech which he delivered to the regular session of the General Assembly in 1960 which was distinguished by the unprecedented number of heads of government in attendance. Without openly violating the canons of non-alignment, he sought to shift the balance of public attention from threats to world peace arising from the entrenched antagonism between the global powers to an allegedly more deep-rooted source of international tension. He maintained that:[11]

> Imperialism and colonialism and the continued forcible divisions of nations – I stress those words – is at the root of almost all international and threatening evil in this world of ours. Until these evils of a hated past are ended, there can be no rest or peace in all this world.

In this speech, in which Sukarno indicated that Indonesia's tolerance over West Irian had come to an end, the failings of the United Nations were represented as a product of that same Western system which had given rise to imperialism. By way of remedy, he suggested the incorporation of the *Pancasila* (the five philosophical precepts of the Indonesian state) in the Charter of the United Nations, and that its headquarters be transferred from New York to a site either in Asia or Africa or Geneva. The speech marked a considered bid to lead the so-called emerging nations on whom he called to break with the past and 'To Build the World Anew'; this was the title of his address.

A more explicit elaboration of Sukarno's international outlook was presented at the first conference of non-aligned states which convened in Belgrade in September 1961. In a speech entitled 'From Non-Alignment to Coordinated Accumulation of Moral Force Toward Friendship, Peace and Social Justice Among Nations', he expounded a considered critique of the structure of the international system. In addition, he now challenged the orthodox doctrine of the non-aligned movement itself, which had been identified with the views of Jawaharlal Nehru, supported by Nasser and Tito. They had conceived of non-alignment as a positive response to the Cold War rivalry between the United States and the Soviet Union. This rivalry was regarded as the principal threat to world peace, given the danger and consequences of a nuclear exchange. Sukarno set his face against this interpretation of the pathology of the international system. He argued:[12]

> Prevailing world opinion today would have us believe that the real source of international tension and strife is ideological conflict between the great powers. I think that is not true. There is a conflict which cuts deeper into the flesh of man and that is the conflict between the new emergent forces for freedom and justice and the old forces of domination, the one pushing its head relentlessly through the crust of the earth which has given it its lifeblood, the other striving desperately to retain all it can trying to hold back the course of history.

The conventional view of non-alignment had been predicated on the assumption that post-colonial states, acting as a third force, would not only avoid the entanglements of the Cold War but also serve as a vehicle for conciliation and mediation capable of moderating international tensions. In Sukarno's schema, there was no room for such a third force, because the international system in his interpretation comprised a bipartite structure which reflected an endemic conflict between justice and injustice without any possibility of coexistence. Although this exposition did not inhibit him from participating in a conventional non-aligned exercise to request both the United States and the Soviet Union to curb their nuclear arsenals and test programmes, he sustained his viewpoint. Indeed, it was expressed in increasingly strident form as the foreign police of Indonesia became more militant. For example, on 17 August 1963 in his annual speech commemorating the proclamation of independence, Sukarno described the world as divided between the New Emerging Forces and the Old Established Forces. The former were described as being composed of 'the Asian nations, the African nations, the Latin American nations, the nations of the Socialist countries, the progressive groups in the capitalist countries'.[13]

In putting forward a revisionist view of international society, Sukarno represented Indonesia as a militantly dynamic member of a constellation of progressive forces charged by history with confronting and confounding the reactionary forces of oppression and exploitation. More to the point, he virtually claimed the leading role in this constellation and sought to underpin this claim through state visits and international public occasions. With Chinese finance, he enjoyed minor success subsequently in giving the New Emerging Forces institutional form when Jakarta served as the venue for the first Games of the New Emerging Forces or, in acronym, Ganefo. Success was denied, however, in his attempt to promote a second conference of African and Asian states, as a preliminary to holding, in Jakarta, the first ever conference of the New Emerging Forces. Apart from the rhetorical and romantic quality of exhortation and deployment of symbols which served an important domestic political function, the revisionist view of the international system articulated by Sukarno had a direct relationship to the prosecution of Indonesia's foreign policy goals. His theory of international relations constituted a moral claim expressed in terms of distributive justice, which had been denied to the Republic. Moreover, he sought to set unrealized national objectives over West Irian and later Malaysia within a moral context, in which diplomatic support would be forthcoming from other progressive and deprived states. In addition, the major powers, but more particularly, the United States, which enjoyed greatest leverage over Indonesia's adversaries, might be persuaded to act to Jakarta's political advantage because of their global competitiveness.[14]

During the period of Guided Democracy, the foreign policy of Indonesia assumed a rumbustious quality which reflected Sukarno's temperament and the frenetic nature of domestic politics. None the less, there was a strong line of continuity in its actual practice which originated with the experience of attaining independence. It has been suggested earlier that because a formative experience of engaging great power support had resulted in political success, it gave rise to a propensity to apply this tried formula on behalf of the independent Republic. The essence of this formula was that, through diplomacy, Indonesia would not only parade internationally the merits and justice of its cause but would also demonstrate how its realization would serve the interests of a great power moved by Cold War considerations; in each case, the United States. The application of this formula with mixed success may be observed in Indonesia's prosecution of disputes over West Irian and the advent of Malaysia, which constituted the major foreign policy issues of the period of Guided Democracy. Its application was distinguished, however, by a coercive element which had not been present to the same extent during the struggle for independence. It was marked also by the assertion of public values which were not in congruence with those upheld in Washington – in contrast to the period of national revolution. Those values were a product of the ideological dominance which Sukarno exercised and which were expressed, above all, in the notion of continuous revolution. Revolution was a sacred symbol which entered all sectors of public life and served a domestic political purpose. One indication of the extent to which Sukarno's thought was actively inculcated into Indonesia's foreign service was provided by an address to a departmental indoctrination course delivered by Dr Subandrio in February 1962. He explained to his colleagues that they should understand that they were conducting two aspects of diplomacy: 'conventional diplomacy and diplomacy as an instrument of revolution, the one complementing the other, each giving content to the other'. He made explicit his preference for revolutionary diplomacy:[15]

> Therefore, should it, for instance, be necessary to choose between a candidate diplomat who is skilled only in the technical knowledge of diplomacy, and a candidate who understands only this second aspect of diplomacy, my choice would fall upon the second candidate, since technical knowledge can be learned in six months, but for true understanding of this second aspect conviction and realisation are needed and these cannot be taught.

Subandrio's injunction echoed faithfully the rhetoric and values of his political master.

Confrontation over West Irian

Two foreign policy issues dominated the period of Guided Democracy, against a background of apparent leftward drift in domestic politics and a corresponding alignment internationally, especially in relations with the People's Republic of China. These two issues, which virtually succeeded one another as touchstones of nationalist faith, were West Irian and Malaysia . They exemplified, in different ways, the imperialist influences which Sukarno was determined to expunge from Indonesia's environment. He had described West Irian as 'a colonial sword poised over Indonesia'. His determination to secure its adhesion to the Republic was almost certainly reinforced by the recent experience of regional rebellion. Moreover, it could be argued that as long as the Dutch retained control of the territory, a threat would be posed to the integrity of the socially diverse and distended archipelagic state. The separate existence of West Irian challenged the territorial *raison d'être* of the Republic based on the historical unity of the Netherlands East Indies.[16] Accordingly, West Irian was perceived as the fundamental symbol of nationalist fulfilment. In additon, it constituted a matter of personal prestige. Time and time again, Sukarno had committed himself to recover the territory within a limited period of time. Ultimately, he proved successful.

The inauguration of Guided Democracy absorbed most of his political energies, so that Sukarno could give serious attention to West Irian only after he had consolidated his domestic position by mid-1960. In his strategy for restoration of the territory, he employed a method of coercive diplomacy to engender a sense of international crisis. In the process, the competing attentions of the Soviet Union and the United States were skilfully engaged. In due course, the latter found itself obliged to calculate the political costs of denying Indonesia's national demand. It should be appreciated that the claim to West Irian was perceived and represented as a truly national demand which enjoyed undoubted popular support, despite its exploitation by Sukarno. In addition, its militant pursuit served the interests of the armed forces in justifying an expanding budget and huge arms transfers, as well as a dominant role in public life. For its part, the PKI had no alternative but to support nationalist agitation in the hope of accelerating an anti-imperialist drift in foreign policy which might serve its domestic political advantage. In this respect, the West Irian issue constituted a common denominator of political interests and served to underpin the fragile system of Guided Democracy.[17]

The vociferous campaign to recover the territory, which had reached one peak at the end of 1957, catered therefore for a variety of political purposes. For example, one author has observed that 'Whatever genuine national indignation over New Guinea there might have been behind it, this frontal attack on Dutch business was essentially a manoeuvre in the internal struggle for power'.[18] If also a diversion in a period of economic hardship and political competition, the issue of

West Irian constituted the external symbol of the continuation of the revolutionary struggle. Such ceaseless struggle was the essence of Sukarno's public message. As a national symbol of relentless struggle, West Irian was sacrosanct and an inviolate instrument for political mobilization and solidarity. None the less, it was not sufficient for Sukarno to rally support and contain internal rivalries by making West Irian the centrepiece of his public utterances on foreign policy. He was obliged to demonstrate progress in pursuit of a claim which he had made a test of his own credibility. The expropriation of Dutch assets and the expulsion of Dutch nationals had produced a transient electric effect and had provided also an important stock of patronage with which to purchase political support. And yet, despite the financial loss and human distress, the Dutch adjusted resolutely to the traumatic experience without impeding the evident progress of their national economy. With political resilience they responded to Indonesia's exercise in intimidation by going ahead with preparations for internal self-government in West New Guinea with open encouragement from Australia.[19] In addition, the action against Dutch assets and nationals had served as the precipitating factor in regional rebellion in which the prinicipal outer islands of the Republic, and not just West Irian, had escaped the control of the central government.

In effect, the reassertion of control by Jakarta over Sumatra and Sulawesi was linked to the restoration of West Irian. In order to accomplish the first priority, it became necessary to display and deploy a military capability which could be used to accomplish the second. Although Sukarno never authorised taking West Irian by storm, such a prospect was central to the practice of coercive diplomacy which he employed in order to encourage diplomatic influence to be brought to bear on the recalcitrant Dutch. It would appear that Sukarno had set in train negotiations for arms transfers from the Soviet Union in the course of his first visit to Moscow in August/September 1956.[20] His object was not only to underpin Indonesia's claim with military substance but also to create Western alarm at the corresponding alignment of his government, which could be channelled into pressure against the Dutch. A credit of US$100 m. served as collateral in negotiations with East European allies of the Soviet Union which bore fruit in time for initial arms deliveries to be employed in putting down the regional rebellion. For example, jet fighters from Czechoslovakia played an important role in denying the rebels air superiority in the eastern archipelago.[21] If by the middle of May 1958 the US Government had relented in its attitude to its Indonesian counterpart by making provision for the supply of light arms for infantry battalions and aircraft parts, a steady flow of heavier equipment came from Czechoslovakia and Poland. Sixty jet fighters and twenty bombers from the former and two destroyers, two submarines and torpedo craft from the latter had more direct relevance for a military campaign to recover West Irian. The flow of heavy military equipment increased concurrently with a growing warmth in relations with Moscow. Nikita Khrushchev visited Indonesia in February 1960 with a credit worth US$250 m. in his baggage, and also bestowed a good measure of impact aid including a 200-bed hospital. The campaign to liberate West Irian which had intensified during the course of 1960 assumed a more intimidating character in the following year, when General Nasution led two arms-purchasing missions to the Soviet Union where he concluded agreements for additional credits to the order of US$450 m. The cumulative expenditure on arms transfers gave Indonesia a substantial military establishment. By the end of 1961, much of the complement of aircraft and naval vessels purchased had arrived including MiG-19 fighters and TU-16 long-range bombers, as well as a Sverdlov class cruiser and missile-firing patrol vessels. Indonesia had become the largest non-communist recipient of military aid from the Soviet bloc and the largest recipient of economic credits after India and Egypt.[22]

The dramatic moves at the end of 1957 had been a mixed blessing but had not intimidated the Dutch; nor had Subandrio's threat of 'confrontation', described as a contest of power in all fields, uttered at the onset of Guided Democracy in July 1959. The Dutch responded by despatching military reinforcements to West New Guinea. In August 1960, President Sukarno announced a break in diplomatic relations with The Hague as a riposte to Holland's flag-showing dispatch of its only aircraft carrier, the *Karel Doorman*, with destroyer escorts to New Guinea waters. This measure also did not constitute an effective exercise of pressure but came as an anti-climax in the wake of the expropriation of Dutch assets. The threat to break off diplomatic relations with Japan if the *Karel Doorman* was permitted to call at Yokohama was an indication of Indonesia's determination, but failed to impress the Dutch. In the circumstances, it became necessary to mobilize more effective pressure. As at the time of independence, the position of the United States was decisive because, unlike the Soviet Union or the Afro-Asian states, it was able to exercise leverage on the Netherlands Government. Sukarno set out to transform the US government's attitude over West Irian from a formal neutrality by intensifying the practice of coercive diplomacy. Underlying the combination of limited probes below the threshold of a *casus belli* and dramatic political gestures was a threat to act in a way that would damage the security interests of the United States in South-East Asia. He had long impressed American ambassadors with this prospect. For example, John Allison briefly *en poste* between 1957 and early 1958 records 'Our interest lay more in keeping Indonesia out of the Communist camp than in worrying about ruffling the feelings of the Dutch'.[23] His immediate successor, Howard Jones, has indicated a sense of empathy with Sukarno's overall strategy in explaining that 'Only a clear threat to the peace of the area, of such a nature as to force American involvement in a conflict in which we had no interest, would move Washington'.[24]

If Sukarno could not move the government in The Hague directly, he would do so by moving that in Washington. However, the Eisenhower Administration was not susceptible to such a strategy, being influenced by a strong sense of personal distaste for the Indonesian President. Despite its more accommodating attitude from the middle of 1958, it none the less refused to supply heavy military equipment in response to a request through General Nasution in October 1960. It was only with the advent of the Kennedy Administration in January 1961, which coincided with the despatch of an Indonesian arms-purchasing mission to Moscow led by General Nasution, that American attitudes began to change. In April, President Sukarno visited Washington and was received with cordiality by the new incumbent of the White House. President Kennedy indicated a willingness to send an aid survey team to Indonesia to prepare a report on possible assistance for the country's eight-year economic plan. Although West Irian was not mentioned in the joint communique and there was no formal indication of any reappraisal of America's position towards the dispute, a representative of the US government was conspicuously absent from the ceremonial convening of the Dutch-inspired New Guinea council which took place in the same month as Sukarno's visit to Washington. Although this gesture indicated that the United States did not wish to be identified with Dutch plans for self-government, progress in that direction created a sense of urgency for Indonesia. It has been pointed out that 'a markedly anti-Indonesian Papuan nationalism was arising'.[25] The prospect of some kind of independent status for the western half of the island by the end of the decade foreshadowed a possible decline in Afro-Asian support for Indonesia's cause, which had been attracted on the ground that the dispute was over the residual presence of colonialism. In the circumstances, Sukarno sought to heighten the sense of crisis. During the course of 1961, the prospect of a military solution was indicated without repudiating resort to diplomacy. Indeed, Indonesia took the issue of West Irian to the United Nations in October without success, but derived satisfaction from the rejection by the General Assembly of a Dutch proposal for trusteeship status for the territory.

The Dutch initiative reflected a growing sense of international isolation and also an awareness of the demerits of sustaining an expensive commitment to West New Guinea in the light of the shift in the balance of local military advantage and the attendant prospect of armed conflict. Holland's desire to be relieved of responsibility after twelve years did not constitute a willingness to transfer the territory to Indonesia. UN endorsement of the trusteeship proposal would have had the ultimate effect of forestalling the extension of Indonesian sovereignty. In this abortive exercise, the Dutch had been assisted briefly by Malaysia's Prime Minister, Tunku Abdul Rahman, who indicated interest in a UN role while seeking to mediate in the dispute. Dr Subandrio retorted 'We cannot accept anything less than a complete transfer of sovereignty from the Netherlands to Indonesia'. In Jakarta, evident resentment was expressed at the lack of absolute support from a neighbouring head of government, whose credentials were suspect because he had not led a revolutionary struggle for national independence. In effect, Tunku Abdul Rahman had fallen victim to an internal Indonesian conflict. His diplomatic venture reflected apprehension on the part of Defence Minister and Army Chief of Staff, General Nasution, at the incessant agitation and bellicosity over West Irian which appeared to be serving the political interests of the PKI.[26] None the less, the episode left a legacy of bad feeling between Jakarta and Kuala Lumpur which revived with the onset of confrontation across the Strait of Malacca.

By the end of 1961, a sense of impending climax seemed to envelop the dispute over West Irian. In December, Sukarno issued a People's Triple Command for the Liberation of West Irian, known in the heroic acronymic language of the time as Trikora. This symbol of intent displayed on the anniversary of the Dutch second 'police action', authorised total popular mobilization. A military command charged with liberation was established, accompanied by increased infiltration by sea and parachute drops into West Irian. Concurrently, Subandrio reaffirmed the application of confrontation in all fields 'which means we will confront the Dutch hostility with a similar attitude in the political, economic and if necessary in the military field'.[27] The concept of confrontation, introduced over two years previously, indicated Indonesia's commitment to a coercive diplomacy. The term was to be revived when Malaysia replaced West Irian as the object of anti-imperialist rancour.

Although Sukarno threatened war, he did not have recourse to it. None the less, by promoting an amosphere of crisis, he succeeded in so alarming the US Government that it felt obliged to undertake a decisive initiative to resolve the dispute to Indonesia's advantage.[28] Ambassador Jones has offered an insight into the coercive diplomatic mode adopted by Sukarno:[29]

He was a master at painting himself into a corner and waiting for someone to rescue him. In this situation with the help of the Russians, he created a real threat of war.

President Kennedy had called on Indonesia and the Dutch not to use force. Sukarno's response had been to demand that the American Government intervene in the dispute in order to prevent a 'use of force' provoked by Dutch attempts to set up an independent Papua.[30] Moreover, in January 1962, he dispatched Subandrio to Washington to point out to the American President the prospect of domestic communist advance if the dispute was not resolved in Indonesia's favour. In the event, he succeeded in attracting the kind of third-party intervention he had long sought. In February, Robert Kennedy, the Attorney General and the President's brother, travelled to Jakarta and The Hague with the object of promoting negotiations between the two sides. Prior to the visits, the Dutch had been informed that they could not rely on America's assistance should a physical confrontation occur over the territory. In consequence, a corresponding shift occurred in the attitude of the Australian government which further weakened the diplomatic position of the Dutch whose Prime Minister had already indicated a willingness to enter negotiations without any preconditions.

Robert Kennedy's mission was a diplomatic success. He secured Sukarno's agreement to Indonesian participation in negotiations with the Dutch under the auspices of U Thant, then acting Secretary-Geneal of the United Nations, but with a senior American diplomat in attendance as mediator. The format for negotiations reproduced the diplomatic circumstances in which Indonesia had attained independence, with the striking difference that the armed strength of the Republic now made it more of a force on its own behalf in prosecuting the claim to West Irian. Indeed, the onus for the success or failure of the talks which began outside Washington in March 1962 was placed firmly on the United States. Subandrio has been quoted by his successor as Foreign Minister as pointing out to President Kennedy 'that the problem of war and peace in the Pacific was henceforth in the hands of the President of the United States'.[31] The object of Indonesia's diplomatic endeavour was to impress on the US government that it would be serving its own self-interest in helping to detach West Irian from Dutch control. Adverse consequences would follow from an unwillingness to heed such advice.

The course of the negotiations did not run smoothly. The Dutch attempted to make any transfer of the territory conditional on the receipt of satisfactory assurances over self-determination which the Indonesians viewed as a matter which had been settled in 1949. The talks were suspended within three days when the Indonesian side made it clear that they were prepared only to discuss the transfer of administration in West Irian. Overshadowing the negotiations, which were conducted by Ellsworth Bunker, the American mediator, was the prospect of a military assault on the territory. From April up to August

when formal discussions were concluded at the United Nations, intermittent infiltration, as well as a spectacular parachute drop over the
town of Merauke, served to sustain the atmosphere of crisis. In July, an
open deployment of Indonesian forces for invasion took place. Adam
Malik, then Ambassador to Moscow, has claimed that 'By July 1962, the
strength of the Indonesian Armed Forces had already reached the point
that a full-scale invasion of West Irian could be successfully
performed'.[32] The two delegations returned to the conference table in
July, by which stage Ellsworth Bunker had succeeded, by protracted
personal diplomacy, in fashioning a compromise agreement which
incorporated the principle of a transfer of administration to Indonesia.
The Indonesians accepted an indirect mode of transfer and provision
for some expression of self-determination by the Papuan population. A
final accord was concluded on 15 August 1962, which allowed Sukarno
to parade his undoubted triumph in his annual Independence Day
address. The central feature of the agreement was provision for an
initial transfer of administration to UN authority (effective from 1
October) and then for a final transfer to Indonesian control after 1 May
1963. In addition, it was stipulated that an 'act of free choice' with UN
advice, assistance and participation would take place before the end of
1969 in order to determine whether or not the inhabitants of the
territory wished to remain subject to Indonesian jurisdiction. A
subsequent compromise permitted the Indonesian national flag to be
hoisted in place of the Dutch flag beside that of the United Nations on
31 December 1962, which served to redeem Sukarno's public promise
that West Irian would be restored to Indonesia by the end of the year.

A face-saving agreement concluded through American diplomatic
intervention and mediation had brought to a close a bitter dispute which
had compounded the sour relationshp between Indonesia and Holland
obtaining on the morrow of independence. At one level, the realization
of the longstanding claim marked the fulfilment of a legitimate nationalist aspiration perceived as an integral part of the struggle for
independence. The dispute over West Irian had served also as a catalyst
in accelerating the pace of internal political change and in inaugurating
a pattern of politics kept in unstable equilibrium by revolutionary
expression, if not revolutionary practice. For President Sukarno, whose
personality and ideological formulas dominated this pattern of politics,
the West Irian settlement constituted a personal triumph. Of undoubted significance was the fact that this achievement had been
accomplished by coercive diplomacy. The ultimate sanction of unleashing the armed forces had proved unnecessary. West Irian had been
restored to the Republic, in great part, by Sukarno's ability to use
Soviet arms transfers to persuade the government of the United States
of the political utility of persuading, in turn, the Netherlands govern-

ment to revise its adamant opposition to transferring the territory to Indonesia.[33] A variant of the diplomatic technique, tried and tested at the culmination of the independence struggle, had been employed with corresponding success. However, the essential nature of the political system of Guided Democracy had not changed as a consequence. Sukarno had demonstrated that his political skills and revolutionary fervour could secure national goals. The triumph over West Irian sustained him at the pinnacle of the political system. And yet his apparent dominance in political life was not underpinned by a power structure. Accordingly, his propensity to indulge in revolutionary romanticism was reinforced because of the need to contain the centrifugal political forces which comprised Guided Democracy. His international outlook was strengthened because of domestic political priorities.

Sukarno's international horizons extended beyond the inhospitable mountains and forests of West Irian to the imperialist citadels of the international system. A senior State Department official directly concerned with the negotiations between Indonesia and Holland has commented that the lesson of West Irian for the Indonesians was that it was possible to force the Old Established Forces to accommodate to nationalist aspiration: 'They were now familiar with the techniques of "confrontation diplomacy" and those techniques had worked'.[34] Diplomatic success over West Irian did not dull Sukarno's appetite for further revolutionary triumphs. Indeed, in so far as the mode of its realization was an expression of the nature of Guided Democracy, a return to mundane political priorities would have undermined Sukarno's personal dominance. In August 1960, he had declared 'I am crazed, I am obsessed by the Romanticism of Revolution', and then admonished 'Let there be none among us who seek to amend or to modulate the revolutionary spirit'. Apart from personal inclination, it served Sukarno's political purpose to sustain a sense of drama and crisis in public life and to uphold a romantic revolutionary spirit which all groups in society were obliged to respect and endorse or suffer the risks of political excommunication. Furthermore, given the fragile balance of internal forces which made for immobilism in domestic policy, the most fruitful field for pursuing 'the romanticism of revolution' was in foreign policy.

Domestic Imperatives and Foreign Policy

An immediate opportunity for engaging in this endeavour arose within days of the settlement of the West Irian dispute. Jakarta had been chosen as the venue for the Fourth Asian Games. In July 1959, the

Soviet government had allocated the equivalent of US$12.5 m. to cover the costs of constructing a stadium with a capacity for 120,000 spectators, as well as auxiliary sports centres. The Japanese had been prevailed upon to build a new hotel. The occasion had warranted extensive road developments in the vicinity of the games site and was being treated as of national importance. It served an important symbolic purpose in that Sukarno could demonstrate to the ill-fed and ill-clad inhabitants of the capital and its environs that Indonesia enjoyed considerable international standing. Though the Soviet Union had advanced a great proportion of the finance for the spectacle, in addition to providing substantial arms shipments, the close relationship between Jakarta and Moscow, which had been inspired by the imperative of West Irian, had passed its peak. Concurrently, a progressive improvement had begun to take place in relations with the people's Republic of China from a low point in 1959 when the government in Peking had reacted stormily to attempts by the Indonesian army to implement a government decree prohibiting alien (i.e. resident Chinese) participation in retail trade outside of the major cities. It has been suggested that the manner of the military administration of this decree constituted an attempt by the army to pick a quarrel with China which could be used to domestic advantage in rivalry with the PKI.[35] At the height of the dispute, Foreign Minister Subandrio, who had travelled to China to try to mend diplomatic fences, was summoned from his hotel bed in the early hours and reportedly threatened by his counterpart, Chen Yi, to the effect that 'if Indonesia did not rescind its anti-Chinese measures, Peking would call on the Singapore Chinese to launch a trade boycott to bring Indonesia economically to its knees'.[36] Both governments found it politic to back away from confrontation and to bury their differences, exemplified, on the Indonesian side, by ratification of the dual nationality treaty of 1955 in January 1960.

The revision of relations between Indonesia and China occurred in the context of the public emergence of the Sino-Soviet conflict. That conflict had its roots in China's resentment of the willingness of the Soviet Union to give up shared international goals and to accommodate itself to coexistence with the United States based on fear of nuclear war. It may be argued that by embarking on a policy that was dignified later by the term *détente*, the Soviet Union had relinquished its credentials for membership of Sukarno's New Emerging Forces. Indeed, the Soviet Union, in public doctrinal debate with China, began to identify itself with an international order which Sukarno wished to challenge. From its position in this theocratic political feud, the People's Republic emerged as a reliable champion of Indonesia's international outlook. Its government espoused a global revisionism and a militant opposition to imperialism which matched and endorsed the revolutionary rhetoric of the government in Jakarta. Sukarno had never exhibited Sino-phobic tendencies; nor, in his attempt to promote internal unity and solidarity, had he sought to exploit the deep-seated resentment of the resident Chinese community. His first visit to China in October 1956 had been somewhat of a revelation. His impression of a state which had freed itself unaided from a semi-colonial condition and which had established a structure of authority which engendered discipline and economic progress is believed to have reinforced his conviction that a Guided Democracy was an appropriate remedy for Indonesia's fragmented and debilitated condition. By April 1961, relations between Indonesia and China had recovered sufficiently for Foreign Minister Chen Yi to pay a visit to Jakarta where he signed a treaty of friendship. China, from a position of relative international isolation, was receptive to Sukarno's proposal to convene another conference of Asian and African states in which it would participate, unlike the forthcoming conference of non-aligned states. In June, Sukarno paid another visit to Peking following a stay in Moscow. In October the Chinese government granted Indonesia loans worth over US$30 m. in addition to credits worth US$41 m. allocated in 1958 and 1959. By the time the Asian Games were held in Jakarta, the evident political harmony between the two states made the relationship with China of special importance. Indeed, when anti-Chinese riots occurred in West Java in May 1963, the government in Peking turned a blind eye.

Just prior to the opening of the games, a dispute arose between the Indonesian Organising Committee and the Asian Games Federation over the participation of athletes from Taiwan and Israel. Although assurances had been provided that political criteria would not be used to deny entry to any national team, up to a week before the opening of the games invitations had not been received in either Taipei or Tel Aviv. In effect, the Indonesian Organising Committee had its hands tied. The Foreign Ministry was not prepared to issue visas to conspicuous representatives of Old Established Forces and to alienate patrons among the New Emerging Forces. Moreover, in the case of Israel, there was Muslim opinion to consider. A member of the executive committee of the Asian Games Federation from Taiwan was put back unceremoniously on a plane for Bangkok after arriving in Jakarta on a flight from the Thai capital without a visa. The repercussions of this incident were felt immediately. The Israeli team withdrew from the games rather than be humiliated either by being refused entry or by studied indifference to its entreaties for a visa by the Indonesian Organising Committee. Patronage of the games was withdrawn by the International Olympic Committee, while the International Amateur Athletics Federation threatened to withdraw recognition if visas were not granted. In the event, the Fourth Asian Games were opened officially on time and with due ceremony by President Sukarno in the absence of teams from Taiwan and Israel because Japan, in particular, was not prepared to jeopardize a burgeoning economic relationship by boycotting the occasion.

The matter did not rest there. M. N. Sondhi, an Indian vice-President of the Asian Games Federation, sought to have the status of the games nullified. This initiative was construed as a personal insult to Sukarno and a national insult to Indonesia. In consequence, Sondhi was subject to inspired intimidation and was obliged to leave the country. India's embassy was attacked by a rented mob while its competitors were booed, as was its national flag during the closing ceremony. This unsavoury episode reflected, as well as contributed to, a growing coolness in relations between Indonesia and India which also had a personal dimension. Sukarno and Nehru had ceased to share a common outlook. There had been profound differences between the two national leaders at the first meeting of non-aligned states in Belgrade. These differences became more acute, concurrently with the Sino-Indian conflict and the progressive intensification of the Sino-Soviet dispute, as Indonesia and India found themselves parties to competing structures of alignment.

The element of personal insult to Sukarno and the Indonesian people over the Sondhi affair was magnified to the proportions of a *cause célèbre*. Even a bitter opponent of Sukarno who was imprisoned by his Administration has endorsed the prevailing conventional wisdom which was governed by the heady atmosphere of romantic cant.[37] The consequences of the affair served as a self-fulfilling prophecy in the Indonesia of the time. For example, the suspension, in early 1963, of Indonesia's Olympic Committee by the International Olympic Committee, which prevented participation in the Olympic Games in Tokyo in 1964, was interpreted and represented as imperialist-inspired and as a justification for persisting along the revolutionary path of the New Emerging Forces. Sukarno seized the opportunity presented by this rebuff to challenge the international sports establishment by sponsoring a revolutionary Games of the New Emerging Forces (in acronym, Ganefo) which was held in November 1963 in Jakarta with the Chinese government providing the necessary financial support. The games took place with sufficient participation to make the enterprise a political success. It was not exactly an athletic occasion; many states sent unofficial teams in order to avoid being excluded from the Olympic Games. None the less, the New Emerging Forces were given a measure of institutional existence in the form of a sporting spectacle, which was sustained with the establishment of a Ganefo Federation which held a further meeting in Cambodia.

China's evident approval of Indonesia's conduct at the Asian Games was reinforced at the end of the year. Early skirmishes in September along the Sino-Indian border had culminated in a demonstration of the superiority of Chinese arms in October. This armed encounter was significant not only for the open transformation of a relationship which had appeared cordial for almost a decade but also because of the studied neutrality of the Soviet government, much to the anger of its socialist counterpart in Peking. If the neutrality of the Soviet Union was deemed to favour India, that displayed towards the war and its outcome by Indonesia appeared to favour China. Indonesia's position of conspicuous neutrality was adopted without any apparent consideration for the great services which India's Congress Party and government had rendered to the Republic during the testing days of the struggle for independence, as well as for India's consistent support for Indonesia's claim to West Irian. The reluctance of the Indonesian government to be identified with any position which might offend China was only too evident during its participation in an inconclusive conference of six non-aligned states which convened in Colombo in December 1962, ostensibly to proffer their good offices to the contending parties. In the same month, Indonesia took the first, if tentative, steps along the road of an anti-imperialist crusade in which Chinese diplomatic support assumed increasing importance.

There had been a strong presumption in Washington that Indonesia's foreign policy would be restored to a calmer course once legitimate nationalist aspirations over West Irian had been satisfied. From this perspective, the West Irian episode had been a one-off expression of irredentism which would be overtaken by a strong commitment to economic stability and development and a corresponding reduction of the political role of the PKI. After all, had not Sukarno told the US Ambassador in Jakarta that 'if the United States would change its position on West Irian, he would throw out the Communists'.[38] In June 1962, an aid review mission led by Professor D. D. Humphries of Tufts University had presented recommendations to Presidents Kennedy and Sukarno which provided for the disbursement over five years of approximately US$250 m. in grants and loans. With this attractive prospect in view, it was expected that Sukarno would indicate a revision of public priorities. In his speech on Independence Day 1962, in which he lauded the triumph of West Irian, he promised to reverse the process of economic decline which had afflicted Indonesia since before the advent of Guided Democracy. Apprehension that he might reject such a course rose in December 1962 when an abortive rebellion in the British protected Sultanate of Brunei in Northern Borneo engendered a revival of the practice of coercive diplomacy similar to that employed over the issue of West Irian. The Brunei revolt and the wider issue of the legitimacy of the prospective Federation of Malaysia, to which it gave rise, was, in a sense, fortuitous in so far as Indonesia became engaged, once more, in confrontation.

If Brunei provided an opportunity to return to confrontation,

Indonesia may be said to have resumed its practice because the initiative to incorporate Malaya, Singapore and Britain's colonies in Northern Borneo (as well as Brunei, initially) within a wider federation was construed as inspired by colonial interests. Indonesia's hostility to Malaysia has also been explained in terms of apprehension that 'the new state that would emerge would inevitably become a second China dominated both politically and economically by the Chinese'.[39] Such arguments and others will be considered in the next chapter. However, no such analysis can provide a complete explanation of why Sukarno's Indonesia ultimately did not take the road to economic stability and recovery but persisted in tilting at the windmills of the international system. A sufficient explanation must take into account the nature and condition of the political system of Guided Democracy which was inherently competitive and unstable.

It has been argued that the mode of prosecution of the campaign to recover West Irian, which was itself an expression of revolutionary ideology, not only served to accelerate political change from liberal to Guided Democracy, but also facilitated the maintenance of its fragile structure over which Sukarno presided. Irrespective of whether Sukarno dealt with the PKI and the armed forces as well as other elements in the political system according to some preconceived design or on an *ad hoc* basis, there is no doubt that the Indonesian President justified his own political pre-eminence because of the need to overcome external challenge and encirclement through revolutionary expression and action. In this context, the prospect of an economic stabilization scheme as recommended in the Humphries' Report constituted a mixed blessing from Sukarno's point of view. Guided Democracy, of which he was the principal political beneficiary, lacked an institutionalized base. Sukarno exercised less than total political dominance by a Byzantine practice of manipulation and by upholding romantic revolutionary criteria for the exercise of power. Wholehearted acceptance of the Humphries' programme in the prevailing political climate posed an undoubted risk of a fundamental revision in these accepted criteria. The criteria demanded as a result of giving priority to economic stabilization and development were not those which called for the political talents exhibited by Sukarno. Moreover, such a programme would entail a conspicuous economic dependence which would oblige Indonesia to coexist with the reviled Old Established Forces. Sukarno had maintained that such coexistence was not possible.

The dilemma posed was evident as, during the course of 1962, the Indonesian economy underwent a progressive deterioration. The country had accumulated massive external debts amounting to more than US$1,000 m. Its foreign exchange reserves were severely depleted, and it was short of basic foodstuffs. Although Sukarno did not

73

appear to perceive an imminent prospect of economic collapse, he must have appreciated that he was approaching a crossroads in policy choices. Would he live just for the political moment and disregard the consequences of policies which ran down the infrastructure of the economy, or would he settle for a more mundane political existence in which those with technocratic qualifications would assume charge of economic affairs? Although a return to confrontation was not preordained or a foregone conclusion in the circumstances of the time, Sukarno's political disposition and temperament, as well as the condition of Guided Democracy, were fundamental obstacles in the way of an alternative course. In this context, it is worth recalling the observation by the US Ambassador on Sukarno's reaction to the news that the transfer documents for West Irian had been signed:[40]

> I had anticipated an enthusiastic even exuberant reaction. Not so. Sukarno nodded thoughtfully, spoke quietly to those who were with him. It was not an exultant moment. I had an odd feeling, as though I were witnessing a scene in which a beloved member of the family were leaving home. Sukarno would miss West Irian, I thought. He had won a victory but he had lost an issue.

The implication of Ambassador Jones' comments was that Sukarno needed an equivalent issue. Indeed, it may be argued that only such an issue would enable him to indulge his political romanticism and to contain the centrifugal political elements encompassed within the system of Guided Democracy. Furthermore, he also needed to sustain Guided Democracy in unchanged form, because only a system of that kind gave him the scope for revolutionary self-indulgence which he appeared to crave. The unstable equilibrium of Guided Democracy was sustained because its competitive elements were obliged to defer to received nationalist and revolutionary doctrine expounded and interpreted by Sukarno. Such doctrine could only assume an anti-foreign form if it was to fulfil its intended domestic political functions. There is no doubt that the issue of Malaysia fitted Sukarno's requirements and served his needs. It enabled him to justify his recurrent theme of, and attachment to, continuous revolution. This much was evident in the peroration of his speech on 17 August 1963, at which juncture the continued prosecution of confrontation against Malaya was still in the balance:[41]

> In my speech 'A Year of Victory' I have already explained that our victory last year was only 'the beginning of Victory'. What is the use of a beginning if there is no continuation? In fact even, there is no such thing as 'the final victory'! Also after we have entered the Garden of Eden of a just and prosperous society, we still have to continue the struggle.

4 From Confrontation to Confrontation

It has been suggested in the previous chapter that Indonesia's revival of the idiom and practice of confrontation just five months after the settlement of the West Irian dispute was, to an extent, fortuitous. An abortive uprising in the British-protected Sultanate of Brunei provided an opportunity to challenge the legitimacy of the projected Federation of Malaysia. Malaysia was perceived and depicted as an unrepresentative alien-inspired polity designed to perpetuate colonial economic and military interests in South-East Asia which, by their nature, posed a threat to the viability and regional role of Indonesia.[1]

Without discounting the element of opportunism in reviving a mode of foreign policy which had served the domestic political requirements of Guided Democracy, it should be understood that informed Indonesian attitudes towards Malaysia were influenced not only by Sukarno's revolutionary ideology but also by the Republic's actual experience of attaining independence. In an early expression of support for the rising in Brunei, Sukarno had voiced a widely held point of view:[2]

> We were born in fire. We were not born in the rays of the full moon like other nations. There are other nations whose independence was presented to them. There are other nations who, without any effort on their part, were given independence by the imperialists as a present. Not us, we fought for our independence at the cost of sacrifice. We gained our independence through a tremendous struggle which has no comparison in this world.

Recollection of the Dutch attempt to impose a federal structure in order to undermine the primacy of the Republic would have been sufficient reason to engender mistrust of Malaysia, given its constitutional form and external patronage. Malaya's progress to independence, which was to be replicated by that of Malaysia, served to generate suspicion of its political credentials. That suspicion was founded also on support provided from Malaya and neighbouring British colonies for the cause of regional rebellion in Indonesia in the late 1950s. For example, Dr Subandrio claimed in 1964 that 'From the beginning both "Malaysia" and Malaya had been utilised by the British as instruments to undermine Indonesia's revolution'.[3] At the outset, however, Indonesia was estopped by self-denying ordinance from objecting to the advent of the new federation because the announcement of its prospect was made almost fifteen months before the Dutch conceded the transfer of administration in West Irian. It is important to point out also that latent resistance did exist to confrontation on the grounds of misplaced priorities and doubts over its efficacy. Such resistance did not have the opportunity for public expression until fundamental change had taken place in Indonesia's domestic political circumstances.[4]

The initial reaction by the government of Indonesia to the public proposal on 27 May 1961 by Malaya's Prime Minister, Tunku Abdul Rahman, that Malaya, Singapore and Britain's colonial possessions in Northern Borneo (including Brunei) might be incorporated within a single political frame was neither truly sympathetic nor truly discouraging.[5] There was no public acknowledgement of the communal calculations which motivated the attempt to contain a predominantly Chinese Singapore within a wider polity with a non-Chinese majority. Relations betwen Indonesia and Malaya had not warmed with the latter's independence in August 1957. As indicated above, from the perspective of Jakarta, the mode of attainment of independence and the political identity of the successor governing elite suggested a feudal establishment reminiscent of the class which had been decimated by social revolution in Northern Sumatra after 1945.[6] Natural suspicion was aggravated by Malaya's initial equivocal stance over West Irian in 1957 and further reinforced by its covert support for regional rebellion in Sumatra and Sulawesi. A measure of rapprochement occurred in April 1959 when the two governments concluded a treaty of friendship which was signed on Indonesia's behalf by Prime Minister Djuanda and not Sukarno. Between the two heads of government, there were major differences in background, experience and personality which proved to be an important obstacle to good relations in a region where personal ties count for much.

The sponsors of Malaysia regarded Indonesia as an interested party to the proposed political changes in maritime South-East Asia. Indeed, the British government, which became the patron of the undertaking, felt obliged to consult its counterpart in Jakarta. In August 1961 Lord Selkirk, Britain's Commissioner-General for South-East Asia, based in Singapore, travelled to Indonesia to discuss the Malaysia project at an early stage in negotiations. Dr Subandrio revealed subsequently that he had informed Selkirk that 'We appreciate that Britain wanted to dispose of her colonies and that in what way it was done was up to Britain and the people concerned'.[7] In November 1961 he placed on public record his government's absence of objection to the formation of Malaysia in a letter to the *New York Times* which wished the Malayan government well 'if it can succeed with this plan'.[8] Moreover, he did not feel obliged, on that occasion, to make any reference to the extension of the Anglo-Malayan Defence Agreement to the new federation. This expression of welcome to Malaysia, which was reaffirmed in the UN General Assembly, was not completely free from reservations. Indeed, it could not be taken completely at its face value because mention of Malaysia had only constituted a postscript to a reasoned argument in support of Indonesia's claim to West Irian. The disclaimer over Malaysia was intended to deny the prospect of any other claims to territories contiguous to Indonesia. At that juncture, the Indonesian government could not afford to express public opposition to the proposed federation because of the risk that any ensuing controversy might prejudice its case over West Irian, then the object of growing American diplomatic interest.

Until the uprising in Brunei in December 1962, the only explicit opposition to the formation of Malaysia from within Indonesia had been expressed by the Central Committee of the Communist Party in December 1961. The significance of such opposition was less in its timing than in its terms, which foreshadowed the idiom in which Sukarno was to reject the legitimacy of the new federation. It was described as 'a new concentration of colonial forces on the very frontiers of Indonesia' and 'an unacceptable colonial intrigue'. The PKI had a natural antipathy to the prospect of Malaysia which was represented openly in Kuala Lumpur as a bastion against communism in South-East Asia. Indeed, it also had good reason to seek to ensure that the public rejection of this 'form of neo-colonialism' became an integral part of the litany of nationalist orthodoxy. During the course of 1962, the balance of domestic political advantage began to move in favour of the PKI as Sukarno succeeded in manipulating loyalties within the armed forces to serve his own ends. This trend became more pronounced in the following year and especially so in 1964.[9] However, there was every reason for the PKI to try to sustain the frenetic climate of Indonesian politics in the year in which the West Irian dispute had been settled because of a general expectation that an attendant outcome would be the implementation of measures to promote economic stabilization. Such measures were linked to the prospect of a receipt of credits from the International Monetary Fund and a Western aid consortium which would almost certainly influence the pattern of external alignments and have corresponding political consequences. It is unclear whether or not Sukarno was seriously interested in a change of economic course which would have entailed admitting the primacy of values and skills not in tune with his ideology or personality. In August 1962 he gave the impression of such interest without discarding his romantic ideology. The absence of open interest in the advent of Malaysia, beyond a statement by Dr Subandrio that Indonesia could not remain indifferent because the territories involved shared a common border, might be construed as a disposition towards moderation. On the other hand, before the Brunei revolt there was little basis in internal dissension within any of the parts of the prospective federation which might have justified a campaign of public opposition.

The outbreak of a rebellion in Brunei on 8 December 1962, which spilled over into adjacent Sarawak as well as into British North Borneo (Sabah), attracted a sympathetic public response from within Indonesia. The rebellion was mounted by supporters of the *Partai Ra'ayat* (People's Party) which held all elective seats but a minority position in the Legislative Council. Its leader was A. M. Azahari who had taken part in Indonesia's national revolution and who had retained political associations with the Republic. With evident popular support, *Partai Ra'ayat* announced its opposition to the entry of the Sultanate into Malaysia and advocated, as an alternative, the formation of an independent state of *Kalimantan Utara* (North Borneo) which recalled an erstwhile suzerainty once exercised by Brunei. Military training and some supplies had been provided from across the Sarawak border in Indonesian Borneo but without clear indication that such assistance had been authorized officially from Jakarta. It has been suggested that the rebellion itself caught Jakarta's leaders unprepared.[10] The uprising was shortlived. Mobile police units were deployed from nearby Jesselton (now Kota Kinabalu) in Sabah, while British troops, including Gurkhas, were flown in from Singapore. Effective resistance was overcome within a week.[11]

In a response to the events in Brunei at a banquet in honour of Yugoslavia's vice-President on the following day, Sukarno claimed that what was taking place in Northern Borneo could not be separated from the movement of the Newly Emerging Forces. This remark served as a cue for expressions of sympathy and support for the rebellion from a variety of political sources. The Minister of Information, Ruslan Abdulgani, called on the press to side with the people who were fighting for their independence. The PKI and its mass organizations, other political parties and the Foreign Affairs Commission of the Parliament added their exhortations, while the Chief of Staff of the Armed Forces, General Nasution, called for vigilance against the neo-colonialism which ringed Indonesia. Comments by Malaya's Prime Minister which implied Indonesian complicity in the rebellion fuelled a growing agitation and provoked an angry riposte from Dr Subandrio. For his part, Sukarno reaffirmed his support for the struggle of the people of North Kalimantan which was said to represent 'the firm attitude of the Indonesian people against colonialism, imperialism and war'. By the end of the year, the linked issues of Brunei and Malaysia had become the subject of a process of political mobilization, by then characteristic of Guided Democracy. The Minister for Basic Industries, Chaerul Saleh, assumed the leadership of a national committee of solidarity with the North Kalimantan People's Revolution. On 20 January 1963, Dr Subandrio publicly reinstated the term confrontation to define Indonesia's policy towards Malaya. He asserted in justification that 'Malaya had openly become a henchman of the imperialists and had acted with animosity towards Indonesia'. In the middle of the following month, Sukarno made explicit and explained his opposition to the formation of Malaysia:[12]

> Why do we oppose it? Because Malaysia is a manifestation of neo-colonialism. We do not want to have neo-colonialism in our vicinity. We consider Malaysia an encirclement of the Indonesian Republic. Malaysia is the product of the brain and efforts of neo-colonialism. Correspondents, mark my words, Malaysia is to protect the safety of tin for the imperialists and Malaysia is to protect the rubber for the imperialists and Malaysia is to protect oil for the imperialists. For this reason, we are determinedly opposed, without any reservation, against Malaysia.

In his statement, Sukarno also reaffirmed that Indonesia would 'carry out a policy of confrontation against the Malaysia idea' in the political and economic fields but omitted reference to any military dimension. In the same speech which took as its theme the encirclement of Indonesia, he reasserted the primacy in political life of Nasakom (the acronym which endorsed a harmonious integration of nationalist, religious and communist forces) without which Indonesia's unity was said to be impossible. There was an evident connection, at least in part, between the revival of confrontation and its utility as an instrument with which to maintain coexistence between the turbulent rival political forces of Guided Democracy. Indeed, those rival forces had good domestic reasons to support a resumption of confrontation against a new external foe even if, in each case, a measure of ambivalence was indicated. The armed forces had been deprived of a custodian role in defence of the Republic not only by the West Irian settlement but also by the earlier elimination of the threat posed by regional rebels and the *Dar ul-Islam* movement. A revival of confrontation would eliminate the prospect of a major reduction in military budgets, which had been foreshadowed early in 1963, and would also serve to shield a position of privilege in economic life which was increasingly resented by the public at large. The PKI saw an opportunity also to place itself in the mainstream of nationalist agitation. Its patriotic credentials would, therefore, not be questioned but enhanced by the fervour of its anti-Western pronouncements.[13] Intense political rivalry, to which Sukarno was also a party, had created a climate in which the issue of Malaysia could be exploited for particular advantage. In this context, confrontation may be interpreted as the external expression of the very nature of Guided Democracy serving as a common denominator for political elements joined in adverse partnership. Yet, if the issue of the advent of Malaysia was less clear cut or even compelling than that of West Irian, it was not totally artificial or fabricated.

The credentials of Malaya, let alone Malaysia, were suspect as viewed through the prism of Indonesia's experience. Its very independence was tainted by the manner of its attainment and by the close residual economic and military relationship with its former colonial power. Accordingly, from the perspective of Jakarta, there was no reason to assume that its government enjoyed popular support. Indeed, opposition to its expansion into Malaysia was only one manifestation of an underlying resistance to 'the marriage between Malay feudalism and British imperialism'.[14] Whether or not the proprietorial attitude assumed by the Indonesian government masked expansionist intent, revealed for an instant just prior to the proclamation of independence, remains unproven.[15] Certainly evident was a resentment of a revision of political boundaries in the vicinity of Indonesia which reconfirmed the legacy of colonialism in determining the territorial basis of state succession. Indonesia, in terms of population and scale as well as experience, had adopted a role of regional leadership which was not acknowledged in Kuala Lumpur. Its government, under Sukarno, held a strong presumption that it was entitled to be a party to territorial changes, especially where defence arrangements gave a former colonial power the right to use proximate bases as it deemed necessary for 'the preservation of peace in South-East Asia'. Such a presumption was made explicit in a reasoned official statement in October 1963 which remarked:[16]

> Such a provision in a bilateral agreement between the United Kingdom and Malaysia which arrogates to itself the right to include other areas beyond those of the contracting parties without the consent of the respective Governments concerned, cannot be interpreted but as having disguised ulterior motives towards the immediate neighbours of the projected Malaysia. For reasons of national security, Indonesia cannot have any alternative but to oppose such a British-Colonial inspired Malaysia.

Such a view was a legacy, in part, of external involvement in regional rebellion, reinforced by Britain's retention of a military base in

Singapore. The incorporation of that island-state into the wider federation constituted an additional source of Indonesian concern and mistrust. Singapore was the object of complex attitudes. With its predominantly Chinese population, it was regarded as the parasitical locus of capitalist enterprise in the region, which attracted smuggled raw materials from Indonesia and so drained the Republic of hard currency. In addition, it was viewed as a potential source of political subversion because of an alleged umbilical attachment by its majority community to their country of origin. The prospect of Singapore participating in a wider federation whose borders would extend across the South China Sea to march with Indonesian Kalimantan aroused anxiety within the armed forces, who regarded Indonesia's resident Chinese community as a source of finance and support for the PKI.

As suggested above, the adoption of a policy of confrontation in opposition to the advent of Malaysia had its roots in a mixture of motives which ranged from crude opportunism to genuine conviction that the projected federation was not only an artificial construct but also a vehicle for nefarious intent. The resumption of confrontation as an instrument of foreign policy matched the political mood and requirements of Guided Democracy and enabled Sukarno to sustain the momentum of symbolic revolution which had been arrested by the settlement of the West Irian dispute. The practice of confrontation had most direct significance for Indonesia in Northern Borneo where, it was alleged, a struggle for liberation was under way. Sympathy and material support were extended to that struggle, although the government in Jakarta never advanced a territorial claim to any part of Northern Borneo; nor did it recognise the government declared by Azahari in December 1962. Moreover, up to the actual inauguration of Malaysia in September 1963, and even beyond, it tempered its hostility to the federation with intermittent exercises in practical diplomacy which suggested that an accommodation might be reached. Correspondingly, the priority of economic stabilization was not rejected immediately. On the contrary, in May 1963, concurrent with expressions of animosity towards and diplomacy over the terms of the formation of Malaysia, Sukarno introduced necessary domestic measures which constituted a precondition for the receipt of foreign credits. These measures, which included raising the price of basic foodstuffs and fuels, were less than popular and aroused opposition channelled, in great part, by the PKI. In the light of such domestic measures which were tuned to important international sources of economic assistance not disposed to countenance a revival of full-blooded confrontation of the kind prosecuted against the Dutch, it would not be advisable to represent the adoption of confrontation against Malaysia as necessarily preordained. None the less, the nature of Guided Democracy and its ideological ambience, as well as the historical experience of the Republic, made for a disposition towards such a mode of conduct. It is, of course, possible that Sukarno himself may have regarded Malaysia, in terms of its constituents and patronage, as a straw man which would be easily blown over by the furious wind of the New Emerging Forces. In other words, the earlier triumph over West Irian may have blurred his sense of judgment to the extent that he thought that he could feed from the hand of the Old Established Forces and bite it at the same time.

Coercive Diplomacy

Irrespective of an evident ambivalence as to the precise purpose of confrontation with Malaysia, one evident object was to question the legitimacy of its original form and manner of establishment. The practice of confrontation corresponded to the pattern of coercive diplomacy employed against the Dutch. One difference of geographical context was that only a barely defended land border of some one thousand miles separated the Borneo territories of the prospective federation from access from Indonesian Kalimantan. Accordingly, armed infiltration was easier to mount and was more readily used as a means of intimidation and to provoke unrest than as a signal of impending invasion. In this military exercise, elements of Indonesia's armed forces were employed as a stiffening component for members of the so-called Clandestine Communist Organisation of Sarawak and the remnants of the Brunei uprising. Drawn primarily from the Chinese community of the colony, and represented as the National Army of North Borneo, these ill-trained insurgents conducted armed incursions across the common border with most action taking place in Sarawak. The first incident of significance following the Brunei revolt took place in April 1963 when some thirty infiltrators attacked a police post three miles within Sarawak's First Division. A cross-border campaign of mixed intensity was sustained for over three years until the end of confrontation was negotiated in the middle of 1966. If the geographical context of confrontation was different in the case of Malaysia, so also was the balance of military forces. Britain's commitment to the defence of the federation, both before and after its formation, did not waver. Resolute and skilful response, bolstered by military support from Australia and New Zealand, associate alliance partners, provided effective countervailing power which was never matched from the Indonesian side.

Confrontation was distinguished from the outset by equivocation and contrived ambiguity. Armed incursions into Northern Borneo were supported in moral terms as the activities of freedom fighters, without any admission of responsibility. Initially, the Sukarno administration sustained an expectation that it would give up a romantic militancy for a sober-minded attempt to restore the viability of a neglected economy from which US$225 m. had to be prised in order to service foreign debts for both military and economic aid. In March 1963 the government had promulgated an Economic Declaration which gave the impression that a serious effort was under way to meet conditions advanced by the International Monetary Fund as a prerequisite for external support. As indicated above, regulations implementing this declaration came into force in May and served to suggest Sukarno's willingness to embark on a fundamental change of economic course. Yet hostility towards Malaysia did not abate. Moreover, an evident diplomatic attempt was undertaken to seek the postponement of its formation – set down for 31 August 1963 – in the expectation that an alternative format more acceptable to Indonesia might be established. In the process, the government of Indonesia was successful in securing its acceptance as a party with recognised standing in negotiations over the advent of the new federation.

One factor in ensuring that success, which arose from a difference in political circumstances from that of the West Irian dispute, was the independently motivated opposition to the formation of Malaysia by the government of the Philippines which had advanced a territorial claim to the greater part of the colony of Sabah in June 1962.[17] Indonesia's relations with the Philippines had been correct rather than cordial ever since the abortive attempt at Baguio in May 1950 to promote a Pacific Pact. Its government had not endeared itself to Jakarta by adhering to the South-East Asia Collective Defence Treaty in 1954; nor had it promoted its Asian identity by defending the record of the United States at Bandung in 1955. Furthermore, the administration of President Garcia had been involved in supporting the regional rebellion in Sulawesi. In terms of economic structure and external alignment, the Philippines was a perceived client of the Old Established Forces. And it had become a party to limited regional association with Malaya and Thailand within the Association of South-East Asia (ASA) in 1961 whose membership Indonesia had rejected.

Irrespective of any reservations over the credentials of the Philippines, it served Sukarno's purpose to attract the support of a close ally of the United States in opposition to the advent of Malaysia at a time when there was still a prospect of securing economic assistance through Washington's good offices.[18] Sukarno had held discussions with President Diasdado Macapagal in Manila in November 1962, when the issue of Malaysia was believed to have been raised. Although Macapagal had been careful to dissociate himself from Azahari who was in the Philippine capital at the time of the Brunei revolt, he indicated his opposition to the formation of Malaysia in January 1963, one week after Dr Subandrio had announced the revival of confrontation. With the government of the Philippines engaged as an active diplomatic party to the dispute, it became possible for the Indonesian government to seek to exploit a triangular pattern of negotiations in which Malaya would be in a minority and, hopefully, susceptible to the joint pressures of its two adversaries.

The initiative in this diplomatic exercise was taken by the Philippine government whose vice-President and Foreign Minister, Emmanual Pelaez, called for a meeting of the three heads of government in February on his return from talks in London on his country's claim to Sabah. Conversations to this end were conducted between Filipino and Indonesian officials, with Australia increasingly active in a diplomatic role in an attempt to moderate tensions. In early March, the occasion of a meeting of the United Nations Economic Commission for Asia and the Far East (ECAFE) in Manila was used to fashion an agreement between President Macapagal and Dr Subandrio that a meeting between the three parties should be held at ministerial level, preceded by discussions between officials who would draw up an agenda. Preliminary talks began in mid-April and survived the onset of the military dimension of confrontation which, apart from incursions across the common border in Borneo, involved attacks by gun-boats on Malayan fishing vessels and violations of air space.

Indonesia's involvement in regional diplomacy was matched by a wider undertaking in which its representatives sought to influence opinion at Third World gatherings. A clear purpose behind persistent attempts to depict the very idea of Malaysia as illegitimate was to promote a sense of international isolation which would reinforce the minority position of the Malayan government in regional negotiations. For example, at a meeting of the Afro-Asian People's Solidarity Organisation in Tanganyika in February 1963, from which representatives from Malaya and Singapore were excluded, the Indonesian delegation appealed for support for the 'revolutionary government' headed by Azahari and called for opposition to the incorporation of the Borneo territories into Malaysia. The projected federation was depicted as a neo-colonialist scheme which sought to deny the people of Northern Borneo the right to self-determination. Parallel, if still modest, support was obtained from Liu Shao-chi, the President of China, during a visit to Jakarta in April. He signed a joint communique which warned the people of North Kalimantan against 'falling into the trap of neo-colonialism in the guise of Malaysia'. Against a background of sustained diplomatic belligerence, the meeting of the three foreign ministers was postponed until June with attendant concern that postponement might well be a prelude to the collapse of the talks.

Concurrently, in an address to an Afro-Asian Journalists Conference in Jakarta, Sukarno returned to the theme of the New Emerging Forces. He pointed out:[19]

> It is also in this context that we interpret the struggle of the people of North Kalimantan, rejecting the formation of Malaysia as at present envisaged, trying instead to ensure that they achieve full national independence.

This hostile reference to Malaysia was made almost in passing, however, and was tempered by sufficient qualification not to exclude the prospect of some accommodation over its formation.

The element of unpredictability in the initial phase of Indonesia's conduct of confrontation was sustained. After Sukarno had stepped on to the soil of West Irian to inaugurate the transfer of administration from United Nations authority, and then after having been proclaimed President for life by the People's Consultative Assembly, he engaged in an exercise in personal diplomacy which appeared to transform the political climate in which the dispute over Malaysia was being prosecuted. Towards the latter part of May, he conferred with President Macapagal in Manila and endorsed the idea of a meeting of heads of government. This proposal was confirmed when, at short public notice, Sukarno met with Malaya's Prime Minister, Tunku Abdul Rahman, in Tokyo at the end of the month. They reaffirmed a common faith in the treaty of friendship between their two governments and agreed to settle national differences in a spirit of neighbourliness. This unexpected meeting raised hopes that the contention surrounding the advent of Malaysia might be overcome. The sense of conciliation engendered by Sukarno's conduct at this juncture was matched by the pragmatic spirit displayed in concurrent negotiations in Tokyo over the status and terms of operations of American-owned oil companies in the archipelago. A new agreement was reached with Sukarno's endorsement, which was signed in Jakarta in September. It ensured continued access to valuable foreign exchange on a more fruitful basis for Indonesia. In the wake of the initial implementation of the economic stabilization scheme, American optimism over Sukarno's disposition was encouraged. Such optimism reinforced subtle diplomatic pressures for concessions on the part of Malaya in order to permit the Indonesian President to sustain an economic course which had provoked the open opposition of the PKI. Playing on common Malay values was an instrumental part of Indonesian diplomacy. The government in Kuala Lumpur was made conscious of its obligation to assist in fashioning a settlement which would save Sukarno's face in the light of his public opposition to Malaysia.

The rapprochement in Tokyo between Sukarno and the Tunku made possible the convening of a tripartite ministerial meeting in Manila in the first week of June, charged with working out the general terms of an accord which would be the subject of discussion between the heads of government at the end of July. The report and recommendations of that meeting were published after the conclusion of the subsequent summit. Its content reflected the unwillingness of the Malayan government to compromise on any point of principle over the formation of Malaysia and its concern to secure the acceptance by Indonesia and the Philippines of the legitimacy of the new federation. None the less, given the diplomatic setting, concessions by Malaya were inevitable and were made in the form of a declaration of adherence to the principle of self-determination for the peoples of non-self governing territories. It was in this context that Indonesia and the Philippines stated that 'they would welcome the formation of Malaysia provided the support of the people of the Borneo territories is ascertained by an independent and impartial authority, the Secretary General of the United Nations or his representative'.[20] For its part, the Philippine government reserved its position on the inclusion of Sabah within Malaysia, subject to the final outcome of its territorial claim. In addition, all parties proffered support for a plan advanced by President Macapagal for a 'Confederation of Nations of Malay origin' which had been conceived as an alternative to Malaysia and predicated on a common anti-Chinese sentiment. While Malaya had been obliged to accept an independent verification of self-determination as a precondition to any endorsement of Malaysia and also membership in a grouping distinguished by ties of race and culture, its deputy Prime Minister, Tun Abdul Razak, also committed his government to a dominant theme of Indonesia's foreign policy. The third article of the document which became known as the Manila Accord stated 'The Ministers were of one mind that the three countries share a primary responsibility for the maintenance of the stability and security of the area from subversion in any form or manifestation in order to preserve their respective national identities'.

For Indonesia, such a formal commitment constituted an important, if symbolic, diplomatic success. Two governments in alliance relationships with Western powers, and guilty of complicity in support of regional rebellion within its archipelago, had endorsed a prescription for regional order which excluded a role for outside states. Such a formula would be augmented in due course as Sukarno sought to build on initial concessions. The preliminary meeting constituted a tangible diplomatic achievement for Indonesia in another respect. The formation of Malaysia had been made the subject of regional negotiations and not left to the exclusive ministrations of Malaya and its patron colonial power. Dr Subandrio, acting on Indonesia's behalf, had skilfully widened the bounds of legitimate involvement in the dispute to include the United Nations, which had also been a feature of the West Irian settlement. In the wake of the Manila meeting, the Indonesian government demonstrated that it would act as the rightful guardian of Malaya's commitment to political rectitude. The sword of confrontation was unsheathed whenever it appeared as if the government in Kuala Lumpur was not abiding by Sukarno's interpretation of what had been agreed in the Philippine capital.

A prime example of the employment of this diplomatic technique occurred in July. On the 9th, representatives of Malaya, Singapore, Sarawak, Sabah and Britain (but not Brunei) reached a final agreement in London on terms for the formation of Malaysia, whose inauguration was confirmed for 31 August 1963. Sukarno responded with fury to this decision, notice of which had been communicated to his Foreign Minister when in Manila. He accused the Malayan Prime Minister of a breach of faith and claimed that the signing of the London agreement, prior to what he termed as a United Nations plebiscite to ascertain the wishes of the people of North Borneo, contravened the accord concluded the previous month. Accordingly, he renewed his open opposition to Malaysia and introduced a more aggressive term into the lexicon of confrontation by affirming a determination to *ganjang* or crush the federation. He also raised doubts about attending the tripartite summit arranged for later the same month in Manila.

Despite persistent doubts as to whether or not Sukarno would attend, the meeting of the three heads of government convened in Manila at the end of July. It was too important a diplomatic event for Sukarno to forgo. It provided an opportunity to deal with the Tunku independently of British support or pressure and with Philippine backing. The Manila summit offered a prospect of tying him down to a formula which might well obstruct the establishment of Malaysia. Indeed, Sukarno had announced his intention of going to Manila 'to continue confrontation to frustrate the effort of colonialism and neo-colonialism to set up Malaysia'. Moreover, the occasion was seen as likely to enhance his standing within the competitive political context of Guided Democracy. His pre-eminence within Indonesia was a function, in part, of the kind of diplomatic role which he assumed in Manila. In the Philippine capital, he attracted greater deference from President Macapagal than did his Malayan counterpart and adversary and, all in all, appeared to dominate the occasion.

The conference, however, was in no sense a ritual formality. It was marked by hard bargaining over the terms of conducting the test of opinion in Northern Borneo. The need to communicate with and secure the assent of U Thant, the UN Secretary General, made it necessary to extend the proceedings. Sukarno had pushed, initially, for a full-fledged plebiscite but compromised on a reaffirmation of the terms of the ministerial accord, with the added bonuses of a reference to the historic General Assembly resolution of December 1960 on colonialism and the inclusion of the expression 'fresh approach' as a description of the exercise in self-determination. The terms of that exercise were limited to an examination and verification of recent elections in Sarawak and Sabah; above all, to ascertain whether Malaysia had been a major, if not the main, issue. Provision was included also for Malaya to secure Britain's cooperation to enable observers from the three countries to witness the activities of the Secretary General's mission. Sukarno did not seem enthusiastic over the achievements of the summit. Although in Singapore and in London the agreements reached in Manila attracted the pejorative epithet of 'a South-East Asian Munich', Sukarno had not been able to tie the Tunku down to more than a limited period of delay to enable the process of ascertainment to take place, and this it was assumed generally, would barely arrest the progress to Malaysia.

If the actual terms of agreement reached at the summit did not meet all Sukarno's expectations, some of the accompanying understandings must have given him satisfaction. For example, it was agreed that initial steps should be taken towards the establishment of the Macapagal plan in the form of an association described in acronym as Maphilindo. This admixture of abbreviations of the names of the three states was coined by Dr Subandrio as a flattering gesture to President Macapagal and conceded by Tun Razak at the ministerial meeting in June in the hope that it would further facilitate the acceptance of Malaysia by Indonesia and the Philippines. By agreeing to participate in the formation of Maphilindo, Malaya had identified itself with a process and institution which paid deference to that part of the Manila Accord reiterated in a joint statement by the three heads of government,[21] namely that:

> the responsibility for the preservation of the national independence of the three countries and of the peace and security in their region lies primarily in the hands of the governments and the peoples of the countries concerned, and that the three governments undertake to have close consultations (*mushawarah*) among themselves on these matters.

The joint statement went beyond this affirmation and in a subsequent passage articulated, from Sukarno's point of view, the spirit of the occasion:

> The three Heads of Government further agreed that foreign bases – temporary in nature – should not be allowed to be used directly or indirectly to subvert the national independence of any of the three countries. In accordance with the principle enunciated in the

Bandung Declaration, the three countries will abstain from the use of arrangements of collective defence to serve the particular interests of any of the big powers.

Whether lip service or not, in some respects Sukarno could claim that he had inducted Malaya and the Philippines into the ranks of the New Emerging Forces.

It is impossible to know with certainty whether Sukarno conceived of the Manila Agreements as merely a diplomatic device which would permit a graceful toleration of Malaysia, or as a means of delaying or even denying its advent altogether. For example, explaining in his Independence Day speech of 1963 why his government opposed Malaysia, he stressed that Indonesia was a country which gave priority to peaceful settlements; Indonesia did not turn its back on negotiations, especially between neighbours, and especially also between 'a Malay nation and another Malay nation'. He even indicated satisfaction with the results of the Manila summit and gave the impression that he would be content with any ultimate outcome. He pointed out that:[22]

> Whatever may happen shortly in North Kalimantan two things become clear: a. Indonesia is no longer treated like the dummy Togog and allowed just to look on alone at alterations to the status quo in the region around it, especially if those alterations concern its safety. b. Indonesia is recognised as having the right and a primary responsibility to guard security and peace in the region together with its neighbouring states, the Philippines and Malaya.

On Sukarno's return to Jakarta, however, his government had announced that the policy of confrontation would continue despite the conditional settlement reached in the Philippine capital. It sought also to widen the scope of those conditions by insisting on dispatching a team of thirty observers to accompany the Secretary General's mission in Northern Borneo, which provoked the opposition – perhaps intentionally – of the British government, still the sovereign power there. In addition, landing rights were sought for Indonesian military aircraft to transport the observers. Negotiations over these issues, in which Indonesia attracted Filipino support, served to delay the dispatch of observers. By the time the matter had been resolved by a compromise which permitted four official observers and four clerical assistants in each team, seven days had elapsed from the onset of the UN investigation. In the event, the observer teams were only able to witness the closing stages of the UN survey and, accordingly, reserved the right not to be associated with the findings of hearings in both Sarawak and Sabah before their arrival. If the controversy over the observers had begun to dissipate the goodwill apparently engendered by the Manila meetings, an initiative by the Malayan government served to transform the diplomatic climate and to present Sukarno with an ideal justification for reverting to active confrontation.

When it became apparent that the UN mission would not be able to complete its hearings before the date set initially for the inauguration of Malaysia (i.e. 31 August 1963), the government in Kuala Lumpur, under pressure from Britain and its prospective federal partners, felt obliged to nominate an alternative date. Justifying its action on legal constitutional grounds and on advice that the findings of the UN mission would be made known by 14 September, the Malayan government announced on 29 August that, irrespective of those findings, the new federation would be established on 16 September 1963. This announcement was made even before the Indonesian and Filipino observers had arrived in Northern Borneo. The impact of the announcement was muted at first. Dr Subandrio did not raise any objections on being informed privately by Ghazalie Shafie, the permanent head of Malaya's Foreign Ministry, of his government's intention. An official protest was presented by the Indonesian government on 3 September, but this *demarche* was not accompanied by any orchestrated campaign of denunciation which would not have been beyond the means of the Foreign and Information Ministries to organise in concert. With evident good political sense, Sukarno held his fire. He may have had some expectation that the Secretary General's findings would challenge the legitimacy of Malaysia and so uphold Indonesia's objections. On the other hand, Malaya's premature initiative provided him with a valid basis for not accepting the formation of the new federation, irrespective of the Secretary General's judgment. He chose not to exploit the opportunity of the latter course until the report on the UN survey was published.

The Secretary General published his report on 13 September. He found that 'there is no doubt about the wishes of a sizeable majority of the peoples of these (Northern Borneo) territories to join in the Federation of Malaysia'. None the less, he felt obliged to make specific reference to Malaya's announcement of a new date for the establishment of Malaysia and commented:[23]

> This has led to misunderstanding, confusion and even resentment among other parties to the Manila Agreement which could have been avoided if the date could have been fixed after my conclusions had been reached and made known.

This pointed admonition became virtually the centrepiece of Indonesia's justification of its refusal to accept the formation of Malaysia. Sukarno gave the impression that he had been deceived and humiliated. He told one of his biographers that 'I was infuriated. The Indonesian government had been tricked and made to look like a dummy'.[24] Whether it had, in fact, been the subject of trickery or self-deception, the response of the Indonesian government was unequivocal. On 16 September Subandrio summoned Malaya's ambassador and informed him that he would not enjoy diplomatic status as the representative of Malaysia which had been proclaimed that day.

Indonesia's refusal to recognise or treat with a representative of Malaysia and Malaysia's response by formally declaring a breach in diplomatic relations between Kuala Lumpur and Jakarta inaugurated a new phase in confrontation. Within Indonesia, the initial expression was a frenetic mobilization of urban multitudes, especially in Jakarta where inspired fury was directed at the British embassy and, to a lesser extent, that of Malaya. The British embassy was burned to the ground in the conspicuous absence of security forces, while British-owned houses were ransacked in a manner suggesting that a prepared list had been made available to mob leaders who were not always in control of their followers. Sukarno's own sense of anger and pique was obvious, although it cannot be certain that he readily countenanced a blatant breach of diplomatic convention. None the less, the conduct of the Jakarta mob was perceived outside Indonesia as the manifestation of a feverish political process which he was well able to manipulate and dominate.

Confrontation Intensified

The refusal to accord recognition to Malaysia with its attendant domestic disorder marked a further turning point in Sukarno's conduct of foreign policy. Whether he had any alternative but to unleash irrepressible domestic forces which had built up because of economic deprivation or whether he had countenanced a gesture which had got out of hand. Sukarno had crossed a Rubicon of his own making. The revival of active confrontation was accompanied by expropriation of British and Malaysian economic assets. In addition, in an heroic act of self-inflicted punishment, economic ties with the new federation, including Singapore, were severed, which meant that half the country's exports were deprived of their traditional outlet to international markets. The response from Washington to the furore in Jakarta was almost certainly expected. The US government made it known that it would withhold, at least for the time being, all new aid programmes to Indonesia. America's allies and associates were informed that there was no purpose in convening a special meeting of a Development Assistance Board at which several governments, including that of Japan, had been

91

expected to pledge about US$250m. in credits to cover Indonesia's current balance of payment deficit as a measure in support of its stabilization policy. This action was reinforced by the suspension by the International Monetary Fund of a US$50m. standby credit granted in July. The abortion of the stabilization scheme was the price that Sukarno was obliged to pay for unleashing the force of a revolutionary tide which he had inspired and then dammed for a time. Politics took priority over economics, in part because Sukarno's dominance over the competitive structure of Guided Democracy was less than complete and he was not prepared to make the effort and risk the consequences of continuing with stabilization measures contingent on a moderate foreign policy.

It is worthy of mention that, if Sukarno had appeared to have burned his diplomatic boats, the US government did not terminate its economic association with Indonesia altogether or interfere with the operations of American-owned oil companies. Although it withheld military supplies, it continued current economic assistance of over US$70m. a year, including surplus agricultural produce. Apart from reservations about the practical utility of Malaysia, the US government wished to sustain lines of communication with Indonesia's armed forces, which were regarded as an essential anti-communist bastion in a state perceived to be of critical strategic importance in maritime South-East Asia. Ironically, also, Indonesia began to repair its relations with the Netherlands, with whom diplomatic ties had been re-established in March 1963.

President Sukarno had made a decisive choice for Indonesia which removed any element of equivocation from his expression of hostility towards Malaysia. In a speech in Yogyakarta in late September, he indicated his preference for the slogan '*ganjang* (crush) Malaysia'. He justified continued opposition to the federation because 'we are convinced that Malaysia is an imperialist scheme, that Malaysia is neo-colonialism'.[25] He made great play of the act of bad faith on the part of the Malayan Prime Minister in announcing the date for the formation of the new federation before the UN mission had completed its task. Indeed, much was made of this transgression by Indonesian diplomats. For example, L. N. Palar, permanent representative to the United Nations, speaking before the General Assembly on 30 September 1963, stressed that 'the fixing of Malaysia Day for 16 September was done irrespective, I repeat irrespective of the findings of the United Nations Secretary General's Team'.[26] Sukarno went further and asserted that Indonesia could not accept the judgment of the Secretary General 'because the procedures agreed on in Manila were not followed properly'. Accordingly, he demanded that the wishes of 'the North Kalimantan people' be ascertained again as a precondition for

Indonesia's acceptance of Malaysia. He thus placed the onus for moderating tension across a common border in Borneo and in the Strait of Malacca on the government in Kuala Lumpur. He had also freed himself from external obligation, and could justify the active resumption of confrontation which received unreserved public approval.

Armed penetration of Sabah and Sarawak had continued during the period of tripartite diplomacy. A major cross-border raid had been launched towards the end of August in an attempt to demonstrate the strength of opposition to Malaysia within Northern Borneo to the UN mission. Following the breach in diplomatic relations between Jakarta and Kuala Lumpur, cross-border actions were intensified and Indonesian troops began to play a greater role in the insurgency; none the less, it made no headway and certainly failed to foment internal unrest. In the face of effective containment by British forces deployed in Northern Borneo, the Indonesian government was obliged to persist with wider diplomatic initiatives also. However, one marked difference in context from the prosecution of confrontation over West Irian was the evident lack of enthusiasm on the part of the Soviet Union for Indonesia's militant course. A number of factors had contributed to Moscow's reluctance to endorse confrontation of Malaysia, whose assumption of Malaya's seat in the United Nations it had not felt the need to oppose. Irritation at Indonesia's tardiness in keeping up payments for credits which had financed arms transfers had been aggravated by its position on international issues in which Soviet interests were involved. For example, the Indonesian government had not been responsive to Soviet attempts to secure participation in Afro-Asian gatherings at which Chinese delegations were represented. A Soviet delegation had not been able to take part in an Afro-Asian Journalists' Conference which convened in Jakarta in April 1963. Moreover, a growing resentment was exhibited at the progressive alignment of the PKI and the Indonesian government with their Chinese counterparts. Indonesia, in company with China, had not endorsed the partial nuclear test ban treaty signed in August 1963, which was regarded in Moscow as a major diplomatic achievement. Given its evident propensity for *détente*, there was no indication that the Soviet Union was willing to be associated with armed intimidation in Northern Borneo in the way in which it had underpinned that exercise against the Dutch in West Irian.

Diplomatic Initiatives

The only diplomatic partner at hand for Indonesia, apart from China, whose support was also a mixed asset, was the Philippines. Although diplomatic ties between Manila and Kuala Lumpur had been broken, its government's interests were not identical with those of Indonesia. Alarm had been indicated at the violent sequel to the break in relations between Jakarta and Kuala Lumpur. And enthusiasm had waned visibly in Manila at the prospect of being drawn more directly into the arena of regional confrontation. In early January 1964, Sukarno visited the Philippine capital in order to solicit support for a greater expression of solidarity against Malaysia. Assistance was proffered over the Philippine claim to Sabah and an offer was made to reroute Indonesia's trade through Filipino ports. The two Presidents expressed their conviction that the crisis over Malaysia could be solved 'by a firm adherence to the spirit and principles of the Manila Agreements'. However, the cautious private response from President Macapagal did not match Sukarno's expectations and left him disgruntled.

At this juncture, he received what seemed to be a diplomatic windfall which generated expectations such as had preceded the process of settlement in the West Irian dispute. On 13 January, it was announced in Washington that the Attorney General, Robert Kennedy, would meet President Sukarno in Tokyo. This announcement reflected, in part, America's concern at the military situation in Borneo and at the contingent prospect of a Malaysian request for assistance from Australia and New Zealand. Such a request could have led to circumstances in which US obligations under the ANZUS Pact might have been invoked. The decision to dispatch Robert Kennedy as President Johnson's emissary recalled the role which he had played two years previously when the United States had sought to mediate in the West Irian dispute. If, in fact, the object of the exercise was primarily to find a task to occupy the energies of the still grief-stricken brother of the recently assassinated President,[27] in Indonesian eyes the initiative conformed to the kind of diplomatic format which had served their interests on previous occasions. The United States gave the impression that it was responding to a situation of crisis to protect its own interests but that it might well be obliged to advance those of Indonesia in the process.

President Johnson's initiative constituted the most that Sukarno could have hoped for in circumstances where the military dimension of confrontation was of diminishing utility. At an initial meeting in Tokyo in January, Robert Kennedy was at pains to emphasize the limited role of his government in the dispute over Malaysia and that any solution had to be found and applied by Asian countries acting alone. This kind of approach appealed to Sukarno, who appeared to resume a cordial relationship with the Attorney General. It would seem, that the US initiative was construed as a sign of partiality, and even softness on the issue, for Sukarno began to advance demands for the withdrawal of

British troops, not only from North Borneo but also from Singapore, as an integral part of any settlement. Of concurrent significance was the evident hostility of the PKI to the diplomatic exercise. Within Indonesia, they inspired further seizures of British enterprises. For his part, Sukarno gave no intimation of a willingness to announce the end of confrontation or to withdraw armed infiltrators from Northern Borneo before the resumption of negotiations. In Kuala Lumpur, which Kennedy visited before travelling to Jakarta to meet Sukarno again, there was strong insistence that respect for Malaysia's integrity and a recognition of its sovereignty were essential preconditions for a return to the conference table.

Kennedy, none the less, succeeded in overcoming obstacles to a resumption of talks. On 23 January Sukarno issued a ceasefire instruction to the Indonesian troops along the Borneo border, making it clear that 'this order of ceasefire is part of the ceasefire implemented by all parties concerned'. He then announced that he would participate in a further tripartite meeting of heads of government, to be preceded by talks at foreign minister level. He stipulated, however, that his government was not prepared to recognise Malaysia as a precondition to the resumption of negotiations and that the conference would be based on the Manila Agreements. On the day the ceasefire was announced, Dr Subandrio told a mass rally in Jakarta that Indonesia would continue with its policy of confrontation against Malaysia in order to give real independence to the peoples of Singapore, Malaya and North Borneo. The inclusion of Singapore and Malaya as objects of national liberation constituted an extension of the horizons of confrontation.

Dr Subandrio, now also first deputy-Prime Minister, travelled to Bangkok in early February for the foreign ministers' meeting, which was held concurrently with a political working committee comprising ministers and officials. At the latter gathering, Indonesia's position was put forward by deputy-Foreign Minister Suwito Kusumowidagdo, who took up Sukarno's earlier demand that the ascertainment of opinion in North Borneo had to be conducted again. The impression was given that attention to the shortcomings of the earlier survey would be sufficient to appease Indonesian opinion. He maintained:[28]

> We know that Malaysia will come one day but we would like to have proof which we can show to our people to convince those who are not happy with the project that Malaysia is really according to the wishes of the people and that everything was according to what we agreed at Manila.

He also tied this demand to the need to secure a concession which would enable Sukarno to save face. Suwito pointed out that 'the people feel that their beloved Sukarno, Great Leader of the Revolution, has been treated very lightly'. He also brought up the disturbing role of outside forces, specifically alleged British manipulation of the procedure of ascertainment, and restated, in that context, the view that Malaysia was a British neo-colonialist project. Despite a fierce retort from the Malaysian side, great play was made with the claim that 'Malaysia is not a real Asian creation', that it would only be welcome as such, and that the onus was on the government in Kuala Lumpur to demonstrate this quality by, for example, removing British bases and military presence. More concrete discussion then centred on the issue of acknowledge-ment of, and respect for, Malaysia's sovereignty, which the Indonesian delegation refused to countenance.

Indonesia's objective at the inconclusive ministerial meeting in Bangkok appeared to be to employ as many negotiating assets as possible, which would be relinquished only in return for real conces-sions from Malaysia which went to the heart of the dispute. The sole concession Indonesia made was endorsement of the ceasefire, which was necessary in order to exploit the utility of America's good offices. However, apart from such endorsement and agreement that Thailand should undertake supervision of the ceasefire, the talks reached a point of deadlock early on because the Malaysian delegation tied any sub-stantive discussion to Indonesia's willingness to withdraw guerrilla units for Northern Borneo. On his return to Jakarta, Subandrio announced that no withdrawal could take place in advance of a general political settlement. Moreover, a subsequent government statement indicated an intention to supply guerrilla units from the air. Indonesia, in conformity with the past practice of confrontation, did not discard the diplomatic option. The Foreign Minister agreed to return to Bangkok to attempt to secure an agreement which would make possible a meeting of the three heads of government. Ministerial discussions resumed in the Thai capital at the beginning of March but did not advance Indonesia's political objective, apart from keeping open the prospect of a summit meeting. Subandrio maintained that the pace of withdrawal of Indonesia's forces was contingent on the progress towards a political settlement.

At this juncture, in a number of respects, the balance of advantage in the dispute had begun to shift against Indonesia. For example, the common front which had been established with the Philippines weakened visibly with the announcement on 12 March of an agreement on the exchange of consular officials between Kuala Lumpur and Manila. In April, after elections in mainland Malaya, the ruling coalition in Malaysia was returned to office with overwhelming support engendered, in significant part, by the impact of confrontation.[29] Moreover, the meetings between Robert Kennedy and President

Sukarno did not give rise to the kind of US diplomatic intervention which had served Indonesia so well in confrontation with the Dutch. Sukarno's appreciation of this fact was probably responsible for his public outburst directed at the United States 'Go to hell with your aid', made in the presence of Ambassador Howard Jones towards the end of March. Furthermore, at a ministerial meeting in Bandung in April charged with preparing for a second conference of African and Asian states, voices had been raised in support of Malaysia's right to participate.

Confrontation was sustained, nevertheless. In Northern Borneo the ceasefire was punctuated by violations, and in Jakarta there was no let-up in presidential exhortation, exemplified by the People's Twofold Command, or *Dwikora*, which Sukarno announced in the middle of May to a mass rally estimated to number one million. In the meantime, the government of the Philippines had assumed the role of mediator between Indonesia and Malaysia. A special envoy of President Macapagal, Salvador Lopez, later Foreign Secretary, secured Sukarno's agreement to a token withdrawal of guerrilla forces in Borneo simultaneously with the convening of a meeting of foreign ministers, which would precede discussions between the three heads of government. This nominal concession was then transposed into an acceptance of the principle of withdrawal and this, in turn, facilitated preliminary talks in Tokyo. The Malaysian government, however, insisted on verification of withdrawal before its Prime Minister would meet Sukarno. Probably its concern was less to confirm withdrawal than to secure a token demonstration of Indonesia's aggression verified by Thai observers. This exercise was not accomplished until Tunku Abdul Rahman had been in Tokyo for five days.

Preliminary discussions had begun on 18 June and were occupied with the question of the extent and verification of withdrawal. Dr Subandrio sought to argue that his government did not enjoy control over the guerrillas in North Borneo because 'They are fighting for the independence of those people there from colonialism and imperialism'. His point was that the problem of withdrawal was political, not military, which required a return to the spirit of the Manila Agreements. In the event, a communication from Thai observers verified that thirty-two Indonesian soldiers had withdrawn across the border. Independent observers suggested that the undertaking was a contrived piece of theatre and not a military operation. None the less, a meeting of heads of government began two days later. This meeting was the culmination of a series of negotiations which had dealt, essentially, with pre-conditions for talks rather than with identifying points of agreement which might serve as a basis for a settlement. It became evident from the outset that common ground did not exist between the Indonesian and

Malaysian leaders, who both probably regarded their attendance as a public demonstration of good intent to the Afro-Asian community which their governments were courting. Moreover, there was very little time for serious discussion. Sukarno had made known his intention to return to Jakarta by 22 June to greet Anastas Mikoyan, then Soviet deputy Prime Minister, who was soliciting support for his country's participation at the Afro-Asian Conference due to take place in Algeria the following June.

In the course of his first statement, Sukarno declared 'I cannot accept *this* Malaysia because of the undemocratic process of its formation'.[30] Moreover, he maintained that if he had known that Tunku Abdul Rahman had intended to change the date for the formation of the federation, he would not have signed the Manila Agreements. When the three foreign ministers took up the discussion on their own, Dr Subandrio made his government's position quite explicit: 'We must return to the *status quo ante*. We must go back to the formation of Malaysia.' The impasse persisted when they were rejoined by the heads of government. Indeed, when the issue of guerrilla withdrawals once again became a sticking point, Subandrio asserted. 'We are not aggressors since Malaysia is not in existence'. For his part, Sukarno insisted 'All withdrawal is in conformity with the progress of the political settlement.'

The summit meeting was little more than a dialogue of the deaf. It broke up after only one day of discussions and produced only the fig-leaf of an agreement in principle on the establishment of an Afro-Asian Commission which would assume an adjudicatory role. Malaysia, however, would only countenance its formation if Indonesia ceased 'all acts of aggression', while Sukarno's concurrence did not entail any willingness to halt confrontation. Indeed, Indonesia saw no point in giving up its only assets, namely, deployment of guerrillas in Northern Borneo and a refusal to recognize Malaysia as a political fact. Whether subject to self-delusion or not, Sukarno gave the impression that it would be possible to secure public admission by Malaysia's leaders that they had acted as servile clients of a manipulating colonial power. He appeared to believe not only that it would be possible to return to the *status quo ante* but also that Indonesia would be able to play the principal role in revising the format of the ill-founded federation.

The Tokyo talks were an abysmal failure. No tangible advantage accrued to Indonesia from Sukarno's participation. Dr Subandrio's response was to announce: 'Confrontation goes on, crush "Malaysia" continues to be Indonesia's policy . . . and will even be intensified.' His utterance was followed by renewed insurgent activity and the heaviest attack across the Borneo border since armed intervention had begun fifteen months previously. A measure of diplomatic and material compensation seemed in prospect with Mikoyan's visit. He preferred, for the first time, his government's explicit support for Indonesia's cause against Malaysia. He also offered credits for arms; in the event, these were not forthcoming, probably a consequence of his not ascertaining whether the Indonesian government would support the attendance of a Soviet delegation at the forthcoming Afro-Asian Conference or not. At the same time, the US government made explicit its support for Malaysia during a visit to Washington by Tunku Abdul Rahman. Offers were made of military training and sympathetic consideration of credits for the supply of military equipment. Once again, the contrast between confrontation against Malaysia and that against the Dutch over West Irian was evident. Despite Mikoyan's visit to Jakarta, neither the Soviet Union nor the United States was seriously interested in competing for the political affections of Indonesia.

For Sukarno, however, there appeared to be no turning back in a year in which the progress of the radical left seemed relentless, at least as perceived from outside the country.[31] He reaffirmed his commitment to confrontation in his Indpendence Day speech, entitled in a mixture of Indonesian and Italian *Tahun Vivere Pericoloso* (A Year of Dangerous Living) and described by the US Ambassador as 'the most alarming diatribe he had made in many years'.[32] In addition to the revolutionary rhetoric with which the speech abounded, he identified his government increasingly with an anti-American alignment convergent with Chinese, rather than Soviet, interests. He specifically condemned America's 'aggression' against North Vietnam in the wake of the Gulf of Tonkin raid. He also called for the speedy reunification of Korea in a form acceptable to the representative of Kim Il Sung seated on the rostrum. On the question of Malaysia, described as a watchdog of imperialism where opposition had been suppressed in a brutal, cold, inhuman way by the colonialists, Sukarno addressed himself to the British government. He called on it to be realistic and implied that if it took action to liquidate Malaysia by military withdrawal, then compensation for confiscated assets could be considered – a theme to which he returned later in the year. In attacking Malaysia, he also turned his attention to the United States. He claimed that the joint statement issued by President Johnson and Prime Minister Tunku Abdul Rahman was 'really too much' and compared America's preference for Malaysia over Indonesia with its policy of preferring Taiwan to China. He pointed out that 'in the question of "Malaysia", we cannot accept a compromise, let alone a compromise which is not friendly towards us'.

This exercise in political pyrotechnics was intended to persuade Britain and the United States of the trouble he could cause for them if Indonesia was not permitted to have its way over Malaysia. The quality of frenzy in his rhetoric was an indication, however, of the growing

99

sense of frustration arising from the failure of confrontation to produce its desired effect. In addition, Sukarno had begun to face obstacles in his attempt to fashion a grand global design incorporating the theme of New Emerging Forces. In discussing the prospect of the second Afro-Asian Conference, he displayed a note of anxiety. He expressed the hope that the question of 'participants' would not cause a rift among 'the progressive revolutionary forces'. He went on to ask all such forces not to let differences of opinion amongst them 'harm the general struggle to destroy colonialism-imperialism'. This allusion to the issue of Soviet and also Malaysian participation indicated the extent to which the Indonesian President was engaged in an attempt to marshal international forces which Indonesia did not have the capacity to control.

In a series of exhortations, Sukarno commanded all volunteers 'to execute all national-patriotic tasks with the spirit of exalted sacrifice and to give their maximum share to our great struggle, our holy struggle to crush the neo-colonialism of "Malaysia"'. In an endeavour to provide a practical demonstration of the effects of such exhortation, three groups of armed intruders were landed by sea on the west coast of peninsular Malaysia the same day – 17 August 1964. Acts of sabotage had previously been conducted across the Strait of Malacca, but such a blatant military intrusion, if satisfying a craving for revolutionary symbolism, constituted a qualitative change in the practice of confrontation. Presumably the intention was to foment internal disorder in parts of the state of Johore which had been centres of communist resistance during the active phase of the Emergency in Malaya. An even more dramatic step was taken at the beginning of September when Indonesian military aircraft dropped paratroopers into parts of central Johore at the same time as there was a renewal of communal violence in Singapore.[33] The extension of confrontation was irresponsible both in the incompetence of its execution and in the striking failure to evoke any positive popular response. Its effect was to engender an acute sense of regional crisis. A British threat of a carrier-based air strike gave the leadership of Indonesia's armed forces serious cause for concern. It also encouraged them to consider terminating confrontation which appeared to be serving the political advantage of the PKI and drawing the Republic into alignment with China.[34]

Indonesia had pursued confrontation against Malaysia by employing the formula which had been used successfully over West Irian. One object of the exercise in coercive diplomacy was to blur any distinction between the two episodes. By depicting Malaysia as a neo-colonial conspiracy and an Asian pariah, it was hoped to secure vindication of military acts which had been tolerated and even approved in the case of West Irian. Accordingly, Indonesia's representative, Dr Sudjarwo

Tjondronegoro, made no attempt to deny Malaysia's charges when the subject of its armed incursions came before the UN Security Council. Indeed, he declared openly:[35]

> I would not deny that our volunteers, our guerrillas with the militant youth of Sarawak and Sabah, some of whom have been trained in our territory, have entered so called 'Malaysian' territory in Sarawak and Sabah. They have been fighting there for some time. This is no secret . . . And now fighting has spread to other areas in 'Malaysia', such as Malaya.

He went on to argue by implication that as 'independent and sovereign "Malaysia" has never existed for us', the acts complained of could hardly fall under the heading of aggression. This attempt to equate the issues of West Irian and Malaysia failed miserably. The majority of members of the Security Council, including the Ivory Coast and Morocco, were not persuaded that the canons of the UN Charter could be disregarded in so blatant a manner just because one of its members regarded Malaysia as an anachronistic substitute for empire. In the event, Indonesia was only saved from implicit condemnation by the veto cast by the Soviet representative. However, as current President of the Security Council, he had made only nominal objection to Malaysia's effective display in the chamber of captured Indonesian arms. The occasion constituted a major diplomatic disappointment for Sukarno and served to compound his sense of grievance against the United Nations.

Disappointed in the Security Council, Sukarno turned his attentions to the second conference of non-aligned states which convened in Cairo in October 1964 and to which Malaysia had been refused admission. He had made it evident earlier that he was much more interested in promoting a second conference of African and Asian states, but he was obliged not to alienate President Nasser. Moreover, the Cairo conference appeared to present an opportunity to encourage the diplomatic isolation of Malaysia from the so called New Emerging Forces, which might then be expressed formally in an *ex cathedra* edict of excommunication in Algeria in 1965. One can only assume that such an objective, if realized, was intended to persuade the United States to use its special relationship with Britain to oblige the government in London to admit its untenable position over Malaysia and to acquiesce, in return for face-saving sweeteners, in the dismemberment of yet another British-inspired artificial federation. In the absence of an official delegation from Malaysia, the way seemed clear for Indonesia to present its case, without let or hindrance. In the event, Sukarno, with characteristic bombast, overplayed his hand. He sought to impose his concept of the New Emerging Forces on the conference in a speech entitled 'The Era of Confrontation'. His fulminations against imperialism, his denigration of peaceful coexistence and his ridicule of conventional non-alignment succeeded not only in alienating the surviving apostles of that faith, Nasser and Tito, but also Nehru's successor, Lal Bahadur Shastri. Moreover, he did not attract sympathy from American observers with his reference to 'outside imperialist forces disturbing the security of Vietnam, Laos and Cambodia'. His attack on peaceful coexistence also arrested a modest improvement in relations with the Soviet Union. His rhetoric failed to make much impression on the participants and, in addition, he proved unable to secure satisfactory endorsement of confrontation against Malaysia in the final programme of the conference. Indeed, that programme stated *inter alia* that states should not use or threaten force against the territorial integrity of other states and that established frontiers should be inviolable. As an indication of his displeasure, Sukarno did not attend the closing ceremony to sign the final programme.

The Cairo non-aligned conference constituted a turning point in Sukarno's attempt to secure international endorsement of confrontation against Malaysia. A factor which undoubtedly militated against his cause had been the abortive extension of armed incursions to the Malayan mainland. Indeed, President Macapagal of the Philippines, while on a visit to Washington, had felt obliged to speak out publicly against this military venture. In the face of recurrent military and diplomatic rebuffs and an evident inability to bend the political will of governments in London and Kuala Lumpur, Sukarno lashed out in a futile exercise in self-vindication. He engaged in a dramatic gesture in a domestic climate in which the PKI increasingly gave the impression that they represented the political wave of the future. Speculation over Sukarno's health in September, after he had undergone treatment for kidney disease in Vienna, aroused speculation that the Nasakom formula might well give way to a more monolithic prescription. On his return to Jakarta in November after travels that had taken in the Soviet Union, China and North Korea, as well as Egypt, he proceeded to reassert his domestic authority, but in a way which suggested endorsement for the PKI. For example, he ordered the dissolution of an organization called the Body for the Promotion of Sukarnoism which had been set up in August with army backing in an attempt to neutralize the communists. Moreover he gave no indication of relenting over Malaysia. In a speech on Heroes Day (10 November), he insisted that the solution to the problem required a return to the Manila Agreements which had been 'trampled upon' by Tunku Abdul Rahman.

On 30 December, Malaysia was installed for a one-year term as a member of the UN Security Council. This arrangement fulfilled the second part of a gentleman's agreement, endorsed by the Soviet Union, which had permitted Czechoslovakia to serve the first part of the normal two-year term. The Indonesian representative had voiced objections to Malaysia succeeding Malaya in the United Nations in the autumn of 1963, but had failed to attract support in the credentials committee. The matter had not been pursued any further. The day after Malaysia's installation, apparently against the strong advice of Foreign Minister Subandrio and without notifying his government's delegation in New York, Sukarno announced that Indonesia would leave the United Nations should Malaysia take up its place in the Security Council.[36] This initiative was an impulsive attempt to salve a perceived affront to personal and national pride. It was equally a dramatic expression of frustration at an inability to make the United Nations serve Indonesia's political ends. The decision to leave the organization was reaffirmed a week later and confirmed by a letter to the Secretary General in which Indonesia's action was justified as a response to 'another absurd colonial manoeuvre'.

If Sukarno had entertained any expectations that his outrageous gesture would rally international support, he was in serious error, as Afro-Asian states, in the main, interpreted his decision as one of gross irresponsibility. None were willing to follow Indonesia's example. Approval was expressed in the main by the government in Peking with which personal diplomatic exchanges had intensified towards the end of 1964. Indeed, Indonesia's departure from the United Nations appeared to be the final step towards close alignment with the People's Republic. Later in January, Dr Subandrio travelled to Peking with a large delegation and concluded an agreement on political principles with Premier Chou En-lai in which a shared revisionist view was expounded of the international system.[37] China was a natural partner in the circumstances, made more attractive by its detonation of a nuclear device the preceding October. Moreover, there may well have been a personal impulse in Subandrio's vigorous promotion of Sino-Indonesian alignment. He had apparently attracted the support of the PKI as a possible successor to Sukarno and his consummation of the *entente* served to sustain their approval.[38] At a dinner for the Indonesian Foreign Minister, Premier Chou En-lai endorsed Sukarno's proposal for a conference of the New Emerging Forces which he suggested could even become 'another United Nations, a revolutionary one may be set up so that rival dramas may be staged with that body which calls itself the United Nations'.

China's endorsement of Indonesia's repudiation of the United Nations did not advance Sukarno's foreign-policy goal. His dramatic gesture had greatest effect internally where the PKI appeared to be entrenching itself in the face of disarray on the part of the armed forces. The communists had inspired harassment of American consular and information offices leading to the closure of the latter as well as to the departure of the Peace Corps. The momentum of domestic political agitation against imperialism was in contrast to the declining vigour of confrontation with Malaysia. Indeed, Sukarno faced increasing difficulties in his attempts to secure international endorsement of its prosecution. For example, at an Afro-Asian Islamic conference held in Bandung in March 1965, from which Malaysia was inevitably excluded, a draft resolution sponsored by Indonesia and China denouncing the federation attracted minimal support, despite Sukarno's claim that 'we are now storming the last ramparts of imperialism'. At celebrations in Jakarta the next month, commemorating the tenth anniversary of the Bandung Conference, Sukarno's Indonesia failed to attract an expected influx of celebrated Third World figures. Attempts to transform the occasion into an anti-Malaysia festival misfired. The majority of delegates refused to interpret the spirit of Bandung as an obligation to denounce Malaysia. Indonesia's employment of the formula which had been tried and tested in the case of West Irian was unsuccessful because, in the main, members of both the non-aligned movement and the Afro-Asian fraternity refused to perceive Malaysia as a manifestation of neo-colonialism. Indeed, instead of Indonesia being able to promote the international isolation of the federation, it was itself placed in such a position. Its diplomatic strategy against Malaysia foundered with the failure of the Afro-Asian conference to convene in Algeria in June 1965. The coup mounted by Colonel Houari Boumedienne which removed President Ben Bella from office occurred when Sukarno, already en route to the Algerian capital, was in Cairo for discussions with the Egyptian President. Because of anticipated controversy over the unresolved issue of Soviet participation in the conference and concern lest Afro-Asian solidarity be affected by the Sino-Soviet conflict, many governments were only too pleased to use the coup as a pretext to postpone the occasion, initially until November. By that date, a process of fundamental political change was already under way within Indonesia and revolutionary conference diplomacy and the ultimate goal of a meeting of New Emerging Forces enjoyed decreasing appeal.

In the face of recurrent diplomatic setbacks and a failure to demonstrate military success either in Northern Borneo or peninsular Malaysia, and against a domestic background of impending political change, President Sukarno was left with limited resources and options with which to sustain a romantic revolutionary course to which he had become obsessively attached. By this juncture, senior army officers had already begun to have serious doubts about the merits of confrontation and had engaged in clandestine exploratory conversations with Malaysian representatives in Bangkok and Hong Kong.[39] They were not necessarily persuaded of the legitimacy of Malaysia in terms of

Indonesia's nationalist values. None the less, they saw little use in continuing with confrontation because its failure to make any impact had served to demonstrate alleged shortcomings on the part of the armed forces which, in turn, justified demands by the PKI for the arming of workers and peasants as a fifth force (after the Army, Air Force, Navy and Police) to defend the revolution against threats from imperialism. On Independence Day 1965 in the presence of China's Foreign Minister, Chen Yi, Sukarno took up the PKI proposal as if it were his own and promised a decision on the matter in his capacity as Supreme Commander of the Armed Forces. He also promised to defend the Republic's freedom 'with *atomic bombs*', which inspired Western speculation that Indonesia would explode a nuclear device with Chinese assistance.[40]

Apart from growing concern about the internal political consequences of the arrested momentum of the military dimension of confrontation, changes within Malaysia itself had prompted a reappraisal of the perceived security threat posed by the new federation. On 9 August Singapore attained independence. Its membership of Malaysia had become an intolerable source of communal tension. The detachment of Malaysia's Chinese economic and political core gave rise to a greater sense of equanimity on the part of the leadership of the armed forces. And it was contemplated that this example might be followed in Northern Borneo. In conjunction with an easing of anxiety over the projection of overseas Chinese influence there was a corresponding apprehension at the direction of Indonesia's international affiliations. The condition of such affiliations was highlighted by Sukarno when, in his speech on the anniversary of the proclamation of independence, he enthused over 'building an anti-imperialist axis, namely the axis of Djakarta-Phnom Penh-Hanoi-Peking-Pyongyang'.[41] He claimed that 'this axis is the most natural axis, formed by the course of history itself', but its members were not natural political partners of the conservative leadership of the armed forces who regarded China as a primary source of external threat. Whether or not Sukarno had made a commitment which indicated the nature of political succession within Indonesia, or whether he was, once again, seeking to hold out a critical prospect to which the United States was expected to respond, became an academic issue. Domestic political change transformed, within a matter of months, both the character of Guided Democracy and Sukarno's dominant role in the making and conduct of foreign policy.

Domestic Political Change

Indonesia's confrontation against Malaysia was a modest undertaking compared to the fierce and bloody confrontation of domestic political forces which ensued as a result of an abortive coup attempt mounted primarily in Jakarta in the early hours of 1 October 1965.[42] A group of dissident army and air force officers, led nominally by a battalion com-, mander of the Palace Guard Regiment, together with members of the Communist Party, inspired the abduction and murder of six of the most senior army generals, including the commander Lt. General Yani. They seized the radio station in Jakarta and surrounded the presidential palace. They then broadcast the names of a Revolutionary Council whose formation was justified as thwarting an alleged CIA-inspired plot. For reasons still unexplained, Major-General Suharto, then head of the army's strategic reserve located in western Java, was not included in the abduction list. He speedily assumed command of the army and overcame the coup forces within two days.

The domestic political consequences of the abortive coup were profound. The cloak of nationalist rectitude was stripped from the corporate body of the PKI, which was depicted by army commanders and Muslim leaders as having engaged in another attempt to stab the Republic in the back – on this occasion as the agent of China. In addition, because of his inadequately explained presence at the centre of coup operations at an air force base on the edge of the capital, his equivocal public response to the coup attempt as an internal army affair, and even more so, his failure to denounce publicly the murder of the six generals, President Sukarno discredited himself politically. In the face of resolute initiative by General Suharto, he was no longer able to interpose his charismatic person between the PKI and those social, religious and military forces eager to seize the opportunity to liquidate the party together with its affiliated organizations. The failure of the coup attempt undermined the fragile domestic political balance which had been sustained, in part, through a radical practice of foreign policy. With an evident change in the structure of the political system, foreign policy underwent a corresponding transformation which reflected the priorities of Sukarno's successors.

The resolution of political conflict within Indonesia did not occur overnight. The process whereby President Sukarno was relieved first of his executive powers and then of high office took many months, during which General Suharto was careful not to usher in too radical a discontinuity with a foreign policy closely identified with his predecessor. Indeed, in declaratory form, confrontation was stepped up both against Malaysia and against the spectre of imperialism. None the less, the prospect of a major change in external alignment was indicated by the tolerance on the part of the security forces in Jakarta to mob attacks on Chinese diplomatic property which was provoked, ostensibly, by the refusal of the embassy to fly its flag at half-mast as a sign of mourning for the murdered generals. At the outset, however, reappraisal of foreign policy was made subordinate to the revision of domestic political order which was managed through the inspired mobilization of student and Muslim organizations against the communists and, later, Sukarno. Because of the wide measure of popularity which the President still enjoyed, especially in Java, and because of many personal ties which he had established within the armed forces, it became essential to ensure that he was fully discredited politically before many of his priorities in foreign policy were set aside. It should be reiterated that, among the military beneficiaries of the abortive coup, opposition to the formation of Malaysia was quite genuine, even if there was equivocation over its prosecution. Although General Suharto ultimately ended confrontation, a sustained, if formal, commitment to that policy was upheld at a time of considerable uncertainty when it was still less than clear whether or not Sukarno would fall from political grace. Sustained support for confrontation served to demonstrate the progressive nationalist credentials of the armed forces who had been attacked both by the communists and Sukarno as 'bureaucratic capitalists'. Confrontation enabled a symbolic display of nationalist rectitude at the same time as a systematic liquidation of the arch rival of the armed forces, the PKI.[43]

The position of the armed forces is best understood in the context of concurrent attempts by Sukarno and Foreign Minister Subandrio to take the initiative in foreign policy matters, and over confrontation in particular. For example, in December 1965 Subandrio offered to negotiate with the leaders of the constituent units of Malaysia and an independent Singapore on the ground that the secession of the island-state and attendant discontent in Sabah and Sarawak had demonstrated the artificial nature of the federation. In February 1966 Sukarno openly opposed impending Filipino recognition of Malaysia and pressed his case with such vigour that the government in Manila agreed to defer this course of action. Sukarno intensified the public display of confrontation following a cabinet reshuffle in February in which Defence Minister General Nasution – who escaped the abduction attempt the previous October – was dismissed. In the event, confrontation was used increasingly as a means of justification for the pursuit of opposing interests by two contending elements engaged in a bitter struggle for the exercise of domestic political power. In this respect, foreign policy had ceased to serve its conventional function of advancing the external interests of the state; it had become a means of advancing and protecting domestic political interests. As Franklin Weinstein has pointed out:[44]

During this period confrontation was less a manifestation of any deep concern about the fate of Malaysia than a symbol used by competitors for power to protect and enhance their own positions in the power struggle.

That power struggle reached its first stage of resolution on 11 March 1966, when, in the face of *force majeure*, President Sukarno was obliged to transfer all executive powers to Suharto, now promoted to the rank of Lt. General. The next day, the PKI was declared an illegal organization, this act of proscription being justified, in part, by the need to crush Malaysia. Deference to the conventions of confrontation was used as symbolic cover during a reordering of the political system to the advantage of conservative forces led by the military. Foreign policy, however, was not left unaffected. In the middle of March, General Suharto formed a new cabinet and Foreign Minister Subandrio was placed under arrest. Subandrio had been the object of popular attack because of identification with alignment with China, and the Foreign Ministry building had been invaded by rioting students. He was succeeded in office by former Trade Minister Adam Malik, who openly indicated general dissatisfaction with the past conduct and priorities of Indonesia's foreign policy. He was obliged to add, none the less, that a proposal to establish diplomatic relations with Singapore constituted an intensification of confrontation. Indeed, it was construed in that light in Kuala Lumpur where the current condition of Indonesian politics was not yet fully understood.

The actual process of negotiating the end of confrontation was somewhat protracted because that policy served an important domestic political function during the internal transfer of power. After the political changes in March it became possible for Suharto, as Defence Minister, and Malik, as Foreign Minister, to approach the problem despite Sukarno's continued ability to raise objections. Preliminary discussions began in Bangkok at the end of April 1966 between Malik and the Philippine Foreign Minister, Narciso Ramos, with Ghazalie Shafie, permanent head of Malaysia's Foreign Ministry, in secret attendance. At this juncture, the ethic of confrontation was being displaced in Indonesia by that of popular welfare, and Malik had maintained in public that essential economic stabilization would be incompatible with a continued policy of confrontation. Subsequently, Malik met Malaysia's deputy Prime Minister, Tun Abdul Razak, in Bangkok at the end of May, having previously indicated that Indonesia would not insist on a 'referendum' in the Borneo territories. A demonstration of the by now open commitment of the leadership of the armed forces to the end of confrontation was a prior visit by a delegation of eight high-ranking Indonesian officers from KOGAM (Crush Malaysia Command) first to Kuala Lumpur and then to the home of Prime Minister Tunku Abdul Rahman in Alor Star.

The Bangkok talks were a serious exercise in negotiations and not a mere formality. The strong military component in the delegation wished to avoid an agreement which might appear to be a capitulation by Indonesia. In the event, an accord was reached whereby hostilities would end and diplomatic relations would be established, but which made only symbolic concessions to Indonesian demands. The peoples of North Borneo were to be provided with an opportunity to express their views as to whether or not they wished to remain in Malaysia 'by elections as soon as possible'. At Bangkok, Adam Malik committed Indonesia to the establishment of normal relations with Malaysia without the precondition of a prior poll in Sabah and Sarawak. In fact, the Bangkok Agreement concluded on 1 June 1966 marked only the first stage in the termination of confrontation. When Malik returned to Jakarta, Sukarno attacked the accord as a capitulation and resisted its ratification. Moreover, its terms were unacceptable also to the armed forces leadership which maintained that the Foreign Minister had made unpalatable concessions. Accordingly, although the Indonesian government was able to recognize Singapore as an independent state on 5 June 1966, no corresponding recognition was accorded to Malaysia. Further exchanges conducted for Indonesia by military intelligence officers took place over the termination of confrontation. It was only after Sukarno was cut down in political size by the People's Consultative Assembly, which took away his title of President for life and confirmed Suharto in the exercise of executive powers, that the dispute was ultimately laid to rest.

On 11 August Adam Malik and Tun Razak signed a final agreement in Jakarta which provided for the establishment of normal diplomatic relations between Indonesia and Malaysia. It was more explicit about the preconditions for a rapprochement. Malaysia agreed to afford the peoples of Sabah and Sarawak 'an opportunity to reaffirm, as soon as practicable, in a free and democratic manner through general elections their previous decision about their status in Malaysia'. In addition, the Malaysian government agreed to a secret annex whereby the restoration of diplomatic relations was made conditional on elections in Northern Borneo; this was apparently necessary in order to overcome residual opposition from Sukarno and to assuage military pride.[45] Confirmation of the existence of such an annex would seem to have been demonstrated by the delay in the establishment of diplomatic relations between Jakarta and Kuala Lumpur until 31 August 1967, after general elections had been held in Sabah but not Sarawak. This ultimate accord constituted a practical face-saving device serving the domestic political purposes of Indonesia's new masters. None the less, the agreement of August 1966 marked the practical end of confrontation and a clear indication of a new course for Indonesia's foreign policy based on different priorities, though not completely so, from those identified with the rule and person of President Sukarno.

The heady experience of confrontation proved to be salutary for

Indonesia. The prospect of Malaysia had presented a very different problem from that of West Irian but had been treated in a similar manner. Recent historical experience gave rise to the view that the federation was an externally inspired and menacing contrivance which ought not to be permitted in its original form to share the same regional environment as Indonesia. This expression of regional entitlement, or a desire to establish a 'pax Indonesia'[46] was authentic enough, but was sustained also by conflicting domestic interests which even Sukarno's charisma could not reconcile. Indeed, in retrospect, his advocacy of permanent revolution would seem to have been a futile exercise in conflict management. In the event, the resolution of domestic conflict in conditions of economic decline accelerated by confrontation made Indonesia appear a feeble regional giant and Sukarno an empty political vessel. Moreover, the practice of confrontation had reduced access to effective external assistance which had been decisive in the dispute with the Dutch. Ultimately virtually on its own, Indonesia did not possess the capacity in material resources and political will to sustain confrontation as a serious undertaking. The balance sheet of the exercise in coercive diplomacy points to a fundamental disjunction between ends and means which spells disaster for any foreign policy. Sukarno's rhetoric against neo-colonialism could not emulate the effect of Joshua's trumpets on the walls of Jericho. A suitable epitaph to confrontation has been provided by Sudjatmoko, at the time Indonesia's Ambassador to Washington:[47]

It has become quite clear that for all our claims to international leadership we ended up with an even greater dependency on foreign credits and with our freedom of action seriously compromised.

5 A New Course in Foreign Policy

Indonesia's revolutionary practice of foreign policy was inspired and sustained by the pattern of power which distinguished Guided Democracy. With the effective consolidation of a government headed by General Suharto, that pattern was radically revised and its attendant revolutionary expression and symbolism set aside. In so far as foreign policy was inspired by the nature of the domestic political order, then domestic political change was succeeded logically by a new course in foreign policy. It should be understood, however, that the political change inaugurated by Suharto's 'New Order' involved a notable reduction in the degree of pluralism within the system and not an assumption to power by new elements. The armed forces, and particularly the army, which assumed command of the political heights of the Republic, had been a factor of political importance from the onset of national revolution. As an institution, it was imbued with a strong sense of nationalism and a similar view of regional entitlement to that exhibited by Sukarno and his supporters. Moreover, General Suharto employed the same constitutional structure as his predecessor. Indeed, it had been the army which had encouraged Sukarno to introduce Guided Democracy based on the 1945 Constitution in July 1959. That constitution was confirmed as the source of political legitimacy because it suited Suharto's political purpose and also because of his perception of the primary needs of the Indonesian state. Thus, there was not total discontinuity in the structure of the political order in the wake of the abortive coup. Correspondingly, foreign policy was not cast in a totally new mould, especially as the army had shared the experience of national vulnerability which had given rise to deep suspicion of the intent of all extra-regional powers[1].

In principle, Indonesia's foreign policy, as it emerged after the internal transfer of power, reinstated a former course rather than pursuing a novel one. Novelty obtained but it arose, in part, from a change in style and not from the reintroduction of an idiom identified with the view of former vice-President Mohammad Hatta. The rhetoric of Sukarno was repudiated and membership in an anti-imperialist axis revoked, but an underlying continuity was maintained because the new

111

political leadership, although fervently anti-communist, had given up neither opposition to membership of military alliances nor an aspiration to a pre-eminent role in regional affairs. That continuity was qualified in a novel form by a progressive economic association with industrialized capitalist states which was, in effect, an alignment. The traditional idiom of foreign policy served to blur the features of that alignment.

The change of style and emphasis owed much to the leadership of General Suharto who whittled away the political base of President Sukarno. Sukarno was obliged to give up office in March 1967. Suharto succeeded him initially as acting President, and was confirmed in office only in March 1968. General Suharto was a very different public personality from Sukarno. He was an authentic son of Java in spiritual outlook and in his facility for political manipulation. A field commander of distinction during the national revolution, his formative experience had contributed to strongly held views about the need for the armed forces to play a central role in political life in order to sustain a fragile national unity. In contrast to his predecessor, he rejected a flamboyant and heroic style of leadership for one of quiet dignity. Sober, cautious and somewhat colourless as a public figure, he displayed none of those personal qualities which had enabled Sukarno to dominate political life by keeping it in a constant state of ferment. As a private figure, however, he was more dynamic and, where necessary, decisive and ruthless. He outmanoeuvred Sukarno politically and neutralized him with consummate skill. His judgment of the pace of that exercise, and of the degree of public humiliation consistent with political stability, displayed acute sensitivity to the emotional bonds which Sukarno had forged within the armed forces and with the public at large, especially on the island of Java. Popular opinion was mobilized against the first President of the Republic on the ground that he had foresaken one of his own basic axioms, expressed in acronym as Ampera, i.e. the Message of the People's Suffering, namely, provision for their basic needs. Suharto introduced a new course by reversing Sukarno's order of priorities, which has put politics before economics. Suharto would not neglect politics but he sought the achievement of his political ends by promoting a sound economic base and not through mass agitation. Indeed, he was to remark in August 1969 in response to a self-imposed question 'Why is the voice of Indonesia no longer heard abroad?': 'The matter is that we shall only be able to play an effective role if we ourselves are possessed of a great national vitality'.[2] By the turn of the decade, national vitality had been refined into the concept of *Ketahanan Nasional* (National Resilience), which was in fact an extension of the armed forces doctrine of territorial defence.[3]

In 1966, in the wake of the abortive coup, national vitality or resilience was only a vague aspiration. The immediate practical problem was to overcome the economic legacy of the Sukarno era, especially the raging inflation which had exceeded 500 per cent during 1965 with the price of rice rising by 900 per cent. The foreign debt amounted to approximately US$2,400m. It was calculated that, in 1966, foreign exchange earnings and debt service payments would amount to US$430m. and US$530m. respectively.[4] It was essential to be able to reschedule overseas debts and to secure ready access to external sources of economic assistance and investment capital. The conservative political orientation of the post-coup military leadership and practical considerations of international politics determined the search for external affiliations to serve internal economic priorities. Open alienation from China, charged with complicity in the abortive coup, and a sustained coolness in relations with the Soviet Union eliminated any real choice in the search for economic benefactors. There was only one major source of aid and investment available, namely, the Western capitalist states, including Japan whose economic relationship with Indonesia had, in fact, made progress during Sukarno's rule. Indeed, the Japanese government made an early offer of credits and played an important role not only in marshalling economic support for Indonesia but also in assisting the consolidation of Suharto's domestic position.[5] It was well understood in Jakarta that economic assistance supplied through the good offices of Tokyo and Washington would be conditional upon an end to confrontation with Malaysia and an evident acceptance of Western conventions of international conduct. A willingness to conform did not arise exclusively from a constraining sense of dependence, whereby natural political tendencies were curtailed because aid was conditional. It also indicated a conviction on the part of Indonesia's new political masters that the Republic had deviated unduly from its ideal course in foreign policy.

An early indication of the direction of change in foreign policy was provided on 4 April 1966 by Adam Malik in a press statement a week after he had assumed the office of Foreign Minister. Malik had been a *pemuda* during the national revolution and had identified himself with the cause of the ill-fated Tan Malaka, for which he had been imprisoned. He sustained his radicalism with membership of the Murba (Proletariat) Party of Titoist disposition and not the PKI. Sukarno had made him Ambassador to Moscow in 1957, where he served until joining the cabinet as Trade Minister in 1962 after playing a leading role in the negotiations over West Irian. During 1964 he became involved, with army support, in organizing the Body for the Promotion of Sukarnoism in an abortive attempt to counter the growing influence of the PKI. Malik's revolutionary credentials, his proven anti-communism, and his diplomatic experience made him a natural political partner for a military establishment which required a civilian figure as public interlocutor with the outside world. In his press statement,[6] Malik indicated that his government would 'reconsider and re-evaluate the foreign policy carried out by the previous Government' and would be 'guided by the realities existing in the outside world'. This statement was qualified with an interlarding of precepts from the Sukarno era because domestic political conflict had not been fully resolved. For example, on the one hand he announced that Indonesia would 'seek the broadest possible international cooperation', including resumption of membership of the United Nations, and, on the other, he reaffirmed a commitment to hold a Conference of the New Emerging Forces and to continue with confrontation with Malaysia. No greater precision and consistency was indicated when he addressed the Indonesian House of People's Representatives on 5 May to give an account of preliminary negotiations designed to produce a peaceful solution to the Malaysia dispute. Once again, a mixture of themes reflected both change and continuity, with continuity expressed in the need to defer to the idiom of Sukarno and also of common views on regional order. In this latter respect, Malik affirmed that:[7]

> The Government keeps on holding the view that security and peace in South-East Asia are the responsibilities of the countries within the area. Foreign military bases are no positive contribution to peace and security but on the contrary may even threaten said peace and security.

Malik reiterated the government's new foreign policy approach 'adjusted to the demands of the people's deepest hearts' and indicated great interest in repairing a host of international relationships including that with the United States. In the same part of his speech, he called for the withdrawal of American forces from Vietnam while Malaysia was still depicted as a manifestation of neo-colonialism and mention was made, if only in passing, to the New Emerging Forces and the Conference of the New Emerging Forces. China, however, was subject to explicit attack for giving asylum and facilities to 'Indonesia's counter-revolutionaries and subversive elements'. Undoubtedly, the new Foreign Minister was attempting to face different ways at the same time in order to obscure the degree of foreign policy revision. One notable indication of such revision was a concluding remark that 'purgatory (*sic*) steps' had been taken to review the composition of the personnel of the Ministry of Foreign Affairs. Within the next three months, the degree of ambiguity in the expression of foreign policy was progressively reduced. After the first stage in the process of ending confrontation, the constitutionally supreme People's Consultative Assembly promulgated on 5 July 1966 a revised statement of foreign policy objectives from which all associations with Sukarno's international outlook were excluded. Foreign policy was deemed to be based on *Pancacila* and the 1945 Constitution; its character was described as:[8]

> Independent and active, opposed to imperialism and colonialism in all their forms and manifestations, and participating in implementing a world role based on independence, abiding peace and social justice.

This statement combined a traditional formulation with the idiom of Bandung. In practice, foreign policy would be geared to the repair and refurbishment of the economy and the sustained assertion of a regional role devoid of the bombast and belligerency of Sukarno. In this exercise, the army was the dominating influence. Its intelligence officers had played a prominent part in negotiating the end of confrontation. Indeed, Suharto admitted in August 1966 that he, not Malik, had assumed responsibility for ensuring successful conclusion to negotiations over confrontation which had been only partially completed in Bangkok.

The end of confrontation facilitated a revision of foreign economic relations. The first priority was to secure the commitment of the United States, Japan and their trading associates to Indonesia's economic recovery.[9] The new Minister of Economics, Finance and Reconstruction, Sultan Hamengku Buwono, indicated this objective in his first press statement on 4 April 1966, while pointing out 'we will welcome foreign economic aid without strings from all countries'. In this undertaking, while Sukarno remained formally head of government and lip service was paid to his international outlook, the onus was placed on Indonesia to demonstrate good faith. Indeed, only limited signs of encouragement were provided early on by the United States. A small-scale transfer of pharmaceuticals to the army for sale on the open market in November 1965 constituted a token expression of the disposition of the US embassy in Jakarta. It was not until April 1966 that Washington provided credits for the emergency purchase of rice and cotton; corresponding economic gestures were made by Australia, Japan and Britain. The pace of reconciliation expressed in economic relations accelerated after the signature of the initial Bangkok agreement to end confrontation and in response also to a Japanese initiative in May calling for an international conference at which an aid consortium for Indonesia would be established. The Indonesian Finance Minister travelled to Tokyo in June to begin preliminary negotiations on rescheduling external debt and on soliciting external aid. This exploratory exercise was resumed in earnest in the Japanese capital in September after the second stage of the agreement to end confrontation had been concluded. Sultan Hamengku Buwono met representatives of

Western creditor states from whom he secured a commitment in principle to reschedule outstanding debt payments. Towards the end of the month, Indonesia resumed membership of the United Nations. Further evidence of good faith in Western terms was displayed by the government's economic measures introduced in October. Apart from a major cut in military expenditure, great emphasis was put on ensuring a balanced budget; provision was made to increase the flow of exports and serious attention was given to curbing inflation. By this juncture, the government had coopted Western-trained economists from the University of Indonesia and was receiving advice also from the International Monetary Fund.

A second meeting of creditors took place in Paris in December 1966 where progress was made on the terms of debt rescheduling. In February 1967 in Amsterdam, the first of a regular series of six-monthly meetings was convened between Indonesian representatives and the Republic's Western creditors and future benefactors. This Inter-Governmental Group on Indonesia (IGGI) constituted an institutionalised expression of qualified confidence inspired in important part by the prospect of economic opportunity. For the United States and Japan, which assumed the major burden of financial commitment towards the rehabilitation of the Indonesian economy, political motives were also paramount. The Vietnam War was at its peak with no end in sight. Political change in Indonesia had made possible the promotion of compensating stability in maritime South-East Asia. The IGGI was a symbol of political endorsement to serve that end. It became the medium through which grants and loans were dispensed for Indonesia's economic recovery and development, and acted also as a watchdog to monitor the progress of economic performance and to advise an appropriate response in terms of aid. Scrutiny was exercised directly through the active participation of the World Bank which set up a resident mission in Jakarta. In 1967, the IGGI committed credits of US$200m., with the United States and Japan each assuming one-third of that amount. The figure was increased to US$360m. in 1968 and to US$500m. in 1969. Ultimate agreement on a formula for debt rescheduling was reached in April 1970. The conditions of repayment, including thirty instalments over thirty years, were exceedingly generous and indicated the transformation in Indonesia's international standing, especially from the perspective of Washington and Tokyo.

The inauguration of a patently demeaning economic association in which aid was made conditional on policies acceptable to Western creditors reflected the assessment of Indonesia's dire condition by its new rulers. The consolidation of their rule, and the establishment of a viable political order, was believed to be dependent on a measure of economic development which could not be financed, in the short run, from the available resources of the Republic. The contingent external economic association arose not only from the lack of a viable alternative but also reflected a firm commitment to priorities of development, for political reasons, which had been alien to Sukarno's temperament and outlook. It accordingly became necessary and practical to reconstitute the domestic economy so as to inspire confidence on the part of foreign governments and private investors on whom recovery and development would depend. To this end, the government announced its intention to restore all foreign enterprises seized during the course of confrontation. In January 1967, a Foreign Capital Investment Law was promulgated which set out liberal conditions for the engagement of overseas enterprises and funds 'to accelerate the development of the Indonesian economy'. Further indication of the reconciliation of national and external creditor priorities was the formulation of an orthodox five-year plan starting in 1969, under which more than 80 per cent of development projects were to be financed initially from overseas sources.[10]

By early 1967, the government had established its *bona fides* in Western chancelleries and had set the Republic on the path of economic recovery financed by external benefactors. The domestic objectives were rehabilitation and economic and political stabilization which were deemed to be interdependent. Foreign economic policy was directed to serve these domestic ends. The declared international outlook was subject to conscious revision justified by the need to reinstate an independent and active foreign policy after a period of deviation under the previous administration. In a new year message on 31 December 1966, General Suharto, as chairman of the cabinet presidium, pointed out:[11]

In the framework of creating solidarity among nations in the world in general and in Asia-Africa in particular, the arrogant attitude, Indonesian conspicuous leadership, the role of posing as the pioneer, champion and the like we have dropped and replaced by more proper ways of approach based on an equal footing and respect.

This repudiation of Sukarno's grandiose style and pretentious goals was replaced by more modest and practical objectives. Suharto explained:

The Foreign Policy in the phases to come shall be directed to improving international relations in Asia-Africa, including non-aligned countries. The creation of regional stability and cooperation in South-East Asia will get first priority, whilst special attention is to be paid to the problem of war in Vietnam.

Indonesia had visibly changed course at a time when Vietnam had become the dominating issue in international politics because of the scale of the US military intervention. Sukarno had been extremely

117

vocal in condemning that intervention. However, under the government of General Suharto, the United States had become virtually the principal external benefactor of the Republic. Moreover, its military leadership shared a virulent anti-communism with the government in Washington, as well as a common apprehension of the regional role of the People's Republic of China. Yet Indonesia was committed to returning to an independent and active foreign policy expressed in resuming membership of the United Nations and in endorsement of the conventional virtues of non-alignment. But non-alignment and support for America's policy in Vietnam were not compatible, as Suharto well knew. In this respect, Indonesia's foreign policy-makers sought to square the circle, while at the same time taking into account domestic political feeling. A gentleman's agreement appeared to obtain between the governments in Jakarta and Washington, whereby mild token criticism of Washington's policy over Vietnam was readily tolerated because of Jakarta's new orientation. Indeed, the US government was already disposed to such tolerance because it could not quite believe its political good fortune over the unexpected way in which Indonesia had been delivered from communism.

Regional Cooperation

General Suharto's indication of foreign policy priorities served to demonstrate that serious consideration had been given to a practical alternative to Sukarno's nostrum of a constellation of New Emerging Forces. In the course of negotiating the end of confrontation, the Indonesian Foreign Minister and his civilian and military advisers had been in regular contact with their counterparts in Thailand and the Philippines, as well as with those in Malaysia. As noted earlier, the leaders of Thailand, the Philippines and Malaya had acted in concert in July 1961 to establish the Association of South-East Asia (ASA), which was a modest and less than successful attempt to promote regional cooperation among like-minded conservative governments. It constituted a feeble substitute for the South-East Asia Treaty Organisation (SEATO) with which regional members had become increasingly disillusioned. In 1960 Sukarno had rejected an invitation from Tunku Abdul Rahman to join in regional cooperation and had expressed open hostility towards the idea of ASA, whose credentials were questioned. In the event, ASA virtually foundered and its activities were suspended, primarily because of animosity between Malaysia and the Philippines arising from the latter's claim to Sabah. Yet, even before the formal ending of confrontation, the governments in Bangkok, Manila and Kuala Lumpur had indicated their eagerness to revive the practice of regional cooperation, and this bore initial fruit with the convening of a meeting of ASA Foreign Ministers in July 1966. Regionalism had been a subject of discussion during the course of the informal bilateral negotiations between Indonesia and Malaysia well in advance of the first decisive initiative to depose Sukarno. It had also been on the agenda at the formal talks between Adam Malik and Tun Razak in Bangkok at the end of May 1966.[12] A central issue which had to be resolved before a general disposition towards regional cooperation could be translated into a wider institutional framework was the terms on which Indonesia would participate. The principal difficulty was similar to that which had delayed the conclusion of a final agreement to end confrontation; namely, the need for Indonesia to avoid giving the impression of capitulation and an attendant demeaning acceptance of membership in an established association which comprised states whose foreign policies violated values espoused by the Republic.

If the format for wider regional cooperation took time to negotiate, the early enthusiasm of Indonesia had been made public. In a statement before the House of Representatives on 16 August 1966, in which he explained the terms of the agreement bringing confrontation to an end, General Suharto expressed an interest in regionalism in a manner fully consistent with views about regional order which had been current and acceptable before the fall of Sukarno. He promised:[13]

When this 'Malaysia' question has been settled we can step up activities in the field of foreign policy towards the establishment of close cooperation based on mutual benefit between the countries of South-East Asia. We will then revive the idea of Maphilindo in a wider sphere, in order to achieve a South-East Asia cooperating in different fields, especially in the economic, technical and cultural field.

He continued:

If one day an integrated South-East Asia can be established, this part of the world then may stand strongly in facing outside influences and intervention from whatever quarter it may come, be it of an economic nature, or a physical-military intervention. A cooperating South-East Asia, an integrated South-East Asia, to constitute the most strongest bulwark and base in facing imperialism and colonialism of whatever form and from whatever quarter it may come (sic).

Suharto's regional vision expressed longstanding views, held particularly within the armed forces, about the management of inter-state relations within South-East Asia and also about Indonesia's assumption of a primary role in promoting a system of regional order.

119

Indeed, that vision, as articulated in August 1966, has been sustained over time without fundamental revision. In 1966, enthusiasm for regional cooperation was combined with a determination to ensure that any such venture would be established on Indonesia's terms, if within a framework of reconciliation. Hence, the reference by Suharto to reviving the idea of Maphilindo (the brainchild of an incarcerated Subandrio) 'in a wider sphere'. Above all, Indonesia was loath to join ASA with its client-state associations. A fresh start was required so that, as a founder member of a new venture, Indonesia could stamp its own imprint on regional cooperation. Underlying this outlook was a refusal in principle to accept the need for the role of an external power to fill any so-called vacuum created within South-East Asia by the retreat of colonialism. Indeed, the concept of regional power vacuum was alien to a strategic perspective which spanned the administrations of Sukarno and Suharto.

The political transformation within Indonesia meant that in one important respect an identity of political outlook was established between the five South-East Asian governments which had been involved in confrontation, whether as adversaries or as conciliators. The change in the Indonesian political system gave rise to a political conformity which had not existed when ASA was established in 1961. Despite its formal reaffirmation of foreign policy principles based on the avoidance of alliance associations or the provision of facilities for foreign military bases, Indonesia, under the leadership of General Suharto, had joined an informal network of like-minded states spanning South-East Asia and beyond, of which Thailand, Malaysia, Singapore and the Philippines were already members. In that respect, Indonesia constituted a natural, if unequal, partner. Indeed, its great scale, natural resources and population added a dimension to regional cooperation which had not only been lacking but also had made prior undertakings seem feeble. The governments of Thailand and the Philippines responded vigorously to Suharto's expression of interest and sought, initially, to promote a South-East Asian Association for Regional Cooperation.[14] Apart from the problem of devising appropriate terms of reference, it took a little time to convince Malaysia's Prime Minister, Tunku Abdul Rahman, of Indonesia's good intent, especially as the two states had not yet restored diplomatic relations. In the event, the virtues of combining a framework for regional reconciliation with a format for regional order carried the day. Regional cooperation with Indonesia's enthusiastic participation resembled, to some extent, that stage in the development of the Inter-American System when the institutional ecapsulation of the most powerful state in the region was envisaged both as a means to satisfy its natural ambition and also to contain its more objectionable hegemonic disposition. The Indonesian government, the object as well as the beneficiary of this logic, was fully conscious of both the intended functions of regional cooperation from the outset.

On 8 August 1967 in Bangkok negotiations culminated in the establishment of a new Association of South-East Asian Nations (ASEAN) comprising Indonesia, Thailand, Malaysia, Singapore and the Philippines. ASEAN constituted an unparalleled exercise in regional reconciliation at a time of acute polarization in other respects, given the scale of America's military involvement in Vietnam with Thai and Filipino participation. Indeed, because of a concern not to provoke undue suspicion on the part of communist and non-aligned states, the main emphasis was placed on the Association's intended role as a vehicle for economic, social and cultural cooperation. The goal of regional peace and stability occupied a secondary place. If ASEAN could not be said to constitute a fusion of contrasting political cultures, given the domestic political change in Indonesia, its terms of reference revealed a blend of international outlooks and a strategic perspective which linked the Sukarno and Suharto administrations. In a preamble to the ASEAN Declaration the five governments committed themselves to the Indonesian-inspired view that: [15]

the countries of South-East Asia share a primary responsibility for strengthening the economic and social stability of the region and ensuring their peaceful and progressive national development, and that they are determined to ensure their stability and security from external interference in any form or manifestation in order to preserve their national identities in accordance with the ideals and aspirations of their peoples.

They also affirmed that:

all foreign bases are temporary and remain only with the expressed concurrence of the countries concerned and are not intended to be used directly or indirectly to subvert the national independence and freedom of states in the area or prejudice the orderly procedures of their national development.

What is notable about this terminology is that, in certain essential respects, it is identical, word for word, with that employed in the documents of the Manila Agreements of 1963 which reflected the foreign policy values of Sukarno's Indonesia. These values had been sustained by the new political regime which had persuaded its prospective regional partners that the ideal of regional autonomy need not be incompatible with the goal of regional security. It was evident, however, that considerable persuasion was needed to secure an incorporation into the ASEAN Declaration of views which were not only held strongly in Jakarta but which were also required to justify close association with regional states which had not long before been depicted as agents of imperialism. The Philippines and Singapore, in particular, resisted Indonesia's formulation. When Adam Malik reported to the Indonesian House of People's Representatives on the outcome of the Bangkok meeting, he revealed:[16]

> It were (sic) especially those principles on stability and security and on foreign military bases put forward by Indonesia in a draft to the members long before the meeting was to start that appeared to give rise to thorough and extensive discussions.

He also felt obliged to state that 'The participation of Indonesia in the formation of ASEAN does not mean that the Government will deviate from her active and independent foreign policy'.

This apologetic six months after Sukarno had been removed from office and Suharto had been appointed acting President indicated that foreign policy was not a mere mess of potter's clay which could be moulded at will into any shape according to the dictates of the government of the day. Moreover, in matters of regional interest, the Suharto Administration did not match its evident economic dependence with a corresponding submissiveness. A revision of external affiliations, based, in part, on economic requirements, did not give rise to a corresponding compliance. It skilfully combined a commitment to regional conciliation with a determination not to abdicate priorities deemed essential to the promotion of a viable regional order. Indonesia's approach to regional reconciliation, which was completed with the establishment of diplomatic relations with Malaysia at the end of August 1967, was marked by a strong element of continuity. In the process, principle had been upheld despite open affiliation with 'Old Established Forces'. Moreover, in his report to the People's Consultative Assembly in March 1968, President Suharto was explicit in stating that ASEAN had been formed 'at Indonesia's initiative'.[17]

Within ASEAN, initial relationships were mixed, as exemplified by the different quality of contact with Malaysia and Singapore. In the case of Malaysia, the idiom of restored blood-brotherhood was carried over from the end of confrontation into practical bilateral cooperation before the formal establishment of diplomatic relations. In March 1967 a security arrangement was concluded by means of a little publicised exchange of letters between Jakarta and Kuala Lumpur. This arrangement confirmed even earlier military cooperation in joint counter-insurgency operations along the common border in Northern Borneo against predominantly ethnic Chinese communist bands which had been encouraged under the Sukarno administration as instruments for the prosecution of confrontation. Malaysia's response to Indonesian interest in cooperation was encouraged by personal contacts established in the course of the negotiations leading to the end of confrontation, and also by a growing impression that, even from the Malaysian perspective, confrontation had been a mistake because Indonesia constituted a nation of kith and kin whose national outlook ought to be emulated. A propensity to merge international outlooks was indicated in an accord between the two states delimiting their common territorial sea boundary in the Malacca Strait, which was confirmed by treaty in March 1970, and the following year in the adoption of a joint challenge to the customary legal status of that waterway together with the Strait of Singapore. Moreover, relations between Indonesia and Malaysia were not affected by the latter's residual military links with Britain, Australia and New Zealand. In a context where change was under way in the balance of influences bearing on the regional environment, tacit approval was indicated of the decision by the British Conservative government, which came to power in June 1970, to revise the policy of its Labour predecessor and retain a modest military presence in South-East Asia within the framework of a consultative Five Power Defence Agreement, to which Malaysia and Singapore became parties. Toleration of this initiative reflected concern at the dangers of communal conflict within Malaysia and between Malaysia and Singapore, which the Five Power Defence Agreement was intended to mitigate. The considerable improvement in relations between Indonesia and Malaysia was, none the less, not totally free from all legacies of the past. For example, the government in Jakarta had reservations about the national spirit of the federal state because of its lack of common experience with Indonesia and also because of the substantial Chinese component in its population.

Indonesia's early post-confrontation relationship with Singapore was strained, even though diplomatic recognition had been accorded to the island-state before final negotiations over the end of confrontation were concluded with Malaysia. One source of strain was the acute sense of vulnerability exhibited by the government of Singapore as the government of a conspicuously Chinese Republic, which was alarmed by the effusive expression of Malay blood-brotherhood which had attended the end of confrontation. In consequence, it felt obliged to inject an abrasive element into close regional relationships in an attempt to ensure that its recently acquired sovereign status would be accorded due respect. Relations between the two countries passed through a stormy stage in October 1968 when the Singapore government ordered the execution of two Indonesian marines found guilty of acts of murder and sabotage during confrontation, despite a personal plea for commutation of sentence by President Suharto. The furore which erupted in Indonesia, with the sacking of Singapore's embassy in Jakarta, in reaction to the hanging of the marines indicated just how close anti-Chinese feelings were to the surface and the corresponding view of Singapore as a conspicuously Chinese entity. It has been suggested that during the attendant crisis, domestic political forces sought to exploit the emotional issue to the advantage of political parties like the PNI, which had suffered from undue identification with Sukarno.[18] The Suharto government responded to the public outburst with moderation, conscious that more was at stake than just relations with Singapore. Adam Malik, with evident support from President Suharto, refused to contemplate any substantive riposte. Superficial undertakings were given to reduce Indonesia's dependence on the port and financial facilities of Singapore, with whom unofficial barter trade had revived to the disadvantage of the Indonesian exchequer, and which was much resented. In effect, the issue was allowed to die down. Indeed, over time, the ability of Singapore to demonstrate its anti-communist credentials and to display a congenial pragmatism in regional cooperation produced a growing sense of tolerance. Singapore's fear of Indonesia, arising from differences in identity, scale and experience and the view that the archipelagic state was a slumbering political vulcano, was not matched in Jakarta, where the strategic perspective gave rise to horizons well beyond the minuscule city-state. The issue of the marines, however, was not forgotten by President Suharto who retained a sense of personal insult. Prime Minister Lee Kuan-yew made an act of personal contrition on his first official visit to Jakarta – not until May 1973 – when he scattered flower petals over the graves of the two executed marines in the Kalibata Military Cemetery.

Within ASEAN, Indonesia assumed a cautious role, conscious of the sensitivity of the smaller regional partners to any revival of grandiloquent design at their expense. Attention was given to conflict management, and at a meeting in Jakarta in October 1968 a successful attempt was made to promote a cooling-off period to contain the revived dispute between the Philippines and Malaysia over Sabah, which had placed a major strain on the cohesion of ASEAN. Concurrently, a marked improvement took place in relations with Indonesia's near neighbour Australia which had been affected adversely because of confrontation over West Irian and Malaysia.[19] With the formation of ASEAN in August 1967, Suharto's government had set well in train a process of international rehabilitation. It had attracted the special consideration, benefaction and economic appetite of the Western world, especially Japan and the United States, while seeking to avoid an obtrusive political relationship. This revision of external affiliations had come as a direct consequence of the internal political changes flowing directly from the outcome of the abortive coup in October 1965. Correspondingly, external affiliations with the communist states were revised adversely.

Relations with the Soviet Union had deteriorated visibly during the course of confrontation against Malaysia. The high point of Indonesian-Soviet *entente* had been reached during the earlier confrontation against the Netherlands but gave way to a less cordial association as both the PKI and the government in Jakarta entered into close alignment with the Communist Party and the government of China respectively. Indeed, Soviet annoyance with Sukarno's regime became increasingly evident during 1965 because of its unwillingness to support Moscow's participation in the abortive Afro-Asian Conference.[20] By October 1965, relations between the two countries were little more than correct. Indeed, there was a measure of mordant irony in the bloody aftermath of the abortive coup in so far as some of the arms supplied to the Indonesian Army by the Soviet Union may well have been used to decimate a Communist Party aligned with its Chinese counterpart. In fact, the PKI had long had reservations about the burgeoning relationship between Indonesia and the Soviet Union and its nexus in arms transfers, because of apprehension at just such a prospect. Any sense of satisfaction derived by the government in Moscow from the political outcome of the abortive coup was qualified by the evident re-alignment of Indonesia with the West and also by the volume of debt outstanding. Of the total amount of foreign debt outstanding at the end of 1965 (approximately US$2,400 m.), nearly US$1,000 m. worth was owed to the Soviet Union and its East European allies. Although the Soviet government expressed criticism through the media of the repression of the PKI and the execution of its leaders, no attempt was made to sever relations. The scale of debt outstanding was probably one consideration. More to the point, there appeared to be little advantage in relinquishing an established diplomatic foothold in a state which had displayed fierce antagonism towards China. Although aid projects were suspended and payments in cash demanded for military spare parts, a temporary moratorium on debt repayments was concluded at the end of 1966, which was followed, ultimately, in August 1970 by a long-term rescheduling agreement on virtually the same basis as that worked out with Western creditors. Even before then, a limited allocation of aid credits from Eastern Europe had been granted, while a Soviet technical mission paid a visit to Indonesia in August 1969.[21]

The evident Soviet willingness to maintain a residual relationship matched the priorities of Indonesia's Foreign Minister. Adam Malik was conscious of the need to project a semblance of balance in foreign policy and to avoid any impression that the Republic had swung from one political pole to the other. General Suharto was persuaded of the value of being able to counter criticism that Indonesia had rejected an authentic independent and active foreign policy, especially while the influence of Sukarno still endured. Early on during the process of the internal transfer of power and before the initial agreement to end confrontation, Malik had expressed publicly his government's heartfelt appreciation of 'the understanding shown by the Soviet Union as regards the new developments in Indonesia'. The relationship with the Soviet Union, however uneasy, was cultivated up to a point because it served as an important symbol of non-alignment. In a speech in August 1969, President Suharto placed great stress on Indonesia's determination to refuse aid if strings were attached. He pointed out that, although considerable economic assistance was being received from the 'Western Bloc', 'this should not be interpreted that we closed the door for aid from the "Eastern Bloc" '.[22] The cooperation of socialist countries was said to be still required. This cooperation has, in fact, been limited subsequently, while tensions in the relationship with the Soviet Union have persisted, partly because the government in Moscow has provided asylum for a faction of the PKI in exile. Moreover, the growing global role of the Soviet Union which encompassed South-East Asia from the late 1960s was construed in Jakarta as an ominous development and a challenge to the goals enshrined in the ASEAN Declaration. Apprehension was shown at the initial deployment of a Soviet naval squadron in the Indian Ocean in March 1968. The proposal by Leonid Brezhnev in June 1969 for the establishment of a collective security system in Asia met with a negative and frosty response. Malik seized the opportunity to employ the logic of non-alignment and maintained that Indonesia would endorse such a system if it enjoyed the support of all major powers, not just one. The Soviet Union came to be regarded with increasing suspicion because it was a global power which had begun to demonstrate a capability to project its military strength within the maritime bounds of Indonesia. Moreover, it had not responded sympathetically to the advent of ASEAN, which had been conceived in Jakarta as a collective vehicle through which might be promoted a regional order which could exclude the undue intrusion of external powers like the Soviet Union.

If relations with the Soviet Union remained correct, though uneasy, following the abortive coup of 1965, those with the People's Republic of China were transformed because of alleged Chinese complicity in that episode, and also because of resentment on the part of the armed forces and the Muslim factions at the association between the two governments which was blamed on Dr Subandrio. The Chinese diplomatic community in Jakarta and in consulates outside became the object of inspired demonstrations and physical attack. So much so, that all technical assistance personnel were withdrawn by December 1965.

From the onset of the internal transfer of power in March 1966, a deliberate attempt was made to destroy the axis which Sukarno had proclaimed only just over six months previously.[23] However, pressure from hard-line military factions to sever diplomatic relations was resisted by Adam Malik, with Suharto's support, until the excesses of the Cultural Revolution and Peking's endorsement of a revolutionary line for the insurgent remnant of the PKI resulted in the withdrawal of a depleted embassy staff from the Chinese capital in October 1967. It has been pointed out that Malik employed the term 'frozen' to describe the state of diplomatic relations between the two countries 'with the objects of obstructing any attempt to establish relations with Taiwan and of holding out the prospect of "normalization" in the future'.[24] A trade mission from Taiwan was received in September 1969 but Malik insisted that it was without prejudice to Indonesia's 'One China policy' which had not been revised. Malik and his Foreign Ministry colleagues were of the opinion that it did not make political sense to contract out of diplomatic association with a state of the international standing of China, but they were unable to prevail over the view of the Ministry of Defence and Security which regarded such an association as an unnecessary risk in the light of previous experience. Moreover, because a prime justification for the dominant position of the armed forces in the political life of the Republic had been their role in quoshing an externally-inspired plot, an early restoration of diplomatic relations with China would have undermined their credibility.

In the event, diplomatic relations have remained suspended, despite the rapprochement between China and the United States and the establishment of diplomatic ties between China and three of Indonesia's ASEAN partners. In the autumn of 1971, the prospect of the People's Republic securing the Chinese seat in the United Nations appeared imminent. Indeed, Adam Malik had made a public statement to the effect that the entry of the Peking government was a foregone conclusion and that it would ease relations with his government. All indications suggested that Indonesia's delegation would vote for the Albanian resolution providing for the expulsion of the Taiwan government and the seating of that from Peking. However, concern among the military establishment in Jakarta lest such action indicate a lack of appreciation of US aid and so alienate Congress prompted President Suharto to dispatch a senior military intelligence officer to New York to advise the Indonesian delegation. In the event, they voted for the US resolution which required a two-thirds majority to sanction the expulsion of Taiwan's representative, and then abstained on the decisive vote. Apart from embarrassing the Foreign Ministry, the abstention aroused public criticism in Jakarta because Indonesia

127

appeared to have deferred to American wishes and, in so doing, had isolated itself from the vast majority of non-aligned states.

Although intermittent ministerial contact was re-established with China after the conclusion of the Vietnam Peace Agreements in January 1973, a combination of factors have combined to keep the relationship 'frozen'. Above all, there has been resentment in Jakarta at the refusal by the Chinese Communist Party to renounce support for the PKI or to revoke asylum for some of its leading members who were members of a delegation visiting Peking in October 1965. Within the Ministry of Defence and Security, a longstanding fear has persisted that China would seek to exploit a resumption of diplomatic relations to manipulate the economic position of the overseas Chinese community in Indonesia to political advantage. Moreover, the leadership of the armed forces has not been persuaded of the practical utility of restoring diplomatic relations. There has also been reluctance to offer any leverage to Muslim opponents of the Suharto Administration who have been outspoken in their opposition to the return of a Chinese diplomatic mission to Jakarta.[25]

In its practice of foreign policy, the Suharto Government sought to maintain a viable balance between continuity and change which would serve to reconcile the imperative of development and the element of aspiration in the independent and active formula. For the new military leadership, repudiation of the rhetoric and affiliations of the New Emerging Forces did not mean any less concern for the integrity and unity of a distended and socially diverse archipelago. In its approach to one piece of unfinished business left over from the Sukarno Administration, there was evident continuity. The armed forces had been involved, up to a point, in the campaign to recover the territory of West Irian from the Dutch in the early 1960s. The leadership had been of one mind with Sukarno over the need to keep the territory within the bounds of the Republic, despite the commitment under the terms of settlement that its inhabitants would be allowed to decide their political future by the end of 1969. Apart from the longstanding conviction that West Irian constituted an integral part of the Republic because it had been an integral part of the Netherlands East Indies, there was apprehension lest the political separation of the territory should stimulate secessionist activity elsewhere in the archipelago. Although the Indonesian government permitted the holding of a so-called 'act of free choice' in the territory, what transpired was a contrived ritual exercise and not a true test of opinion because of a determination that no challenge should be permitted to the integrity of the Republic.

During the period between December 1949, when Indonesia attained independence, and August 1962, when the Dutch agreed to relinquish administrative control of West New Guinea, a local nationalism had been fostered and native Papuans had been inducted into the bureaucracy and the rudiments of political life. The transfer agreement effected through US diplomatic intervention and under UN auspices was not welcomed in the territory. Indeed, when Indonesia assumed its administration in May 1963, armed resistance was encountered led by a Free Papua Movement which persisted despite military response, including the use of air power. Before the fall of Sukarno, the Indonesian government had shown little inclination to honour its commitment in the transfer agreement; a plebiscite was said to have become 'superfluous'.[26] However, the rise of Suharto and Indonesia's resumption of UN membership produced a change in public attitude as a matter of practical necessity rather than genuine inclination. Accordingly, the 'act of free choice' was conducted in July and August 1969. It took the form of a crude exercise in political stage-management in which the overseeing representatives of the United Nations were denied full opportunity to adjudicate on the true merits of an undertaking in which village notables voted by 1,025 to nil in favour of continued union with Indonesia.[27] The report of the UN mission on the test of opinion was not without reservations. When it came before the General Assembly with an implicit endorsement of Indonesian rule, it was subject to criticism, especially from a number of African delegations whose governments had come to perceive a measure of ethnic affinity with the Papuans in what became known as Irian Jaya. On the issue of the 'act of free choice', however, the armed forces and the Foreign Ministry were of one mind in facing the outside world. The principle of self-determination was deemed to be secondary to the priority of ensuring the integrity of the Republic. President Sukarno had once represented Holland's possession of West Irian as a denial of the completion of the Indonesian revolution. His successor in office was no less determined to consolidate its territorial completion. President Suharto announced the incorporation of West Irian into the Republic as its twentysixth province on 17 September 1969. Moreover, his government went on to conclude a boundary agreement with neighbouring Papua-New Guinea, Australia acting on its behalf in advance of its independence in 1975. Despite that agreement, differences have arisen with the administration in Port Moresby, because of cross-border insurgency mounted by the Free Papua Movement which has provoked Indonesian counter-measures.

Change in Regional Environment

The West Irian issue had possessed an evident external dimension but had been treated, essentially, as a matter of internal security.

Indonesia's management of the 'act of free choice' had been virtually free from constraint; limited diplomatic objections were ignored. The completion of the national revolution in territorial terms constituted an exceptional undertaking. Indonesia's success in this endeavour stood in contrast to its inability to exercise decisive influence within its own regional environment beyond the limited enterprise in regional co-operation which ASEAN constituted at the time. When Indonesia helped to form ASEAN in August 1967, the regional environment was dominated by the scale of US military intervention in Indochina. The Indonesian government held mixed views on this intervention. The apparently unflagging US commitment offered assurance to a ferociously anti-communist administration which had only recently achieved the virtual destruction of the PKI. On the other hand, US military intervention constituted an extreme example of the regional phenomenon to which the Indonesian government was opposed in principle. Moreover, while military action on the part of the United States had arisen from a policy of containment directed, above all, at the People's Republic of China, the government of Indonesia drew a distinction in terms of threat between China and Vietnam and did not hold to the notion of a monolithic communism. When Indonesia joined ASEAN, it was close to a suspension of diplomatic relations with China, not Vietnam. Recent experience pointed to China as the principal source of external threat, and not the country which was the object of US military intervention. Indeed, within Indonesia, there was a strong sense of affinity with Vietnam engendered by a perceived parallel experience in challenging colonial rule and this diluted the impression of communist dominance of the movement for national unification. During the Sukarno era, diplomatic relations had been established with the Democratic Republic of Vietnam and a mission accepted from the National Liberation Front of South Vietnam, and this had prompted the Saigon government to sever diplomatic ties. Those relations were not suspended with the fall of Sukarno, nor were relations formally repaired with the government in South Vietnam. Indeed, Indonesia maintained an embassy in Hanoi during the period of intense American bombing and made abortive attempts to mediate in the conflict. The relationship with Communist Vietnam was sustained after October 1965, although subject to strain because Indonesia's recurrent calls for a halt to the bombing were regarded as no more than token declarations. None the less, the diplomatic link was useful because it served to uphold the claim to an independent and active foreign policy.

Indonesia's participation in ASEAN also took place concurrently with significant changes in the regional environment which generated doubts about the merits of the United States as a *de facto* ally. Only a month before the formation of the Association, the British government had announced its intention to withdraw its military presence from Malaysia and Singapore. In January 1968, notice was given of an accelerated withdrawal. The following March, as if in consequence, a small Soviet naval squadron undertook a tour of the Indian Ocean entering the sea space from the Straits of Malacca and Singapore. Whatever sense of alarm was generated by this naval intrusion, the dramatic events in Vietnam at the end of January 1968 had more profound regional repercussions. The historic Tet offensive may have been a military failure, but it succeeded in breaking the political will of the US government. It was responsible, because of its domestic impact, for the virtual abdication from office of President Johnson and for the associated decision to restrict the bombing of North Vietnam and to consider peace negotiations. The evident US unwillingness to continue with an open-ended conflict and the concurrent deterioration in Sino-Soviet relations paved the way for President Nixon's enunciation in July 1969 from the island of Guam of a statement indicating a fundamental reappraisal of US policy in East Asia. Such a reappraisal was confirmed two years later when Nixon's national security adviser, Henry Kissinger, appeared unannounced in Peking, much to the consternation of the government in Jakarta. By February 1972, when President Nixon made his historic visit to China, Indonesia's regional environment had been subject to a process of change in which the Republic had not participated and there had also been no corresponding enhancement of its capability to play a decisive regional role. Slogans exhorting national resilience and formulas for regional order were no compensation for its impotence as a regional bystander. Moreover, military capability had been consciously neglected in order to avoid disturbing regional partners and alienating Western creditors.

In the main, pragmatism prevailed over declaratory policy and development was placed before the priority of a regional role. An attendant consequence was a willingness on the part of the military-dominated government to pay deference to civilian virtues in order to modify any external estimate that it was merely another junta. Although for practical purposes foreign policy was subject to the control of a military establishment, a civilian face was presented to the outside world because of the importance of restoring international confidence. Foreign Minister Adam Malik was a civilian, while the intellectual luminary Sudjatmoko assumed the key diplomatic post of Ambassador to Washington. These circumstances made for an inevitable intra-bureaucratic tension over the making of foreign policy and, in particular, over competition for the ear and authority of President Suharto. The expression of such tension assumed increasing importance because of the changing nature of the regional environment. In this respect, although the Foreign Ministry was relegated to a

131

secondary status vis à vis the Ministry of Defence and Security and various intelligence agencies, Malik, through his personal relationship with the President, was able to moderate a military propensity to regard foreign policy in terms of stark alternatives which were likely to frustrate or favour communism.

The impact of change in the regional environment, the evident limitations to Indonesia's capability to influence that environment, and tension between the Foreign and Defence Ministries converged at the turn of the decade. The cause was the violent course of events in Cambodia following the deposition of the head of state, Prince Norodom Sihanouk, in March 1970. Cambodia was viewed as the soft underbelly of South-East Asia and a likely source of threat to Indonesia's security. Threat was not contemplated in conventional terms. For example, although the People's Republic of China was viewed with the greatest apprehension, it was not considered as posing an imminent threat, given its limited ability to project military power at a distance. President Suharto's military advisers conceived of the problem of security primarily in terms of inter-related processes of regional subversion and insurgency which might coincide with a corresponding process within Indonesia. Such a mode of challenge, in the light of most recent experience, was regarded as communist-sponsored and directed and appeared plausible in the late 1960s in respect of Eastern Java and along the common border with Malaysia in Kalimantan. In other words, the Suharto government entertained its own version of the 'Domino Theory' conceived as continuous political erosion within its outer defence perimeter. With this strategic perspective in mind, it became alarmed at the onset of conflict in Cambodia.

Perched precariously on the sidelines of the Vietnam War, Cambodia had maintained a tolerable, if conditional, independence by a practice of accommodation with the Vietnamese communists. From 1969 public challenge on the part of Prince Sihanouk himself to Vietnamese exploitation of Cambodian territory as an active sanctuary had highlighted an issue which his domestic opponents used to justify his removal from office while he was out of the country. The coup was led by the Prime Minister, General Lon Nol, formerly Commander of the Cambodian armed forces. Apparently impressed by the deposition of Sukarno, he had established contact with a group of Indonesian intelligence officers before acting against Sihanouk. The interest of the Indonesian armed forces in Cambodia was mixed. They were keen to encourage Lon Nol to employ their military doctrines, while association with a state enjoying a neutral status and reputation was regarded as a decided political advantage. Indeed, Cambodia had been visited by President Suharto for that very reason during his first foreign tour in

1968.[28] An ulterior motive on the part of those intelligence officers who cultivated the relationship was a desire to transfer Indonesia's stock of outmoded rifles to Cambodia as part of a package arrangement under which the United States would replace them with modern M16s.[29] This interest was pursued when Cambodia became an additional theatre of war in the wake of Prince Sihanouk's deposition. The reaction of the Vietnamese communists to this episode had been hostile. Their diplomatic missions in Phnom Penh had been sacked; their troops enjoying sanctuary across the Cambodian border had been presented with an ultimatum to withdraw. The Vietnamese response was to lend active support to a National United Front set up in Peking with Prince Sihanouk at its head in opposition to the Lon Nol administration which had attracted speedy American recognition. This front, which initially enjoyed only limited support within Cambodia, served as a political shield for Vietnamese armed intervention in the east of the country from the end of March. Such was the pace and success of that advance that expectation was aroused in April that the capital would soon fall.

The evident disintegration of the small and ill-equipped Cambodian army gave cause for anxiety and also prompted a sense of opportunity in Jakarta. The prospect of communist takeover was viewed with deep concern. At this juncture, a group of intelligence officers proposed dispatching an expeditionary force to aid the Lon Nol government. Apart from an evident interest in exploiting the crisis to secure modern small-arms from the United States, it is difficult to know whether or not any practical military purpose was envisaged. In the event, the United States proved unwilling to finance an expeditionary force or to underwrite the transfer of Indonesian rifles to Cambodia on a replacement basis. Indonesia's military role amounted to the dispatch of an advisory military mission and a token shipment of arms and equipment in April. Subsequently, some Cambodian officers were trained in Indonesia. An additional reason why no active military role was undertaken was that Foreign Minister Malik was able to persuade President Suharto – who was fully conscious of the practical difficulties in the way of military intervention and of the attendant political risks – of the greater advantage of convening an international conference to draw attention to the situation in Cambodia.

Indonesia had adopted a position based on the formal requirement of a neutral Cambodia. An initial response had been to propose the re-establishment of the International Control Commission and to demand that all foreign troops leave the country. In late April, after regional consultations and with the approval of the UN Secretary General, Indonesia issued an invitation to twenty Asian and Pacific governments, including those of Australia and New Zealand, to participate in a conference in Jakarta. Its declared objective was 'to find a constructive formula on how to stop the deteriorating situation in Cambodia and restore peace and security to that country in order to enable the Cambodian people to solve their own problems by themselves'.[30] Apart from seeking to obstruct an adventurous propensity on the part of the more hawkish generals, the prospect of such a conference was attractive because of the opportunity it would provide to demonstrate that Indonesia had resumed an active, and not just an independent, foreign policy. It was contemplated as a diplomatic exercise in the tradition of Bandung for which Indonesia had received recognition and respect.

Adam Malik's intention had been to convene a diplomatic gathering which would be truly representative of Asia. A major obstacle, however, was the fact that Indonesia, in identifying itself with demands for the withdrawal of foreign troops and the restoration of Cambodian neutrality, appeared to be endorsing the authority of the Lon Nol government and also to be siding with the United States. In the event, the Jakarta Conference convened as a conspicuously partisan and committed assembly. It attracted the hostility of the communist invitees; North Vietnam, North Korea, China and Mongolia refused to attend. Moreover, the dispatch of invitations to the governments of Asian neutrals, including India, Burma and Ceylon, was followed almost immediately at the beginning of May by an American and South Vietnamese military incursion into Cambodia. This unfortunate coincidence, which was not anticipated in Jakarta, constituted a major set-back for the Indonesian government, whose ambassador in Washington made a futile protest. The act of intervention served to destroy the credibility of the impending conference as a non-aligned occasion. It came to be regarded as an American-inspired diplomatic adjunct to an armed incursion which aroused much fury within the United States. The list of actual participants served to confirm this view for those governments who looked on the event with deep suspicion and hostility. Representatives from the five ASEAN states were joined by America's allies, Australia, New Zealand, Japan and South Korea, as well as by representatives from the Royal Government of Laos and South Vietnam. In addition, a delegation from the Lon Nol administration was permitted to attend, though not as a participant. Foreign Minister Yem Sambaur was accorded the right to deliver an 'explanatory' address in advance of the first official plenary session, which further tainted the credentials of the conference and undermined the intended purpose of Indonesia's diplomatic enterprise.

In opening the formal proceedings on 16 May President Suharto not only dealt with the purpose of the conference but also pronounced on the nature of his country's foreign policy. He explained:[31]

For Indonesia, its foreign policy of non-alignment is not identical to non-involvement. That is the reason why Indonesia prefers to call it an independent and active foreign policy because to us foreign policy is not sterile, inanimate or idle. Indonesia's foreign policy is independent in the sense that Indonesia is free from any ties whatsoever, be it military, political or ideological so that Indonesia is truly free to evaluate any problem or event without any influence from any ties, military, political or ideological.

While Suharto's assertion that 'We do not choose confrontation' possessed an obvious appeal to many of the assembled delegates, his attempt to justify the conference on Cambodia by reference to an ideal view of Indonesia's foreign policy drew no sympathy from the conspicuously absent Asian neutrals and communist states. Moreover, the orientation of the conference aroused criticism within Indonesia. However it was represented in Jakarta, the occasion served to reinforce a general international assessment that Indonesia was a member of the Western camp. Indeed, a visit to Washington by President Suharto later in May appeared to confirm that impression.

As a diplomatic occasion, the Jakarta Conference was depicted within Indonesia as the most important undertaking of its kind since the Bandung gathering in April 1955. As an exercise in the projection of influence within South-East Asia, it was virtually a non-event; even the US government displayed only a tepid interest. Praiseworthy but powerless resolutions, including a call for the withdrawal of all foreign troops from Cambodia, were placed in the charge of a three-man mission drawn from Indonesia, Malaysia and Japan, which engaged in a fruitless perambulation to solicit the cooperation of members of the UN Security Council. In convening the conference, the Indonesian government had sought to give notice of an intention to resume an active regional role after an interlude of relative quiescence. The circumstances and composition of the conference marred the impression which Adam Malik had sought to convey. Moreover, apart from its being so evidently a gathering of supporters of the political *status quo* after the fall of Sihanouk, the conference had no bearing whatsoever on the cruel course of events in Cambodia itself. Indeed, in July 1970, the Indonesian government was obliged to reject a Cambodian request for military assistance. Malik remarked 'We have no arms for them. We just pray for Cambodia' – a striking indication of Indonesia's inability from a position of maritime insulation to do more than watch and wait on events which were deemed to affect its security.[32]

All in all, it was a sobering experience for a government which had insisted on incorporating its prescription for regional order in the founding document of ASEAN. When President Suharto addressed the third conference of non-aligned states in Zambia the following September, there was an evident defensiveness in his public justification of the Jakarta meeting.[33] Moreover, his experience on that occasion resulted in a growing sense of distance from the mainstream of non-alignment, which had begun to espouse a quality of radicalism with which Sukarno would have been more comfortable. The crisis over Cambodia, in which rhetoric could not be matched by action, put the concept of non-alignment into practical relief and introduced a measure of doubt as to its utility. Its reaffirmation had been a function of entrenched domestic values and a longstanding conviction that to deviate from them would compromise the independent interests of the Indonesian state. However, the practical business of foreign policy involved operating within identifiable constraints which required distinctions to be drawn between external powers and their associates, even if, in principle, they were all regarded with suspicion. Accordingly, the Indonesian delegation had no inhibitions in opposing the seating of a representative of Sihanouk's government in exile at the conference.

Adam Malik had made explicit that the first priority of Indonesia's foreign policy was to serve its development needs. Accordingly, special account had to be taken of the fact that the major source of development finance was overseas and that it was necessary to ensure external confidence in Indonesia. [34] The domestic economic requirements of the Republic and the political orientation of the military-dominated government had produced a convergence of economic and political interests with those of the principal external benefactors. And yet, an openly aligned anti-communist disposition was inhibited by a deep-seated aspiration to pursue an independent foreign policy which had its roots in the formative national experience. Moreover, a radical tradition tracing its lineal descent from national revolution and the campaign to recover West Irian was part of Indonesia's political culture, despite the transformation of the political system. Foreign policy was therefore subject to competing pulls. The domestic situation and concern over the changes in the balance of external influence in the regional environment disposed the government towards a convergence of interests with the United States and its associates. Indeed, this convergence had produced an informal alignment which, in turn, provoked domestic criticism of an unhealthy over-dependence and a departure from a foreign policy tradition which, if adhered to faithfully, would serve the regional destiny of the Republic. Malik's actual conduct of foreign policy constituted a pragmatic attempt to reconcile these competing pulls.

The Islamic Factor

Domestic constraint on foreign policy was felt in another respect also. This constraint arose from the cultural diversity of the Indonesian state and the attendant unresolved problem of national identity. Although President Suharto had repudiated the public values associated with his predecessor, he had endorsed the national creed which President Sukarno had expounded in June 1945. Indeed, the five principles of *Pancasila* were given a central place in his political system. Fundamental to that creed was the axiom that 'the state is based on divine omnipotence', which meant, in practice, that belief in God did not require adherence to any one exclusive faith, including that of Islam. Although Islam is, in princple, the religious faith of the vast majority of Indonesians, there is, in practice, a considerable variation in adherence to orthodoxy. A communal division exists between those Indonesians whose religion combines pre-Islamic animist and Hindu-Buddhist beliefs and those who follow more faithfully the precepts of the Prophet. Under the sponsorship of the Japanese during their occupation, orthodox Muslim political organizations flourished and developed expectations that an independent Indonesia would conform, in public values, with Islamic principles. These expectations were not fulfilled. Such principles were not incorporated in the constitutional structure of the Republic but were set aside in favour of the pluralist philosophy of *Pancasila*, which catered more readily for the large constituency of nominal Muslims who were concentrated primarily in East and Central Java. President Sukarno echoed the values of this constituency. He had formulated *Pancasila* in an attempt to prevent religious-communal passions from undermining the unity of the nationalist movement. To impose Islam on Javanese whose nominal adherence to that faith was combined with disdain for its orthodox practice was perceived to be a formula for religious strife on a national scale. In the event, organized political Islam had to be content with the provision for religious coexistence which was incorporated in *Pancasila*.

Moreover, the first general elections in 1955 demonstrated that the adherents of political Islam did not constitute a majority of voters. None the less, for those committed to religious pluralism as a means to ensure cultural identity, Islam persisted as a threat. Even before the attainment of independence, the *Dar ul-Islam* (House of Islam) movement had launched a violent campaign in support of a theocratic state, initially in West Java with affiliated insurrections occurring later in North Sumatra and South Sulawesi. Moreover, in the late 1950s, Islamic orthodoxy had been a factor in regional rebellion implicating the Masjumi Party proscribed by Sukarno in 1960. During the first decade of independence, Islam was perceived by the central government as a source of national division. Many senior officers in the armed forces, who assumed positions of importance after March 1966, had spent their formative years in the field in counter-insurgency operations against Muslim

137

rebels. Fear of the political ascendancy of orthodox Islam was a common characteristic of the military beneficiaries of the fall of Sukarno.

Under the leadership of General Suharto, special care was taken not to involve Indonesia in international issues which might lend encouragement to Muslim political ambitions. During the struggle for independence, such a self-denying ordinance had not obtained because of the importance of rallying as much international support as possible to the cause of the embattled Republic. Consequently, a conspicuously devout Islamic deputy Foreign Minister was dispatched to the Middle East to solicit diplomatic backing. After independence, circumstances and attitudes changed. Above all, internal Islamic challenge made for a more circumspect outlook on the part of the national government. Concern with domestic order did not, for example, prohibit public declarations of support for the Palestinians or for implementation of UN resolutions on Palestine, such as that embodied in the final communique of the Bandung Conference. Correspondingly, Indonesia did not recognize Israel; nor did its government contemplate such a prospect. However, support for the Palestinian cause was extended on the ground of the right of national self-determination and not on that of support for coreligionists.

The breakdown of parliamentary democracy in Indonesia was, in part, a product of intra-Islamic rivalry. None the less, the Muslim parties opposed the reinstatement of the 1945 constitution because Sukarno had refused to contemplate its amendment to incorporate Islamic principles. In consequence, he by-passed the Constituent Assembly and imposed the basic document of Guided Democracy by decree. After the event, political expediency governed the attitude of the conservative Javanese-based Nahdatul Ulamma (Muslim Scholars) Party, while the Masjumi was soon proscribed because of its association with regional rebellion. Within Guided Democracy, formal provision for the participation of religious interests in politics was made within the Nasakom formula, but it was religion in the *Pancasila* sense. Moreover, the prevailing ideological climate precluded any prospect of promoting a specifically Islamic cause either domestically or internationally. The refusal to grant visas to Israeli athletes seeking to take part in the Asian Games in 1962 constituted a response to Arab pressure and domestic Muslim opinion, but the issue was not clearly an Islamic one. Like that of Taiwan, it was associated within Indonesia with the rhetoric of the New Emerging Forces. For their part, the forces of Islam became preoccupied with the threat posed by the PKI to economic, as well as to religious, interests and were little engaged in matters of foreign policy beyond ritual support for the two phases of confrontation. It was only with the political transformation in the wake of the abortive coup in October 1965 that Islamic organisation came back into its own. In tactical alliance with the armed forces, Muslims led physical attacks on adherents and associates of the PKI who were slaughtered in tens of thousands. The vanguard role of Islamic groups, including active student bodies, in decimating the communists and in helping to usher in a new political order gave them a strong sense of political entitlement and the expectation that Islam's time had come. Indeed, it has been pointed out that 'Muslims not only confidently looked forward to attaining a political majority but also to the wider practices of an Islamic way of life throughout the country, if not the actual attainment of an Islamic state'.[35] Furthermore, in the ensuing rivalry between Generals Suharto and Nasution for political leadership, Suharto viewed Muslim resurgence and Nasution's attempt to exploit it not only as a challenge to his personal position but also to cultural values which he held in common with Sukarno.

The break between political Islam and the leadership of the armed forces was not long in coming and has not since been repaired. Although Muslim political parties have not demanded a theocratic state, they have resented their minor role in political life under *Pancasila* Democracy and have not given up aspirations for the incorporation of Islamic values into the constitutional structure of the state. Islam's sense of entitlement and expectation has been frustrated and denied because the government has been dominated since March 1966 by a military establishment identified with non-Islamic values. Islam has been contained, if not suppressed, within a political culture which espouses religious pluralism. The symbols of state have not encouraged the mobilization of the faithful. And the conduct of foreign policy has demonstrated a correspondingly negative intent.

In other words, a coreligionist dimension has been consciously excised from foreign policy in order to deny legitimate opportunity for Muslim groups to make claims on the government of the Republic. For example, when the People's Consultative Assembly formally re-affirmed Indonesia's independent and active foreign policy in July 1966, support was extended to the struggle of the 'Arab People of Palestine . . . to establish justice, truth and independence' without any expression of coreligionist sentiment. An even more telling instance was the government's refusal to sign the Charter of the Organisation of the Islamic Conference established in Jeddah in March 1972. Objection was based on the ground that the terms of the Charter gave rise to the conclusion that 'the signatories would be Islamic countries', whereas Indonesia has always insisted, in an exercise in studied ambiguity, that it is neither a theocratic nor a secular state. The practical purpose of Indonesia's position was to avoid any act of international affiliation which might serve to validate the cause or claims of the adherents of Islam within the Republic. In the event, Indonesia was permitted to participate in the activities of the organization without signing its founding document. Subsequently, it has sought to identify itself at Islamic conferences with the principles of Bandung and the non-aligned movement and not those of Islam. Moreover, it has sought to keep the political turbulence of the Arab world at a distance. The Palestine Liberation Organisation has not been allowed to open an office in Jakarta. Such political circumspection has been a striking, if negative, feature of the conduct of foreign policy by the Suharto government, which has sought to define Indonesian identity without reference to Islam.

By the early 1970s, the administration established by General Suharto had changed course successfully in foreign policy, if without rejecting all the priorities of its predecessor. The goals of a viable unitary state, free from internal divisions and external dependence and with a decisive role in the management of regional order, had been sustained. Yet, if in many basic respects the ends of policy had not been revised, the means to those ends certainly had. Externally financed development, especially in oil production, was chosen as the instrument to be employed for the ultimate attainment of a greater prosperity and self-reliance. Greater international standing was attained as an active, if minor, member of OPEC. Regional cooperation with like-minded conservative states had been undertaken in an attempt to promote an autonomous system of regional order based on a willing acceptance of Indonesia's primary role. The relationship between such means and ends was itself complex and placed a strain on the conduct of a foreign policy whose ideal declaratory goals possessed genuine domestic political appeal. Thus, development policies involved a *de facto* alignment, while the deeply held anti-communism of the military establishment meant that the prospect of revolutionary political change in Indochina could not be easily accommodated within the perspective of non-alignment. Equidistance in international politics was a luxury which an enfeebled Indonesia could not afford, even if it was useful to give the impression, in rhetoric, of such a disposition. Deficiencies in miltary capability also meant that continuity in pursuit of goals in foreign policy was combined with paradox in its practice. The source of such paradox was deep-rooted, namely, the inability to reconcile an independent nationalist spirit and an attendant sense of regional entitlement with a weak and vulnerable social and physical state structure. Such paradox was pointed up by Foreign Minister Malik in an interview in August 1971. He explained: [36]

Without leaving out idealism, we will give first priority to business-like rational and objective national interests for the sake of economic development which will bring prosperity and welfare to the whole Indonesian people. Economic cooperation with other countries is

first priority in the order of priorities in our international relations.
... It is clear that the principles of our foreign policy remain
unchanged. Only the tactics in its execution change sometimes.

He went on to say:

Indonesia is attempting to create an area of goodwill, friendship and
cooperation. Indonesia needs close friendly relations and mutual
understanding particularly in South-East Asia so that the limit of
common interests can be projected directly to the eastern border of
India and the southern border of China and Japan.

Paradox or not, Indonesia's new course in foreign policy had begun to
pay dividends, even if the Republic was more of a spectator than an
actor in the theatre of regional relations. Adam Malik gave his interview
shortly before assuming the presidency of the UN General Assembly –
a symbolic indication of the international political rehabiliation of a state
which had revoked its membership of the world organization less than
six years previously.

6 The Management of Regional Order

In August 1966 General Suharto had articulated a vision of 'a co-operating South-East Asia' which would 'constitute the strongest bulwark and base in facing imperialism and colonialism of whatever form and from whatever quarter it may come'. A year later, with the formation of ASEAN, the Indonesian government was successful in transposing that vision to the new association, whose founding members committed themselves 'to ensure their stability and security from external interference in any form or manifestation'. Indonesia's active and unprecedented participation in regional cooperation constituted an attempt to realize longstanding ends through new means. ASEAN was seen as the most appropriate instrument with which to expunge the legacy of confrontation and also to promote a willing acceptance of Indonesia's political primacy within South-East Asia. Moreover, it was perceived as the vehicle through which Indonesia and its cooperating neighbours might provide, in time, for a system of regional order untrammelled by dependence on outside powers. Indonesia's aspiration for ASEAN was indicated by Adam Malik in his claim that the Association expressed:[1]

> the growing determination of the nations of this region to take charge of their own future, to work out problems of their development, stability and security together. It signifies the rejection by those countries of the assumption that the fate of South-East Asia is going to be determined by outside powers.

In the event, the theory and practice of regional order diverged. Initially, cooperation within ASEAN was minimal. Indeed, evident strains appeared within the Association because of the revival of the Philippines claim to Sabah and the execution in Singapore of two Indonesian marines. Furthermore, the sense of strategic perspective which Indonesia sought to impart to ASEAN as a corporate entity did not match the requirements of its memebrs. For example, in the case of Thailand, ASEAN possessed less than immediate relevance to the fundamental security problem of how to manage future relationshps with China and the Democratic Republic of Vietnam, given the

142

uncertainty and increasing domestic liability of reliance upon American countervailing power. Indeed, Indonesia's patrimonial purview, expressed in an intention to assume the role of *primus inter pares* within a new concert of regional states, possessed primarily declaratory significance. In the light of a changing balance of extra-regional influences bearing on South-East Asia, which the government in Jakarta could only observe and not truly influence, Indonesia's regional vision enjoyed limited regional acceptance.

One striking example of both the persistence with which the Suharto government pursued its regional design and the mixed response to this enterprise arose from a joint attempt by Indonesia and Malaysia in November 1971 to challenge the customary legal status of the Straits of Malacca and Singapore. A previous chapter has discussed the major maritime initiative undertaken by the Indonesian government in December 1957 when an archipelagic principle or doctrine was promulgated as an expression of abiding concern for the vulnerable condition of a socially diverse and physically fragmented state. An underlying purpose of that earlier initiative was to establish a recognized legal position in advance of the development of a capability to control access by naval powers into the maritime interstices of the archipelagic state. To this end, if without success, Indonesia had sought to secure recognition of its claimed archipelagic status at the first two UN Conferences on the Law of the Sea which convened in 1958 and 1960. This objective was sustained after the internal transfer of power in 1966. And it was actively pursued in the wake of the establishment by the United Nations of an *ad hoc* committee on the seabed in 1967, which set in train a debate culminating in a decision in December 1970 to convene a third conference on the law of the sea. The *Wawasan Nusantara*, or 'Archipelago Outlook', had been adopted as an integral part of the doctrine of Indonesia's armed forces from 1969. Its notion of 'one territorial unity' possessed an evident maritime dimension, for it had been made clear that:[2]

> The seas and straits must be utilised to bridge the physical separa-
> tions between the islands, regions and the manifold ethnic groups;
> this is also the case with our air space.

Moreover, in March 1973, the constitutionally supreme People's Consultative Assembly affirmed a commitment to the 'Archipelago Outlook' as a guideline of state policy.

During 1971, an opportunity arose for Indonesia to assert a related maritime claim in the case of the Straits of Malacca and Singapore which, apart from providing the shortest sea route between the Indian and Pacific Oceans, also provides a point of entry into its archipelagic waters. As a consequence of its acute interest in ensuring safety of navigation for its supertankers in passage from the Persian Gulf through those straits en route to its home islands, the Japanese government had concluded agreements with the respective coastal states for the conduct of detailed hydrographic surveys. Concurrently, initiative was taken in London at the headquarters of the Inter-Governmental Maritime Consultative Organisation (IMCO) to promote a traffic separation scheme in the congested narrows. In its enthusiasm to ensure safety and freedom of passage, Japan's Ministry of Transport had circulated a draft proposal which referred to the creation of a 'Malacca-Singapore Straits Board' to which Indonesia, Malaysia and Singapore as coastal states would be obliged to submit annual reports. What the Japanese delegate to IMCO had preferred to describe as 'necessary international action' to implement a traffic separation scheme was readily construed as an unwarranted intrusion into a matter falling exclusively within sovereign jurisdiction. In consequence, Indonesia's representative entered a strong protest. Then, attracting the support of Malaysia and Singapore, a delegation from the three coastal states called on IMCO's Secretary-General in London in September 1971. They requested specifically that the UN agency refrain from discussing the problem of navigational safety in the Straits of Malacca and Singapore until the coastal states were prepared themselves to raise the subject at a future meeting.

This *démarche* provided the backgroud to consequent consultations and an initiative on the part of the three coastal states on 16 November 1971. In a public statement, the governments of Indonesia, Malaysia and Singapore expressed their agreement that 'safety of navigation in the Straits of Malacca and Singapore is the responsibility of the coastal states concerned'. Much more significant was the concurrent assertion by Indonesia and Malaysia only 'that the Straits of Malacca and Singapore are not international straits, while fully recognising their use for international shipping in accordance with the principle (*sic*) of innocent passage'. Singapore did not concur but only 'took note of the position' of its coastal state neighbours and ASEAN partners. This joint statement by Indonesia and Malaysia constituted a challenge to the customary legal status of two linked straits used for international navigation which had been assumed by all maritime powers to be governed by the legal regime of unimpeded passage. Its basis as a legal claim arose from Indonesia's extension of the limit of its territorial waters to twelve miles in December 1957 and a corresponding extension by Malaysia in August 1969, and then the conclusion of a treaty between the two states in March 1970 which delimited the territorial sea boundary in the Malacca Strait.[3]

The joint statement by Indonesia and Malaysia reflected, on the one hand, the degree of reconciliation between the two states since the end of confrontation. Initial military cooperation along their common border in Nothern Borneo had been matched by a progressive convergence of outlook on the question of regional order expressed in an evident special relationship within the wider framework of ASEAN. This convergence of outlook was demonstrated in matters of maritime policy to the extent that Malaysia was encouraged and willing to play an active role in articulating the challenge to the customary legal status of the Straits of Malacca and Singapore. On the other hand, the joint statement reflected the wider maritime interests of Indonesia indicated fourteen years earlier with the enunciation of the archipelagic doctrine. Apart from genuine concern about the environmental hazards arising from grounding or collision of oil tankers in the straits, and also the competitive use of the passage between the two major oceans by the superpowers, the initiative which Indonesia inspired derived from a longstanding strategic perspective. This perspective had been acquired in the course of attaining and sustaining the independence and integrity of the archipelagic state. It incorporated elements of the paradox discussed earlier, namely, a sense of national vulnerability combined with one of regional entitlement.

The Indonesian-inspired initiative constituted a presumptuous act, given Indonesia's limited naval capability and the importance of the Straits of Malacca and Singapore as a maritime corridor between major oceans. Indeed, as if to put that initiative in proper perspective, both the United States and the Soviet Union deployed naval squadrons through those straits en route to the Bay of Bengal for an exercise in competitive naval display in the closing stage of the Bangladesh War. In March 1972, the Indonesian and Soviet governments engaged in a rancorous public argument about rights of passage which obscured a more private, if equally determined, protest conveyed by the United States. The unity of interests of the two superpowers over the issue of the legal regime of all straits used for international navigation meant that the Indonesian-Malaysian challenge to the customary legal status of the Straits of Malacca and Singapore had little prospect of success. Moreover, the political disposition of the Suharto administration, and its *de facto* relationship with the United States, was such that Indonesia could not adopt a practical policy of equi-distance towards the superpowers. If, in principle, all superpower naval deployment within South-East Asia was regarded with distaste, and even though, for example, ostensible public concern had been expressed at the construction by the United States of a defence facility on the Island of Diego Garcia in the Indian Ocean, a major distinction had in practice to be drawn between the conduct of the government in Washington and that in Moscow. In a regional environment of some uncertainty, the United

States constituted a security partner, if an informal one. Its strategic requirements, including the underwater deployment of submarines carrying missiles with nuclear warheads through Indonesia's deep-water straits of Lombok-Makassar and Ombei-Wetar, could not be detached totally from Indonesia's security interests. A Soviet naval presence operating within the strategic horizons of Indonesia had become a fact of political life and the US navy constituted the only credible counterweight and had to be tolerated in the interests of *raison d'état*.

The challenge by Indonesia and Malaysia to the customary legal status of the Straits of Malacca and Singapore, if a genuine expression of strategic outlook, did not serve the cause of regional cooperation within ASEAN. Singapore, conscious of its own dependence on freedom of navigation, refused to endorse the challenge, while Thailand indicated concern at the prospect of any interruption of shipping along the only route connecting its western and eastern coastlines. The issue of safety of navigation in the straits was another matter. And here, Indonesia and Malaysia, with Singapore, reached an initial agreement on traffic separation in February 1977 which was endorsed by IMCO the following November. This traffic separation scheme became operative in May 1981 on a voluntary basis. The legal regime of passage, however, could not be negotiated exclusively among the coastal states. In the event, in return for concessions over safety of navigation, Indonesia, with Malaysia, became obliged to accept a regime of 'transit (i.e. continuous and expeditious) passage' in the Straits of Malacca and Singapore which gave the maritime powers the freedom of naval movement on which they had always insisted.

In negotiations at the sessions of the Third UN Conference on the Law of the Sea which began in 1974, it became evident that the Indonesian delegation was more interested in securing legal recognition of its declared archipelagic status than in a revised legal regime in the Straits of Malacca and Singapore. Indeed, the impression was obtained that the joint initiative taken over the straits in November 1971 was intended to establish a prior bargaining position in an attempt to secure satisfactory concessions on archipelagic status. Such concessions were secured at the Law of the Sea Conference because of the skill of the small archipelagic lobby, of which Indonesia was a powerful member, in pressing its case. Success was facilitated by a general acceptance of a 200-mile Exclusive Economic Zone and a reciprocal undertaking to accord a right of 'archipelagic sea lanes passage' which corresponded, in essential respects, with that of 'transit passage'. Archipelagic status was inscribed in the negotiating texts and the draft convention of the Law of the Sea Conference which was approved by majority vote in April 1982. In this process of negotiation, Indonesia was closely aligned with the

Philippines – as ASEAN partner – which also had claimed archipelagic status, but less closely with Malaysia, with whom it had issued its earlier challenge. The government in Kuala Lumpur became concerned at the prospect and consequences of Indonesia's archipelagic waters interposing between its Peninsular and Borneo wings. It was not until February 1982, after protracted negotiations, that Malaysia's apprehensions over freedom of navigation were assuaged. A maritime treaty was signed in which Malaysia recognised Indonesia's archipelagic jurisdiction in return for Indonesia's recognition of Malaysia's right of free passage.

The Indonesian government has enjoyed mixed success in its attempt to underpin the fragile integrity of the archipelagic state by legal means. In the case of the Straits of Malacca and Singapore, relations with Singapore had been strained, while the joint opposition of the two superpowers had not permitted much more than a declaratory challenge to customary legal status. More evident success was obtained over the issue of archipelagic status through an ability to exploit a global trend, although the government in Kuala Lumpur was left with the feeling that it had been used in a joint enterprise over the Straits of Malacca and Singapore in order to serve a larger Indonesian purpose which did not cater for its own interests. Indeed, even before the issue of the archipelagic status had been joined at the Law of the Sea Conference, Indonesia had found it necessary to thwart a Malaysian initiative which threatened its regional vision. Coincidentally, it did so towards the end of the same month in which the joint initiative had been undertaken with Malaysia over the customary legal regime in the Straits of Malacca and Singapore.

A Zone of Peace

When Tun Abdul Razak became Prime Minister in September 1970, the Malaysian government had sought to transform the nature of its foreign policy. At the meeting of non-aligned states in Zambia, he had called on the delegates to endorse the neutralization of Indochina 'and possibly of the entire region of South-East Asia guaranteed by the three major powers, the People's Republic of China, the Soviet Union and the United States'.[4] Apart from a desire to revise a foreign policy which had reflected close association with the former metropolitan power, a prime objective of this proposal was to serve a domestic political purpose by placing dealings with China on a sound intergovernmental footing. The intention was to demonstrate to the alienated among Malaysia's large resident Chinese community and to the predominantly ethnic Chinese Malayan Communist Party that the legitimacy of the government in Kuala Lumpur was recognized and endorsed in Peking.

147

To this end, the government had dispatched an envoy to the Chinese capital in advance of the encouraging appearance there in July 1971 of Dr Henry Kissinger to prepare for President Nixon's historic visit in February 1972. Further encouragement for the realization of its policy was provided in October 1971 when the government of the People's Republic secured China's seat in the United Nations. In contrast to Indonesia, Malaysia voted against the two-thirds requirement for the expulsion of the Taiwan government, and also voted in favour of seating the mainland government while Indonesia abstained.

The differences in position over the China seat in the United Nations between the two closest ASEAN partners was not the first occasion on which their interests had come publicly into conflict. The previous September, the Indonesian Foreign Minister had put forward a reasoned rejection of Malaysia's neutralization proposal which merits reproduction in part. Adam Malik had argued that:[5]

> neutralisation that is the product of 'one-way' benevolence on the part of the big powers, at this stage, would perhaps prove as brittle and unstable as the interrelationship between the major powers themselves.

As an alternative, he suggested:

> I strongly believe that it is only through developing among ourselves an area of internal cohesion and stability, based on indigenous socio-political and economic strength, that we can ever hope to assist in the early stabilization of a new equilibrium in the region that would not be the exclusive 'diktat' of the major powers. However dominant the influence of these powers may be, I think there is and there should be scope for an indigenous Southeast Asian component in the new, emerging power balance of the region. In fact, I am convinced that unless the big powers acknowledge and the Southeast Asian nations themselves assume a greater and more direct responsibility in the maintenance of security in the area, no lasting stability can ever be achieved.
> It is only through such a Southeast Asian presence in the power equation that we can ever hope to persuade the major powers to take into account our wishes and aspirations and the directions and forms in which we want to develop. At this transitional stage, in which the international constellation of forces is moving towards new balances of accommodation, we are afforded an opportunity to contribute our concepts into the mainstream of thinking and searching that is going on. It is a unique opportunity and we should not waste it. Once a new equilibrium is crystallized, we may not be able to do any more.
> To this end, therefore, the nations of Southeast Asia should consciously work towards the day when security in their own region

will be the primary responsibility of the Southeast Asian nations themselves. Not through big power alignments, not through the build up of contending military pacts or military arsenals but through strengthening the state of our respective national endurance, through effective regional cooperation and through cooperation with other states sharing this basic view on world affairs.

It is here that the importance of such an organisation as ASEAN comes to the fore, as basically reflecting the determination of its member countries to take charge of their own future and to reject the assumption that the fate of their region is to continue to be determined by outside powers.

Malik rejected the notion of neutralization, above all because the provisions of the Malaysian proposal were construed to mean that the fate of South-East Asia would continue to be determined by outside powers. As such, it constituted an unacceptable alternative to Indonesia's long-standing regional vision which had been entrusted to ASEAN. Indonesia's opportunity to persuade its regional partners of the merits of its own strategic perspective occurred towards the end of November when the Foreign Ministers of the Association assembled in Kuala Lumpur in an *ad hoc* session and not in a formal ASEAN gathering, prompted by the assumption of China's seat in the United Nations by the government in Peking. Adam Malik appeared in the Malaysian capital accompanied conspicuously by a group of senior military advisers whose prime concern was the prospect of a collective agreement to establish diplomatic relations with the People's Republic of China. There were no differences, however, between Indonesia's Foreign and Defence Ministries over the proposal for neutralization, which they regarded as naive. Moreover, ready support for Indonesia's position was attracted from all the other ASEAN partners who opposed the Malaysian proposal for their own reasons. From Indonesia's point of view, an unstated irritation was the attempt by the Malaysian government to prescribe unilaterally for the management of regional order. Such an initiative on the part of a state deemed, from Jakarta's perspective, to be inhabited by country cousins was regarded as audacious. More fundamentally, the central feature of the neutralization proposal, namely, provision for external power guarantees, was repugnant to the leadership of a government which exhibited a strong sense of regional entitlement. The prospect of external powers (including communist states) being permitted virtual policing rights within South-East Asia foreshadowed a condominium of sorts, which would not necessarily be free from conflict and which would violate the principles enshrined in the preamble to the ASEAN Declaration. Malaysia had sought to turn Indonesia's conception of regional order upside down. In the event, the force of Indonesia's influence prevailed, facilitated by the strong reservations of other governments. Thus, although public agreement was expressed that 'the neutralization of South-East Asia is a desirable objective', the Malaysian proposal was altered in nomenclature and in legal quality so as to appear a diluted version of the original formulation. After much discussion over alternative formulas and under Indonesian guidance, the Foreign Ministers stated their governments' determination:[6]

> to exert initially necessary efforts to secure the recognition of, and respect for, South-East Asia as a Zone of Peace, Freedom and Neutrality, free from any form of manner of interference by outside Powers.

The terminology of the Kuala Lumpur Declaration of 27 November 1971 lacked the legal precision of the concept of neutralization. The Malaysian government had been obliged to concede an imprecise alternative aspiration. The Zone of Peace formula constituted an exercise in creative ambiguity intended to exclude any possibility of justification for external power intervention, which was regarded, by Indonesia in particular, as an intolerable affliction. Despite its intangible quality, it offered scope for the kind of system of regional order which Indonesia had long advocated and which its Foreign Minister had elaborated on the previous September. Indonesia had scored a diplomatic victory of a kind in Kuala Lumpur, if, in part, a negative one. It had been able to set to one side the concept of neutralization and had reinstated its own strategic perspective as the common platform of the ASEAN states, though without making more than a declaratory impact. A consistency of purpose had been sustained but practical application and initiative did not rest with Indonesia and its regional partners. They were obliged to respond to change. Their capability to induce it and to shape it was minimal.

Apart from growing concern at the course of conflict in Indochina, Indonesia was noticeably disturbed by the outbreak of hostilities in South Asia which culminated in the advent of Bangladesh as a new state in December 1971. Two features of that conflict caused apprehension in Jakarta which delayed the extension of diplomatic recognition to Dacca. First, strong private disquiet was expressed at the success of a separatist movement facilitated by an act of direct outside intervention by India. The fear that a precedent might have been established for other parts of Asia was strongly felt in the light of Indonesia's own experience of internal dissent. Secondly, alarm was engendered because of the role of the Soviet Union in helping to promote the dismemberment of Pakistan. The treaty of friendship concluded between India and the Soviet Union in the August prior to the final and decisive act of military intervention also reinforced fear of a regional precedent. Suspicion was aroused towards India for serving as a proxy in a process which Indonesia wished to reverse in the case of South-East Asia. In the wake of confrontation, relations between Indonesia and India had been repaired, in part because the two states shared a common mistrust of China. However, India's willingness to indulge in a classic balance of power manoeuvre utilizing the countervailing capability of the Soviet Union produced a reversion to coolness in the relationship. Moreover, India's confirmation as the primary power in South Asia reintroduced an element of rivalry as memories were revived of Nehru's erstwhile paternalism. One response on the part of Indonesia was to pay greater attention to regional military cooperation, if outside the formal auspices of ASEAN. Though not a substantive intitiative, it indicated that adherence to non-alignment would not be permitted to impose constraints deemed to harm Indonesia's interests. For example, in Manila in February 1972, the Presidents of Indonesia and the Philippines agreed to cooperate in the 'exchange of information, training of personnel and joint patrols and exercises for self defence and the enhancement of national defence capability'. Bilateral military cooperation with a regional partner, itself in a formal alliance relationship with the United States, had ceased to be a matter of taboo, given the adverse changes in the regional environment which had been in train ever since President Johnson had announced his virtual abdication from office in response to domestic protest against the war in Vietnam. From initial military cooperation on a bilateral basis which had begun with Malaysia, Indonesia went on to extend the practice to all its ASEAN partners. Indeed, in the case of Malaysia, in April 1972 the security arrangements entered into in 1967 were so revised as to constitute a tacit alliance in terms of the scope of defence cooperation between the two states.

The element of pragmatism displayed in response to an uncertain regional environment was indicated in a willingness by Indonesia to participate in the International Commission of Control and Supervision (ICCS) which was set up to monitor the Paris Peace Agreements on Vietnam concluded in January 1973. The Indonesian government had responded to the initial suggestion that it play a role in peace supervision in Vietnam made by President Nixon when he visited Jakarta briefly in July 1969. President Suharto's positive response reflected a desire to cooperate with the United States, given its role in promoting Indonesia's economic recovery. Moreover, the Americans had, to a limited extent, resumed military assistance to armed forces which were sadly depleted in equipment. Such assistance had begun again in 1967 on a small scale, with initial emphasis on a civic action role designed to moderate any apprehension among Indonesia's neighbours and to appease its external creditors. For example, provision was made for

151

spare parts for air force transports to enable distribution of foodstuffs and medicines within the archipelago. The United States assumed a more substantive role with the reorganisation of Indonesia's armed forces from the end of 1969. Over the next five years, moderate provision rising to approximately US$45m. helped to refurbish a depleted military machine, while Australia was encouraged to transfer a squadron of Sabre jets, a few aircraft for maritime surveillance and coastal patrol vessels. Such defence aid was designed to facilitate a sense of partnership and to assist in the further consolidation of central government control rather than to augment significantly the country's military capability.

Indonesia's response to President Nixon's suggestion that it play a part in supervizing an eventual cease-fire in Vietnam should be understood in the light of such assistance, and a realization that ideal formulas were hardly sufficient in themselves to provide for regional order. Accordingly, when General Westmoreland visited Indonesia in February 1972 to discuss the prospect of participation in a peace supervision force, his military counterparts expressed interest, if only to secure access to defence aid in return for a willingness to help the United States save face. Only mild comment was expressed when the United States bombed Hanoi and mined the harbour of Haiphong in response to the spring offensive launched by North Vietnam in March that year. Indeed, Adam Malik's remarks were construed widely as an endorsement of US policy. In November 1972, shortly after tentative accord had been reached on a peace agreement for Vietnam, the Indonesian government agreed to participate in the ICCS. Its membership was accepted by North Vietnam in January 1973 after initial resistance. In the event, Indonesia's participation was a mixed blessing, especially as both its Foreign and Defence Ministries expected eventual unification of Vietnam on communist terms. Thus, Indonesia became a member of an impotent body serving as an American nominee. Pride at being the only Asian participant in the ICCS, an opportunity to monitor the culmination of a regional conflict of global significance, and ensuring receipt of much needed military assistance had to be set against a declining standing in the Third World and a disposition on the part of Hanoi to regard the government in Jakarta in a similar light to those of ASEAN partners which had actually sent troops to fight in Vietnam. North Vietnam could only have been antagonized by the Indonesian delegation's walk-out from the conference of non-aligned Foreign Ministers held in Guyana in August 1972 in protest at the seating of a delegation from the Provisional Revolutionary Government of South Vietnam. From the outset, ASEAN had been regarded as a tool of US imperialism and Indonesia's conduct did not give the government in Hanoi any reason to revise its view of the

Association. Accordingly, President Suharto could not have been engaging in anything but wishful political thinking when in Manila in early 1972 he expressed the aspiration that ASEAN would become 'the main asset towards the development of a bigger regional organization covering all the nations of South-East Asia irrespective of political system'.[7]

Indonesia was caught between aspiration and achievement. ASEAN was envisaged as the appropriate instrument for the management of regional order and, indeed, as a foundation on which an even more extensive pattern of regional relationships might be established.[8] The government's sense of regional entitlement was indicated in February 1973 in the cool response accorded to the proposal by the Australian Prime Minister, Gough Whitlam, that an Asia-wide organization be established within which ASEAN would be subsumed as 'a sub-regional organization'. However, refusal to contemplate a proposal which could be realized only at ASEAN's expense was not matched by ability to demonstrate the vitality of an association described by Adam Malik as the cornerstone of Indonesia's foreign policy.[9] ASEAN had not displayed a capacity for growth. Willing candidates for membership were embattled governments who would have brought weakness and dissension within the Association. Moreover, the compromise formula of inviting such governments to ministerial meetings as observers served only to confirm the aligned disposition of ASEAN and, in advance of resolution of the conflict in Indochina, did not augur well for its expansion on a viable basis. The government in Hanoi refused to send an observer to the meeting of ASEAN Foreign Ministers held in Pattaya in April 1973 because American bombing of Cambodia was being conducted from bases on Thai soil. And in 1974 it rejected an invitation to send an observer to the corresponding meeting in Jakarta because of the refusal of the host government to invite a representative from the Provisional Revolutionary Government of South Vietnam. Indeed, at that seventh annual meeting of Foreign Ministers, President Suharto expressed his open disappointment at the limited progress attained by ASEAN, maintaining 'it will remain a very fragile reality unless we concentrate on our constant vigilance and on our common noble dedication'.

Indonesia's sense of frustration at not being able to influence the pattern of regional events was reinforced as individual members of ASEAN went their own way in foreign policy. For example, at the end of May 1974, Malaysia's Prime Minister, Tun Abdul Razak, travelled to Peking where diplomatic relations were opened, much to the displeasure of the military establishment in Jakarta. Moreover, in June and July 1975, the Philippines and Thailand followed suit in the wake of the dramatic culmination of the Second Indochina War. For these somewhat peripheral members of ASEAN, the abiding virtues of the balance of power counted for more than any ideal formulas for regional order which were a product of the unique experience of Indonesia. Ironically, the only ASEAN government which kept diplomatic pace with Indonesia over China was that of Singapore, which announced that it would establish diplomatic relations only after they had been resumed by its counterpart in Jakarta. This self-denying declaration was small comfort to the Indonesian government which could not fail to contrast the scope of its regional vision with its limited role as regional spectator. In the circumstances, its association with the United States became of greater importance. Despite passionately held views about the nefarious intent of all external powers,[10] the prospect of the United States in a phase of strategic decline aroused profound concern. Irrespective of any mixed feelings about US motives and reliability, the likelihood of competition between the Soviet Union and China to fill the vacuum left by an abdication of the US military presence was extremely disturbing.

East Timor

It was at this juncture and in this context that the Indonesian government responded with an act of war to a perceived threat to the security of the Republic which arose within the bounds of its archipelago. The eastern half of the island of Timor in the lesser Sundas group, 300 miles to the north of Australia, had been settled by Portuguese friars in the sixteenth century; formal demarcation of Timor between Portugal and the Netherlands had not been completed until 1913. East Timor, together with the enclave of Oecusse in the western half of the island, had been encompassed within a common political framework during Japan's occupation of the Netherland East Indies but was not included in the territorial claim of Indonesia's nationalist movement after August 1945. Indeed, the eastern half of the island of Timor had not been the object of serious Indonesian attention before political upheaval in Lisbon in April 1974 gave rise to repercussions for all the Portuguese overseas possessions. East Timor had escaped the romantic political appetite of Sukarno because it was a Portuguese possession. Successive Indonesian governments had justified a claim to West Irian on the grounds that all and only the territories of the former Netherlands East Indies constituted the Republic of Indonesia. Moreover, given East Timor's size (only 7,500 square miles), its population (approximately 650,000), its distant location and marginal economic condition, this vestige of empire hardly constituted as attractive an issue as that of

Malaysia for promoting solidarity with which to shore-up the political fragility of Guided Democracy.

Indonesia's interest in East Timor did not constitute an expression of territorial acquisitiveness as such. It indicated deep apprehension at a possible threat to the security of the Republic which might arise from uncertain political change in the adjoining colony. It is possible that the Suharto administration would have been opposed to the emergence of any independent state in succession to Portuguese rule. The advent in mid-May 1974 of a radical political movement with a measure of popular support generated anxiety at the prospect of having to share a common border with an independent state of an unacceptable political identity. Its external affiliations could pose a challenge to Indonesian interests through its very presence at the margin of a fissiparous archipelago. This political movement, which ultimately styled itself the Revolutionary Front for an Independent East Timor (Fretilin), demanded early and complete independence. Its radical rhetoric, its intentional acronymic similarity to Frelimo in Mozambique and its links with leftist groups in both Portugal and its overseas possessions in Africa caused consternation in Jakarta. An early Indonesian response was to cultivate a client political party which sought integration for the colony within the neighbouring Republic. Indonesia's support for the Timorese Popular Democratic Association (Apodeti) established at the end of May was determined by an intense concern with national security. To explain Indonesia's initiatives and ultimate military action in terms of geographic tidiness and Javanese imperialism would be an over-simplification. East Timor was coveted and then seized by force of arms not because the Portuguese half of the island was perceived as an asset or prize but because it was deemed essential to secure it in order to deny its uncertain utility to others. East Timor, at the very periphery of archipelagic Indonesia, attracted serious attention in Jakarta because of the abiding sense of territorial vulnerability arising from geographic fragmentation and social diversity. Such an apprehension was made more acute by the dominant influence of the armed forces in the government of Indonesia. Accordingly, the augury of political change in East Timor after April 1974 conjured up a variety of worst possible cases, including the prospect of a point of entry for hostile forces being opened up into the soft exterior of the Republic and encouragement being provided for separatism within the archipelago.

Initially, the Indonesian government sought to pursue its goal of incorporation by influencing the political process within East Timor. Forcible incorporation was contemplated only as the instrument of last resort because President Suharto did not want Indonesia to be seen to be violating Portuguese sovereignty as long as it was being visibly exercised within a stable context and on the basis of a firm commitment to orderly decolonization. There existed a concern not to tarnish the international reputation of Indonesia in the regard of its benefactors among the IGGI Aid Consortium as the moderate opposite of the country under the rule of President Sukarno. In addition, there was no desire to provoke a sense of alarm among its regional neighbours, and especially its partners within ASEAN. It has been argued earlier that Indonesia's plans for the management of regional order were predicated on an ability to consolidate a store of goodwill built up assiduously within non-communist South-East Asia since the formal ending of confrontation.

A major diplomatic effort was made designed to persuade the Portuguese government to Indonesia's way of thinking. This exercise was conducted not by the Foreign Ministry but by a leading intelligence officer, Lt. General Ali Murtopo, who sought to secure at least tacit consent to a campaign to influence opinion within East Timor, whose political future the Portuguese government wished to have decided by an elected constituent assembly. During the remainder of the year following the assumption of power by the Armed Forces Movement in Lisbon, Indonesia's attempt to promote by overt and covert means the political advantage of its internal client served only to induce a counter-vailing coalition between Fretilin and the Timorese Democratic Union (UDT), a conservative grouping established early in May 1974 which had sought continuing political association with Portugal. This alignment in January 1975, and the absence of political disorder in the territory, denied Indonesia any credible justification for armed intervention. However, during the course of 1975, circumstances arose which provided both justification and opportunity.[11] First, as a consequence of increasing radicalism on the part of Fretilin and an Indonesian ability to play on UDT apprehensions, the association between the two Timorese parties became subject to strain. UDT withdrew from the coalition at the end of May and street confrontations followed between opposing supporters. Secondly, a major breakdown in law and order occurred from August when increasing antagonism between UDT and Fretilin culminated in an inept attempt by the former to seize power. The UDT show of force was short-lived as Fretilin loyalists among Timorese forces in the Portuguese garrison rallied to its cause. By mid-September, Fretilin had established control in the administrative capital, Dili, and had crushed all opposition except along the border with West Timor. The outbreak of civil war not only disrupted Portugal's plan for orderly decolonization but also led to the complete abdication of responsibility by the officials of the reluctant colonial power who retreated to the neighbouring island of Atauro.

With the onset of civil war and sensitive to Western attitudes because of the financial scandal over the foreign debt incurred by its national oil company, Pertamina, the Indonesian government sought initially to promote its political ends through the medium of a collective police action under the aegis of Portuguese sovereignty. But it was unable to persuade either Portugal or neighbouring Australia to countenance participation of troops within a multi-national force, including Malaysia, even though Gough Whitlam had indicated that the best outcome would be for East Timor to become part of Indonesia. After the failure of this initiative which coincided with an evident consolidation of control by Fretilin, Indonesia undertook more direct efforts to protect its interests. The nature of these efforts was indicated in late September when a Fretilin spokesman claimed that unidentified forces had crossed into East Timor from the Indonesian half of the island. In effect, Indonesian forces had assumed an insurgent role acting as the military arm of Apodeti and UDT. The object of this covert military exercise was to challenge the territorial position of Fretilin in order to frustrate any claim which the Front might present to the outside world for recognition of sovereign status. Indonesia also took diplomatic action to this end. Portugal not only refused to recognise any exclusive claim by Fretilin but, in a joint statement, issued on 3 November after talks in Rome between its Foreign Minister, Melo Antunes, and Adam Malik, also appeared to endorse Indonesia's right to be a principal party to the conflict. From this juncture, the die appeared to be case in East Timor as Fretilin found itself obliged to take the inevitable step of asserting, unilaterally, an independence which the Indonesian government could legitimately deny, on the ground that the rights of its two internal adversaries, whose political standing was still recognised by Portugal, had been violated.

Fretilin proclaimed the independence of the Democratic Republic of East Timor on 28 November 1975. The next day its internal adversaries augmented by the addition of two more Timorese parties – Trabalhista and Kota – were mobilized to declare East Timor an integral part of Indonesia. On 1 December their representatives met in the western half of the island with the Indonesian Foreign Minister, who promised his government's support and announced that the solution to the conflict now lay on the battlefield. An authoritative statement by the Indonesian Minister of Information, Mashuri, issued on 4 December signalled the prospect of decisive intervention.[12] This intervention did not follow immediately but was almost certainly delayed because of a concurrent brief visit to Jakarta by President Gerald Ford and Dr Henry Kissinger. Their presence in the Indonesian capital gave rise to understandable speculation about the extent of consultation and even collusion with the American President and his Secretary of State on the imminent military enterprise. In the event, they were spared the embarrassment of being in Jakarta while the invasion of East Timor was proceeding. This invasion began on 7 December, the day after their departure, and was justified as a response to requests from within East Timor to restore order. An Indonesian government statement maintained that it could not prevent 'Indonesian volunteers from helping their brothers in East Timor in their struggle to liberate themselves from Fretilin oppression'.[13] This act of armed intervention by 'volunteers' resolved the issue of the political future and identity of East Timor. Although it proved to be an incompetent military enterprise while the initial resistance from Fretilin loyalists was vigorous, the balance of military resources and the total absence of any external support for Fretilin put the incorporation of the eastern half of the island within Indonesia beyond any doubt. A provisional government headed by the chairman of Apodeti and recognized by Indonesia was set up in Dili on 17 December; by the middle of February 1976, it was claimed that the island was under effective control. The rest was sheer ceremony, although the unfortunate inhabitants of East Timor were obliged to undergo a harrowing experience. An estimated 100,000 people died as a direct or indirect result of the invasion and counter-insurgency operations.

On 31 May 1976 a plenary session of the newly created East Timor People's Representative Council resolved to integrate the Portuguese half of the island into Indonesia. This resolution was presented as a petition to President Suharto on 7 June who accepted it as an expression of 'a brotherly union'. This ceremonial process was extended with the dispatch of an Indonesian mission 'to ascertain the wishes of the people of East Timor', whose work, so-called, was completed in good time for the formal admission of the twentyseventh province of Indonesia on 17 July 1976. The act of incorporation was accomplished with some evident diplomatic costs, apart from expected hostility from communist and radical African governments sympathetic towards Fretilin. The application of *force majeure* by Indonesia, however disguised, instead of an internationally acceptable act of self-determination, alienated a number of governments, including that of Portugal which broke off diplomatic relations. Objections to the transfer of power were raised within the UN Security Council; it adopted a resolution which recognized the right of the people of East Timor to self-determination, deplored Indonesia's military intervention and called on it 'to withdraw without delay all of its forces from the Territory'. Moreover, some states geographically close to Indonesia adopted a less than friendly attitude. Earlier, in the General Assembly, Australia, where political passions had been aroused by Indonesia's action, had voted in favour of a critical resolution, while newly independent Papua New Guinea, which shared a common border with Indonesia, pointedly abstained. Even the unity of ASEAN was tested when Singapore also abstained, standing apart from all its regional partners in not supporting the Indonesian case. These political responses produced resentment and irritation in Jakarta but were tolerated with some reserve in as far as there was no prospect of Indonesia's possession of East Timor being effectively challenged, and also because the regional opposition was ambivalent.

Virtually all of Indonesia's neighbours had been alarmed at the prospect of an independent East Timor, less than viable economically and in the charge of a Fretilin government. They were, none the less, displeased at the manner of Indonesia's resolution of the conflict. During the Sukarno period, neighbouring governments in Australia and Singapore, for example, had lived with the problem of co-existing with a volatile, and possibly expansionist, Indonesia. By its armed intervention in East Timor it conjured up, if only temporarily, the spectre of a similar phenomenon in the future. In the event, Indonesia's neighbours who formed part of the same general political alignment were obliged, at first privately and then publicly, to come to terms with Indonesia's way of securing its own and their priorities. The extent to which the government of Indonesia was prepared to violate the conventions of the international system and to risk alienating the non-aligned community, and also neighbouring states whose political associations it valued, indicated the importance placed on securing the integrity of the archipelago. Its attendant diplomatic isolation was demonstrated at the meeting of non-aligned states in Sri Lanka in August 1976; the final declaration affirmed the right of the people of East Timor to self-determination in accordance with United Nations resolutions. Over time, the issue of East Timor has become less of an embarrassment for Indonesia within the United Nations, while Australia has accepted the *fait accompli*. However, the episode has served as a continuing irritant in relations between Jakarta and Canberra because the Australian media persistently return to it.

President Suharto justified the act of annexation in terms of self-determination and the abolition of colonialism, claiming that it had taken place in compliance with the free wishes of the people of East Timor. He also revised the longstanding *raison d'être* for the territorial bounds of the Republic. Previously, they had been contemplated with reference only to the struggle against the Dutch. On the eve of Independence Day 1976 he announced to the people of East Timor:[14]

> We do not regard you as newly arrived guests. We look upon you as our blood brothers who have returned to our midst in the midst of the big family of the Indonesian Nation.

Rhetoric aside, Indonesia's military intervention constituted an attempt to secure the perimeter of the archipelagic state. The prospect of an independent radical political entity located at its periphery could not be tolerated. Indonesia was able to deploy sufficient military strength to eliminate it, partly because Fretilin did not enjoy any access to counter-vailing power. Moreover, Indonesia could count on the benevolent private attitude of all the proximate regional states whose interests were advanced by the act of annexation. In any circumstances, a military leader like President Suharto would have been strongly disposed to take action against an independent East Timor. In 1975 the regional environ-ment of the Republic had been subject to adverse change. Apart from the spectacular victories of revolutionary communism in Indochina, an evident strategic decline on the part of the United States appeared on the point of being succeeded by the competitive engagement of the interests of China and the Soviet Union. That competitive engagement was focused primarily in Indochina, where the pattern of power did not indicate a monolithic communism but a fierce antagonism between its Vietnamese and Cambodian varieties. This feature, which modified an anticipated regional polarization, served to mitigate more acute concerns in Jakarta and other ASEAN capitals in the wake of the dramatic end to the Second Indochina War. None the less, East Timor under Fretilin control was perceived as a menace which had to be expunged.

ASEAN Summit

Because of the radical political changes which had overtaken Indochina in the course of 1975, the Indonesian government had been obliged to give up expectations of an expansion of ASEAN to include all the states of the region. Given the ideological orientation of the Association, the membership of communist governments could not be regarded as an asset. Such membership would almost certainly have placed an intoler-able strain on its cohesion. Moreover, there was no enthusiasm for the more likely requirement to make a new start in regional organization – comparable to the replacement of ASA by ASEAN – in order to over-come Vietnam's unwillingness to join a grouping conceived and constructed at the height of the Second Indochina War and regarded as an insidious instrument of US and Japanese interests. Accordingly, Indonesia's regional vision was curtailed in scale.

However, its regional role was enhanced within a limited framework because the direct effect of the communist success in Indochina was to introduce a tangible sense of urgency into the deliberations of ASEAN. Urgency was not displayed as panic but it did give rise to the first ever meeting of heads of government of the Association which convened on the Indonesian island of Bali in February 1976. At Bali, the public values of Indonesia's foreign policy were reiterated, including an injunction against interference in South-East Asia by outside powers. In addition, Indonesia and its regional partners displayed an attempt to promote dual priorities: first, to reaffirm and reinforce a special relationship within ASEAN based on a sense of shared predicament among its essentially conservative governments; second, to use the strength of that relationship to initiate a dialogue with the Indochinese states, above all, Vietnam, in an attempt to establish a set of common assumptions which might serve as a basis for regional order. It has been pointed out above that Vietnam had been viewed in Jakarta as an additional regional partner and not as a natural adversary. A deep-seated apprehension of communism had been moderated in its case because of a belief that nationalism was Vietnam's dominant value, that the government in Hanoi did not possess political-territorial ambitions beyond former French Indochina, and that its proven resolution and vitality would serve to withstand the exercise of undue Chinese influence. Indeed, a longstanding conviction that Sino-Vietnamese differences were more deep-rooted than any ideological affinity had been reinforced by the deteriorating relationship between Hanoi and Peking in the wake of Sino-American rapprochement. It was calculated that if Vietnam could be drawn, however tentatively at first, into a framework of regional cooperation, then the prospect of continuing outside power interference would be correspondingly reduced. Such calculation was consistent with a statement on 'Indonesia's Foreign Policy and ASEAN Regional Cooperation' which had been issued by Indonesia's ASEAN secretariat in 1974. This statement had stressed *inter alia* the importance attached to ASEAN as an indigenous expression of regional cooperation 'which should be developed on the basis of self-reliance to ensure the stability and security of the South-East Asian region from external interference in whatever form or manifestation'.[15]

The two priorities which Indonesia pursued with its regional partners were expressed in public documents signed by the five heads of government. A Declaration of ASEAN Concord articulated the political goals of the member states with prime emphasis on internal security, which took precedence over a reaffirmed commitment to a Zone of Peace, Freedom and Neutrality. The tone for a common position on security had been set by President Suharto when he addressed the opening session of the summit. He refuted the suggestion that ASEAN was a military pact and pointed out:[16]

Our concept of security is inward looking, namely to establish an orderly, peaceful and stable condition within each individual territory, free from any subversive elements and infiltrations, wherever from their origins might be.

161

This view was echoed in the Declaration of ASEAN Concord where it stated:[17]

> The stability of each member state and of the ASEAN region is an essential contribution to international peace and security. Each member resolves to eliminate threats posed by subversion to its stability, thus strengthening national and ASEAN resilience.

The underlying rationale of that statement was that political stability was indivisible among the ASEAN states and, conversely, that any incidence of political instability in any one state would have repercussions for all the others. It constituted an endorsement by the governments of ASEAN of Indonesia's concept of national resilience writ large, namely regional resilience which was contemplated as a major obstacle to external intervention which thrived on intra-regional tensions. The Declaration of ASEAN Concord acknowledged the formal evolution of the Association into a diplomatic community with clearly defined political interests and constituted an attempt to display confidence and cohesion in the wake of profound regional changes.

The second public document promulgated at Bali was a Treaty of Amity and Cooperation in South-East Asia. This treaty set out basic rules of inter-state conduct. It stressed the sanctity of national sovereignty and territorial integrity and made provision for pacific settlement of disputes, while its terms were intended to 'constitute the foundation for a strong and viable community of nations in South-East Asia'.[18] Moreover, the treaty was 'open to accession' by other regional states. Accordingly, it was intended to serve as a political bridge to Indochina and to indicate that regional accommodation could take place on the basis of generally accepted norms of international behaviour, but not at the expense of the separate identity of ASEAN. In other words, Indonesia was not prepared to jeopardize the practical accomplishment of ASEAN which had evolved into a diplomatic community for the sake of a wider regional vision which could not be pursued without radical qualification because of fundamental political change in Indochina.

Indonesia's expectations of reconciling intra-ASEAN priorities with a wider regional vision were quickly frustrated. The governments of Vietnam and Laos, in particular, made explicit their suspicion and hostility towards ASEAN which was depicted as a version of SEATO. It was made abundantly clear that, while a willingness existed to establish good relations with individual members of ASEAN, Vietnam and Laos were adamantly opposed to treating with the Association as a corporate entity. The revolutionary government in Cambodia – renamed Democratic Kampuchea – adopted a similar view, although its attitude was distinguished more by a quality of indifference than by one of positive antagonism. For Indonesia, its membership of and role within ASEAN involved a matter of choice with attendant political opportunity costs. In practice, there was no question of choice, given the ideological disposition of the government in Jakarta and the diplomatic stake already invested in ASEAN. In the circumstances, the hostility which emanated, above all, from Hanoi had to be endured in the hope that a more tolerable relationship would be established in the fullness of time once the bitter legacy of the Second Indochina War had begun to fade. For the present, however, Indonesia was obliged to suffer the strictures of a state which was regarded with fellow feeling because of the historical parallels between the two independence struggles. Such strictures were expressed at the time of the Bali summit in February 1976 and for more than two years subsequently. For obvious reasons, the government in Hanoi refused to accord ASEAN any right to speak on behalf of South-East Asia and to prescribe for the conduct of regional relations in the manner indicated by the documents promulgated at Bali. Indded, a direct clash of interests involving Indonesia occurred at the conference of non-aligned states held in Sri Lanka in August 1976.

Although the government in Jakarta had been less than sympathetic towards Malaysia's neutralization proposal for South-East Asia, the alternative diluted formula of a Zone of Peace, Freedom and Neutrality as promulgated in November 1971 reflected Indonesia's regional priorities. The formula expressed the notion of a regional order based on the endeavours of resident states. The Zone of Peace idea had been endorsed at the previous conference of non-aligned states held in Algeria in 1973. In Colombo, however, the delegation from Laos, acting on behalf of that from Vietnam, opposed the inclusion of the Zone of Peace formula in the final resolution of the conference. Indeed, it was denounced by association because it had been 'issued at the very moment when the ASEAN countries were directly or indirectly serving the US aggressive war in Vietnam, Laos and Cambodia, in complete contravention of the principles of the non-aligned movement'.[19] This *démarche* produced a diplomatic impasse with the result that the Zone of Peace formula did not go forward for plenary endorsement. For Indonesia, the diplomatic confrontation at Colombo was salutary. It demonstrated the extent to which the management of regional order remained an elusive undertaking, However, the hostility expressed by Vietnam and Laos did serve to reinforce the sense of common predicament of the five ASEAN partners. Indeed, President Suharto declared at the second meeting of ASEAN heads of governments held in Kuala Lumpur in August 1977 'We have closed our ranks'. A visible closing of ranks, a modest measure of economic cooperation and the development of bilateral diplomatic links between ASEAN and Japan,

Australia and New Zealand constituted the sum of the Association's response to fundamental regional change. If evident consolidation had been demonstrated by ASEAN, from Indonesia's perspective the momentum of regional cooperation had been arrested. Initiative over the management of regional order had been frustrated. Although determination was exhibited to stand by the Zone of Peace formula in order to display solidarity in the face of communist hostility, any attempt to promote an overarching structure for regional relations would be obliged to wait on events.

The subsequent course of political events in South-East Asia into the 1980s served to highlight further the contrast between Indonesia's regional vision and its limited ability to assume the role of prime manager of regional order. An inability to project power beyond archipelagic bounds was a readily accepted limitation, but a corresponding inability to determine the political direction of ASEAN in regional affairs proved to be more frustrating as Indochina came to be afflicted by its third major conflict since the end of the Pacific War. Before that conflict culminated in Vietnam's invasion of Kampuchea, Indonesia and its ASEAN partners became the temporary beneficiaries of intra-communist antagonisms both within and outside South-East Asia. The surface wartime unity between the Vietnamese and Kampuchean revolutionary movements had become strained from the morrow of success in Indochina. The latter were ferociously obdurate in their refusal to reach the kind of political accommodation exemplified by the subordinate relationship between Laos and Vietnam. Armed conflict between Kampuchea and Vietnam became a matter of public knowledge from the end of 1977 when the government in Phnom Penh broke off diplomatic relations with Hanoi. This conflict became caught up in Sino-Vietnamese and Sino-Soviet rivalries. It was in this context that Indonesia and its ASEAN partners were subject to diplomatic competition for their political affections. China, if not Kampuchea, had endorsed the Zone of Peace formula and had moderated its initially hostile view of ASEAN in the early 1970s. After the communist revolutionary success in Indochina, the attitude of the government in Peking towards the Association became quite benign in marked contrast to that of Vietnam which had moved into closer alignment with the Soviet Union. As Kampuchean-Vietnamese and corresponding Sino-Vietnamese and Sino-Soviet antagonisms intensified, a public change of heart was displayed by Vietnam and the Soviet Union towards the ASEAN states. This change of heart was most clearly demonstrated from September 1978 when Vietnam's Prime Minister, Pham Van Dong, embarked on a tour of every ASEAN capital, including Jakarta.

For those responsible for making Indonesia's foreign policy, the regional environment of the Republic had become increasingly perplexing. With revolutionary communist success in Indochina in 1975, there was immediate concern lest South-East Asia be subject to an acute polarization of states and ideologies which would attract external counterparts. Though the evident absence of a monolithic Indochinese communism was demonstrated, initial satisfaction was erased by an attendant concern that regional intra-communist conflict would be aggravated through the intervention of external powers, namely the Soviet Union and China, who had become identified as patrons respectively of Vietnam and Kampuchea. It was at this juncture that Pham Van Dong visited Jakarta where he went out of his way to provide assurances of his government's good intentions towards its regional neighbours and an explicit commitment to respect Indonesia's independence and to refrain from interfering in its internal affairs. Although the circumstances of his visit engendered a natural scepticism, the Vietnamese Prime Minister gave the impression of wanting to accommodate Indonesia. He appeared willing to reconcile competing formulas for regional order, if not disposed to endorse, without qualification, ASEAN's Zone of Peace, Freedom and Neutrality, to which President Suharto reiterated his government's commitment.[20] Of greatest importance during the visit was Pham Van Dong's apparent ability to convince his hosts that, despite becoming a member of Comecon the preceding June, Vietnam was very much the master of its own political destiny.

The visit to Jakarta by Vietnam's Prime Minister constituted an interesting episode because it served to point up underlying ambiguities in Indonesia's international outlook. On the one hand, a natural apprehension existed of a reunited Communist Vietnam whose military capability was renowned beyond South-East Asia. Moreover, a tangible dispute had arisen between Indonesia and Vietnam over the demarcation of the continental shelf in the South China Sea as a result of which the government in Hanoi had appeared to question the validity of the archipelagic doctrine. On the other hand, this apprehension was mitigated by an alternative view of Vietnam which derived from a sense of shared experience of struggle against colonialism. This point of view was exhibited strongly by Adam Malik who had become vice-President in March 1978 and also by his successor as Foreign Minister, Professor Mochtar Kusumaatmadja, who acknowledged 'a special flavour in our relationship'.[21] Apart from a somewhat sentimental view of Vietnam, coloured by a sense of shared experience, concern over its regional intentions was mitigated also by an intense underlying conviction that Indonesia's natural adversary was China[22] and that an independent Vietnam, and, preferably, a set of independent friendly states in Indochina, should stand interposed between China and the members of ASEAN. Such a view had been reinforced by the strident proprietory position adopted by the government in Peking in response to a mass exodus of ethnic Chinese residents from Vietnam. Moreover, the treaty of peace and friendship concluded between China and Japan in September 1978 was construed as a threat to the burgeoning economic relationship between Indonesia and Japan.

Kampuchea

Whatever sense of satisfaction may have been felt at the end of Pham Van Dong's visit to Jakarta, as well as to other ASEAN capitals, was superseded by growing alarm at the course of the conflict in Indochina. On 3 November 1978 Vietnam concluded a treaty of friendship and cooperation with the Soviet Union similar to that entered into by India and the Soviet Union in August 1971 which had served to neutralize China and had facilitated the dismemberment of Pakistan. One month later, a so-called Kampuchean National United Front for National Salvation was established with evident Vietnamese inspiration and Soviet support to challenge the government in Phnom Penh headed by the infamous Pol Pot. A Vietnamese military offensive was launched against Kampuchea on 25 December 1978, disrupting Indonesia's plans to establish a diplomatic mission in Phnom Penh. This offensive reached a speedy political climax with the investment of the Kampuchean capital on 7 January 1979 and the installation the next day of a government carried into the country in the saddle-bags of the Vietnamese Army.

Once again, a violent conflict whose outcome was of major interest to Indonesia had been resolved with the government in Jakarta in the role of spectator. In 1970, the political impotence of Indonesia had been demonstrated by the abortive attempt to mount a diplomatic initiative intended to restore political stability and sustain the *status quo* in a violated Cambodia. In 1979, the impact of Vietnam's military intervention was even more immediately decisive politically, although armed resistance to its occupation continued. For Indonesia, the circumstances of the overthrow of the Pol Pot regime were doubly disturbing. First, there had been a conspicious and blatant violation of national sovereignty which was in direct contravention of those principles which were at the heart of the Treaty of Amity and Cooperation conceived as a code of conduct for regional states. In other words, Vietnam, using a spurious united front, had overthrown the cardinal principle of the post-colonial system of states. Second, Vietnam had been assisted in this nefarious enterprise by a communist superpower engaged in competition for influence in South-East Asia with its principal communist rival, China. Moreover, the prospect of renewed external power intervention in South-East Asia was confirmed by China's act of military punishment against Vietnam undertaken in February 1979.

The onset and course of the Third Indochina War has served to expose dilemmas in Indonesia's foreign policy. The violation of principle by Vietnam supported by the Soviet Union, and the obligations which have ensued from Indonesia's membership of and commitment to ASEAN, have set up a tension with an alternative disposition. This disposition is governed by a willingness to tolerate Vietnam's dominant position in Indochina and a concern to check the extension of China's influence and to prevent the revival of great power rivalry in South-East Asia. Indeed, from the very outset of this most recent phase of conflict in Indochina, Indonesia has been subject to the competing pulls of principle and balance of power which have found expression within its own bureaucracy. Non-violation of national sovereignty is regarded in Jakarta as the central precept of any system of regional order. Yet, a Vietnam dominant in Indochina, able to fend off the pressures of China, and in no way dependent on the Soviet Union is envisaged also as a starting point for a regionally ordered structure of relations. In this respect, one source of grievance felt towards the United States has been its refusal to treat with Vietnam so that it has had no alternative but to reinforce its close association with the Soviet Union.

In the event, Indonesia experienced considerable frustration as the response to the Vietnamese invasion of Kampuchea came to be dictated by the priorities of the ASEAN state most directly affected by that military action. Thailand, which faced an unprecedented violation of its strategic environment, entered into an informal alliance association with China, which had shown itself to be the only state willing to use force to register disapproval of the Vietnamese invasion. Moreover, Thailand served as a sanctuary in which the residual forces of the Democratic Kampuchean regime (or the Khmer Rouge) could take refuge and be restored to fighting strength as an instrument in a wider strategy of attrition designed to place breaking strain on the society and government of Vietnam. In this exercise, ASEAN assumed a diplomatic role in denying recognition to the successor Heng Samrin government in Phnom Penh and also in upholding the international status of the ousted Democratic Kampuchean government, especially in the United Nations. Indeed, ASEAN assumed the initiative in sponsoring an international conference on Kampuchea held ultimately in July 1981 under UN auspices, which called for the withdrawal of all foreign (i.e. Vietnamese) troops from the country and the holding of free elections to be supervised by the world body. It also sponsored a coalition government of Khmer anti-Vietnamese resistance groups in June 1982.

Indonesia was a reluctant partner in the overall enterprise directed

167

against Vietnam, in great part because ASEAN had been drawn into an association with China in a strategy deemed likely to serve its interests, particularly should Vietnam's independence be undermined. Correspondingly, the Indonesian government perceived, as an alternative adverse outcome of such a strategy, the undue dependence of Vietnam on the Soviet Union. In other words, the strategy conceived by China and Thailand, with support from its ASEAN partners, which was designed to coerce Vietnam into revising its policy over Kampuchea, was contemplated as likely to lead to one of two objectionable outcomes: either a Vietnam subject to China's dominance, or a Vietnam in a client relationship with the Soviet Union. Such apprehension aggavated by Thai disposition and a change of government in Bangkok served as the inspiration for a joint statement which President Suharto issued with Malaysia's Prime Minister in Kuantan in March 1980. This declaration looked forward to a Vietnam free from the influence of both China and the Soviet Union and also took cognizance of Vietnam's security interests in Kampuchea. In effect, it constituted an ideal formulation which did not take account of the existing asymmetry in Vietnam's relations with China and the Soviet Union. Moreover, neither Indonesia nor Malaysia possessed any substantive leverage on Thailand which, because of its geo-political circumstances, had been able to set the tone for ASEAN's policy over Kampuchea. Because ASEAN, including Indonesia, could only perform a diplomatic function which was marginal to the actual withdrawal of Vietnamese forces from Kampuchea, Thailand saw practical reason to cultivate a burgeoning relationship with China and to help sustain its Khmer Rouge client in the conviction that the Vietnamese would only respect superior force.

In the circumstances, any substantive attempt by Indonesia to set ASEAN on a different course could serve only to undermine the cohesion of an association in which it had invested so much by way of political resources. Accordingly, the Indonesian government went along with the prevailing view, if indicating its reluctance and reservations privately. It made only a marginal impact on policy, for example by ensuring the exclusion of the name of the transgressor in early statements deploring the invasion of Kampuchea and by maintaining an intermittent bilateral dialogue with Hanoi through its Foreign Ministry and, importantly, its military intelligence agencies. The circumstances of Vietnam's invasion of Kampuchea and the requirement for Indonesia to stand publicly by Thailand against Vietnam meant that the government was not able to exercise any truly independent initiative over the conflict and, correspondingly, in the management of regional order. On the contrary, that initiative seemed to slip from its grasp from the onset of the Third Indochina War, leaving a deep sense of frustration in Jakarta. Moreover, in order to sustain a necessary consistency in an elusive exercise in regional order, its government has been obliged to uphold the principle of non-violation of national sovereignty which had become the formal standpoint of ASEAN as a corporate entity in February 1976. Accordingly, in a speech in January 1982, President Suharto made this explicit with reference to Kampuchea:[23]

> We reject and we cannot accept the government of some country that is set up by and with the help of armed forces from outside, because that is against the principles of the sovereignty and freedom of states.

The fall of Phnom Penh in January 1979 and the continuing struggle for power in and over Kampuchea serves as an illustrative point of reference with which to contemplate the regional priorities of Indonesia under the leadership of President Suharto. Indonesia had sought to express a moderate sense of regional entitlement through a practice of regional cooperation. That sense of entitlement, however, was not matched by the display of a corresponding capability which could provide necessary assurance to regional partners, especially to Thailand, the most directly affected of all ASEAN states by Vietnam's invasion of Kampuchea. Moreover the governments in Jakarta and Bangkok did not share a common strategic perspective, or a common definition of external threat. Vietnam's military undertaking constituted an immediate threat to Thailand but not to Indonesia in its maritime insulation. Although Vietnam's military action gave rise to evident concern, it did not replace China as the principal, if long-term, source of external threat for Indonesia. In consequence, differences of interest, as well as limitations in capability, made for a political distance between Indonesia and Thailand, even though divergences were accommodated around the principle of non-violation of national sovereignty. Accommodation is not the same as reconciliation. Indeed, reconciliation over divergent interests in Indochina has not been possible because the Indonesian government has held to the private view that Thai policy, while understood, can serve only to intensify a process of competitive external intervention in the affairs of South-East Asia which could well challenge the independence of its resident states. A characteristic expression of such concern was broadcast over Jakarta Radio in a commentary in February 1982. It was pointed out that the problem of Kampuchea was no longer a problem between the groups of forces within that country or a confrontation between Kampuchea and Vietnam but reflected great power rivalry in South-East Asia. It concluded 'If unsolved, the problem will be a great danger because it could lead to direct involvement of the big powers and eventually to their permanent stay in this region'.[24]

This well-established view, combined with a barely repaired

vulnerability, points up the disjunction between aspiration and capacity to influence the regional pattern of power. For example, the course of events in Indochina with its attendant competitive external intervention has not only made an informal security association with the United States indispensable, but has also set up tensions within that relationship. Once again, an element of paradox is introduced as Indonesia's foreign policy establishment has indicated criticism of the lack of resolute leadership displayed by governments in Washington and, at the same time, has expressed evident resentment at an unwillingness on the part of the United States to compete with the Soviet Union for the political affections of Vietnam.

In its pursuit of regional order, the Suharto administration has sustained conceptions of both a spectre and a vision, without being able to do much by way of substance to expunge the one or to promote the other. The spectre is the continuing process of external intervention in South-East Asia whose latest phase has been dominated by Sino-Soviet rivalry. The vision is the exclusion of such rivalry and related intervention and the alternative establishment of a viable structure of regional relations based, primarily, on the collaborative endeavours of resident states, including Vietnam. Evident powerlessness to replace the spectre with the vision has not been accompanied by any repudiation of long established values. A nationalist spirit which was engendered from 1945 has been sustained to the effect that the sense of the Republic's regional destiny had endured without revision. However, the pragmatic disposition which was demonstrated from 1966 has made for a realistic acceptance of the fact of external power interest in South-East Asia and adjustment to the view that the most sensible course is to work to contain external involvement to a tolerable degree.

In the meantime, concurrent with the resumption of major conflict in Indochina, Indonesia has allocated increasing resources to its defence establishment after a period of relative neglect. It has sought to develop a greater self-reliant capability to command its archipelagic perimeter. For example, a series of annual combined exercises were begun in March 1980 in the South China Sea pointedly encompassing the Natuna Islands which provide the baseline for the northernmost point of Indonesia's maritime boundary. Recourse to greater defence expenditure involving the purchase of modern ground attack fighter aircraft and airlift capability, as well as armed patrol vessels for maritime surveillance, will hardly make Indonesia the military master of its immediate environment. Its military capability is limited and the total size of its armed forces is less than 300,000 out of a population of more than 150 million.[25] In strategic terms, the scale and configuration of the archipelagic state are more of a burden than an asset. Moreover, the experience of the Third Indochina War has demonstrated that there is limited competence for influencing regional events. Despite its regional vision, Indonesia has been obliged to occupy the role of spectator until that conflict reaches a point of resolution. Ironically, Indonesia's best prospect of reviving an active regional role would arise should the Khmer Rouge resistance be crushed by the Vietnamese and Thailand be obliged to accept Vietnam's dominance in Indochina. In such circumstances, although in some political difficulty because of its public attachment to the principle of non-violation of national sovereignty, Indonesia would be well placed to act as interlocutor between its ASEAN partners and Vietnam. One obvious basis of convergence would be a more common antipathy to China with whom Indonesia has consistently refused to restore diplomatic relations.[26] Indeed, evidence of determination by its military establishment to block such restoration was indicated in December 1981 when Taiwan's Prime Minister, Sun Yun-suan, visited Jakarta and was received by President Suharto. The Foreign Ministry remained unaware of this impending visit until shortly before Mr Sun arrived. One sequel was China's cancellation of an Indonesian trade mission to Peking which had been planned for several months.

Even if Indonesia were able to begin a fresh dialogue with Hanoi with the object of engaging Vietnam in regional cooperation at the expense of its close relationship with the Soviet Union, its limitations would be only too evident. Should Sino-Vietnamese antagonisms persist, then, although Vietnam would almost certainly welcome a more fruitful relationship with Indonesia and its ASEAN partners, it could not be expected to contemplate it as an alternative to the countervailing one that obtains with the Soviet Union. There is no other adversary of China which can serve as an appropriate makeweight in a balance of power exercise central to Vietnam's security. There lies the rub. Moreover, as long as the Soviet Union enjoys access to naval facilities in both Vietnam and Kampuchea, then the United States will continue to display an interest in competitive naval deployment in and through a region which serves as an important crossroads for sea and air communications. Indonesia does not possess the resources and capability to assert a regional dominance, and the terms of the regional partnership which it has promoted in order to aspire to a position of primacy do not give rise to identical interests, only some shared ones. In such circumstances, the conspicuous disjunction between declaratory policy and its actual practice will remain. The consequence can only be an abiding sense of frustration in Jakarta which is endured by a military leadership which draws on technocratic advice in foreign policy. That policy has been based, in practice, on recognition of national weakness and on a realistic understanding that such weakness serves as the principal obstacle to the pursuit of an independent and active course.

7 Conclusion: Change and Continuity

Nearly four decades have elapsed since the late President Sukarno proclaimed Indonesia's independence. In that period, the Republic has experienced the upheaval of national revolution and a succession of political systems beginning with a febrile Parliamentary Democracy. Parliamentary Democracy gave way to the romantic and volatile authoritarianism of Guided Democracy and this, in turn, was replaced, by a more sober authoritarianism which has styled itself *Pancasila* Democracy.

The course of Indonesia's foreign policy has reflected this uneven political progress. First, changes in political system have given rise to corresponding changes in the idiom of foreign policy. For example, under Guided Democracy, the precept of an independent and active foreign policy was discarded. In its place was enthroned an alternative notion of progressive New Emerging Forces, with Indonesia depicted as their vanguard. That notion was based on a view of the international system totally at variance with the one which had underpinned the original independent and active formula. That formula was reinstated, however, with the collapse of Guided Democracy and has been maintained as official doctrine. Second, changes in political system have been accompanied by changes in the pattern of external associations and alignments. For example, on the morrow of independence, an ideal commitment to an independent and active foreign policy was combined with a qualified disposition towards the Western constellation of states. That tendency was revised during the changing course of Parliamentary Democracy in favour of a more assertive and explicit non-alignment. With the advent of Guided Democracy, and as a consequence of confrontation over West Irian and Malaysia, an association was cultivated with communist states at the expense of the West – first with the Soviet Union and then with the People's Republic of China. Alignment with the latter was reinforced by repudiation of membership in the United Nations. Such a pattern was speedily reversed when Guided Democracy was succeeded by the New Order, or *Pancasila* Democracy, inaugurated by General Suharto. Special relationships were then established with the United States and Japan and an unprecedented initiative was undertaken in regional association in company with conservative neighbouring states.

Finally, changes in political system have been matched by changes in the style of conduct of foreign policy exemplified by the prosecution of Indonesia's claim to West Irian and its challenge to the international status of Malaysia. In the former case, although unwavering in objective, governments during the period of Parliamentary Democracy were content, in the main, to pursue the claim by conventional diplomatic means. By contrast, during Guided Democracy, which was dominated by the personality and pronouncements of Sukarno, a flamboyant coercive diplomacy was adopted. Such practice was employed successfully in the case of West Irian, but not in that of Malaysia. At an early stage in the establishment of the New Order, accommodation with and to Malaysia was reached by informal and formal negotiation. Subsequently, Indonesia resumed membership of the United Nations and its foreign policy has been conducted with greater deference to the conventions of the international system.

If change has been evident, however, it does not constitute the sum of Indonesia's foreign policy. Such change has been more than matched by a strong strain of continuity. That continuity, expressed in international outlook and policy goals, has been the direct product of a shared experience on the part of post-colonial successor elites. A Java-centric view of the regional standing and vulnerability of archipelagic Indonesia which was formed during the struggle for independence has been sustained since its attainment. The political generation whose mental attitudes were affected most deeply by the impact of national revolution have not departed completely from public life. Indeed, both President Suharto and vice-President Adam Malik were actively involved in the independence struggle, if each in different ways.

Nationalist challenge to the restoration of Dutch rule precipitated a protracted and bitter struggle in which the vulnerability of the embryo Republic was exposed and exploited. The experience of upholding independence in both domestic and international dimensions generated an abiding concern for the integrity of a state beset by social diversity and physical fragmentation. That concern was reinforced by a conviction about the country's attractiveness to external interests because of its bountiful natural resources and important strategic location. A common and consistent theme of Indonesia's foreign policy has been the need to overcome an intrinsic vulnerability. Paradoxically, however, a continuous sense of vulnerability has been combined with an equally continuous sense of regional entitlement based on pride in revolutionary achievement, size of population, land and maritime dimensions, natural resources and strategic location. That sense of regional entitlement has been less than consistently displayed in open form; it has persisted none the less.

In the years since the attainment of independence, the spectre of external intervention has haunted the Indonesian state. Foreign policy priorities have been determined accordingly. For example, Sukarno pursued the claim to West Irian for a variety of motives but not least from a suspicion that the Dutch had retained a peripheral foothold from which to assert influence in the event of political collapse within the Republic. He was supported in this endeavour by the leadership of the armed forces which had been engaged, during the 1950s, in crushing Islamic and regional rebellion, the latter having attracted external support. Sukarno appointed as commander of the final phase of the West Irian operation the very man who succeeded him as president. If President Sukarno had questioned the requirement for a test of opinion in West Irian provided for in the settlement of August 1962, his successor, President Suharto, was prepared to tolerate such an exercise only as a formality. The so-called act of free choice conducted in 1969 did not permit an authentic expression of self-determination. It was conducted in a sober manner without the public display characteristic of the Sukarno era, but the priority of ensuring the integrity of the archipelago and of denying any precedent for separatism was firmly maintained. The subsequent conduct of the Suharto administration over the controversial issue of East Timor served to confirm a strong attachment to a strategic perspective which existed before the internal transfer of power in March 1966. Indeed, a sense of strategic imperative overrode deference to the conventions of the international system.

As indicated above, the group of soldiers led by General Suharto who deposed and succeeded Sukarno did not constitute a new political force. They were the product of the same military and political experience attendant on the creation of the Indonesian state out of a Dutch administrative frame. The armed forces had never been fully subordinate to civilian authority during the period of national evolution. After independence, the officer corps, although beset by factional and regional divisions, had exhibited a sense of guardianship towards affairs of state. They derived a perception of political entitlement from their military endeavours during the national revolution and subsequently in holding the post-colonial state together. They played an influential part in inaugurating Guided Democracy and have claimed the right to a political role because of their contribution to the creation and preservation of the Republic. Charged with the defence of the state, they have been more conscious than their civilian predecessors of the innate vulnerability of the Republic, especially to any conjunction between internal dissension and external interference.

The leadership of the armed forces repudiated the domestic and international alignments of Sukarno and claimed that they were restoring the Republic to its true course in foreign policy. That was correct in so far as idiom, outlook and style were concerned but it was contingent on an attempt to recover the confidence of those Western states whose assistance was essential for economic recovery. A necessary concession to secure such assistance was the cessation of confrontation with Malaysia. Accommodation to the reality of Malaysia had been made possible, above all, by domestic political change and facilitated by the prior separation of Singapore from the federation. The armed forces had not differed from Sukarno in opposing the advent of Malaysia, at least not at the outset. As the course of confrontation appeared to serve the interests of the Indonesian Communist Party, and had led on to an unpalatable alignment with the People's Republic of China, the leadership of the armed forces reappraised their interests. Malaysia had been suspect because of the manner of its formation, the conspicuous role of Britain as patron of the undertaking, and also the pivotal position which Singapore appeared to occupy. Its advent was deemed to pose a threat to the security of Indonesia; it offended also against the Republic's sense of regional entitlement. Accordingly, the ending of confrontation in August 1966 marked a break in continuity in the light of a policy enunciated three and a half years previously. For some within the armed forces, acceptance of Malaysia was, initially, a bitter pill to swallow. None the less, the strategic perspective which had contributed to confrontation was not discarded with the settlement of the dispute between Indonesia and Malaysia.

When Indonesia led by acting President Suharto appeared to confirm a change in international course in August 1967 by helping to found ASEAN, it displayed an outlook which had been shared, in part, by the administration of President Sukarno. The special interests which the Indonesian delegation managed to get incorporated within ASEAN's inaugural declaration had been articulated and endorsed at those conferences which convened in Manila in 1963 to deal with the contention aroused by the prospect of Malaysia. The qualified proscription of foreign military bases set out in that declaration reflected one of the basic objections to the formation of the federation. The Manila documents to which Subandrio and Sukarno had put their names also expressed a clear sense of regional entitlement. The incorporation of clauses dealing with regional order within the ASEAN declaration expressed a corresponding outlook. The difference between Manila in 1963 and Bangkok in 1967 was one of context and degree. The constituents of an Indonesian-inspired strategic perspective had been sustained and an unprecedented willingness to engage in regional association indicated an attempt to use alternative means to attain abiding priorities. A recognition by the Suharto administration of the underlying weaknesses of Indonesia has meant a grudging disposition to adjust to prevailing realities. None the less, that administration has persisted with attempts to prescribe for regional order based on a limited and diminishing role for external powers. Such a view was central to the declaration by the ASEAN Foreign Ministers in November 1971 in favour of a Zone of Peace, Freedom and Neutrality, which was incorporated within the Declaration of ASEAN Concord promulgated in February 1976. It was incorporated also in the joint statement issued by President Suharto and the Malaysian Prime Minister, Datuk Hussein Onn, in March 1980, if received without enthusiasm by other regional partners.

Further confirmation of an underlying continuity in foreign policy expressing both a sense of weakness and one of entitlement has been indicated in maritime initiatives. An archipelagic principle was enunciated in December 1957 after the introduction of martial law had suspended Parliamentary Democracy. It was reaffirmed as part of municipal law by decree in February 1960 during the first year of Guided Democracy. It was further incorporated as one of the guidelines of state policy in March 1973 by the People's Consultative Assembly during *Pancasila* Democracy. Moreover, the Indonesian government has pressed its claim to archipelagic status with evident success during the course of the Third UN Conference on the Law of the Sea.

The argument for continuity must not be pressed to the exclusion of all other factors. There are obvious differences between civilian and military-based governments and between a charismatic leader like Sukarno and a cautious military figure like Suharto. Moreover, environmental circumstances change which may require changes in policy. For example, Islam has become a more important factor in foreign policy considerations. During the administration of President Suharto, Islam has burgeoned as an international phenomenon with domestic significance. Accordingly, the government has been obliged to be especially careful to strike a balance in external associations in order to appease domestic Islamic opinion without appearing to enhance its national standing in political terms. Yet, that requirement stems from unresolved problems about the identity of the Indonesian state which were the subject of public debate before the proclamation of independence. The communal divisions which express the absence of a single great cultural tradition have determined the constituencies of political life. They have direct relevance to the conduct of foreign policy. Indeed, they constitute an immutable feature of a fragmented social fabric only matched by a fragmented physical structure. Indonesia in its present form cannot escape it social diversity, in respect of which the national motto 'Unity in Diversity' represents a statement of aspiration rather than achievement. It also cannot escape a geographical configuration which, combined with social diversity, encourages centrifugal political tendencies. Moreover, it cannot escape a location in which fundamental problems of state and nation-building have been heightened by intrusions on the part of external powers.

The dominant theme of Indonesia's foreign policy arises from the interplay of all these factors and the constant, if uneven, attempt by governments in Jakarta to overcome an attendant condition of subordination. The administration of President Suharto has sought to overcome that condition, in part by promoting economic development which, if reversing a conspicuous internal debility, has also aggravated social tensions. In terms of rhetoric, that administration has proclaimed the concept of national resilience which amounts to a call for spiritual, as well as political, self-reliance which has been echoed, to an extent, by ASEAN partners. Like the motto of 'Unity in Diversity', this concept expresses an aspiration rather than an accomplished fact. None the less, the exhortations to both national and regional resilience indicate more than a mere declaratory desire for national and regional self-determination. The government's undoubted objective is to serve as the foundation of a regional grouping of its own promotion which would be independent of the substantive influence of outside powers. It is in this context that the independence of Brunei and its future membership of ASEAN has been welcomed.

In this endeavour, Indonesia faces untold difficulties arising from its own relative weakness and that of its regional partners. Moreover, those regional partners do not necessarily share its strategic perspective to the full. For example, Thailand entertains a very different perception of external threat, and this has been responsible for a pattern of external alignments, incorporating China, which is viewed with deep suspicion in Jakarta. And although Singapore under Prime Minister Lee Kuan-yew has developed a practical working relationship with the Suharto administration, its government has never sought to hide a concern that a regionally determined balance of power might give rise to an unpalatable local dominance. Accordingly, Singapore has indicated a preference for an ordered involvement of external powers which would neutralize both them and any threat posed by a potentially dominant regional state. Furthermore, for all its achievements, ASEAN remains no more than a diplomatic community which has been more successful in accommodating than in reconciling divergent intramural interests. In practical terms, it is a sub-regional association obliged to share an aspirant managerial role with a constellation of Indochinese states in which the dominance of Vietnam is in no way matched by Indonesia's position within ASEAN. In the light of intra-regional polarization since the end of the Second Indochina War, which has been aggravated with the onset of renewed conflict, the Indonesian government has been obliged to moderate its plans for regional order, which continue to be affected also by the competing interests of major and global powers.

Indonesia has never been able to overcome the difficulties involved in confronting problems posed by the intrusion of such powers. For example, should the global powers ever be in accord, then their willingness to act in concert would certainly prove an insuperable obstacle to the realization of Indonesia's regional vision. Indeed, an example of such accord has been displayed over passage of naval vessels through straits used for international navigation and, specifically, over the Straits of Malacca and Singapore. However, should the global powers be at odds, which is their normal condition, then there is a reasonable prospect that they will have competitive interests to pursue in South-East Asia. In such circumstances, a country like Indonesia would be obliged to make a choice if only because it is almost certain to perceive each global power in a different light. This has been the case during the course of its foreign policy since independence. In so far as its pattern of external alignments has fluctuated, this has reflected changing relations with the major powers and has also indicated attempts to employ conventional balance of power techniques.

Under the Suharto administration, the longstanding suspicion of all external powers has been sustained but tempered with an evident pragmatism, especially in relations with the United States and Japan. Indeed, regional circumstances since the end of the Second Indochina War in 1975 have reinforced a strategic dependence on the United States, despite a declining confidence in its ability to resume a military role in South-East Asia. The result has been an evident paradox in attitudes. On the one hand, Indonesia would prefer, ideally, to do without an American military presence just over the horizon as a counter to that of the Soviet Union which has been extended from the Indian Ocean to the South China Sea. On the other hand, because of adverse changes in the balance of external influences bearing on the region, especially the expression of Sino-Soviet rivalry, there has been strong private criticism of the United States as insufficiently resolute in its superpower role and also for placing global priorities before regional ones, especially in dealings with China over the transfer of military technology. In other words, the Indonesian Government would prefer the least objectionable superpower to be on tap and not on top. Preferences, however, have had to give way to pragmatism. For example, during the Carter Administration, irritation at the prominence given to the issue of human rights did not obstruct an extensive release of political prisoners deemed necessary to assuage the political sensibilities of the White House and Congress.

Indonesia's ambivalence towards the United States has been more than matched by its relationship with Japan, which has played an increasingly prominent role in the economic life of the Republic. Given the development strategy which it has employed, the Indonesian government cannot do without Japanese capital investment and technical expertise. Japan is also a major market for raw materials, especially oil and liquified natural gas. Yet Japan and its ubiquitous businessmen are generally perceived as engaged in the exploiting role that the Nipponese forces set out to undertake in 1942. Indeed, a visit by a Japanese Prime Minister in 1974 provided a justification for public disorder in Jakarta. The economic relationship with Japan is endured because it serves the requirements of political elites committed to development policies which rest on Indonesian participation in the international capitalist economy. However, despite the measure of dependence which this might appear to entail, there has been no inclination to endorse America's encouragement of Japan to assume a military role in Asia. Japan is tolerated as a necessary economic partner but is not regarded with any enthusiasm as a prospective regional one. Australia is a less daunting neighbour but is also viewed with mixed feelings of amity and irritation.

Since 1966, Indonesia has maintained unchanging priorities in assessing the merits and demerits of external powers. If the United States and Japan have been regarded with a mixture of forebearance and reserve, the Soviet Union has been contemplated with suspicion because it is a communist superpower which has displayed a growing capability to project military means within Indonesia's maritime bounds. Asylum for exiled members of the PKI and inept attempts at espionage have served to reinforce such suspicion. Moreover, to the extent that a country like India appears to enjoy a special relationship with the Soviet Union, that suspicion has been carried over in relations with New Delhi and pointed up by differences over Kampuchea. Rivalry over competing claims for influence in the Indian Ocean has been mitigated, to the extent that the government in New Delhi has demonstrated a genuine willingness to assume the role of maritime watchdog. In addition, Indonesia shares with India a profound apprehension of China.

It is well appreciated in Jakarta that China does not possess the requisite military capability to pose a threat to Indonesia. The People's Republic is not contemplated in terms of conventional threat but in respect of a presumed access to Indonesia's resident Chinese community. Concern over the political reliability of a Chinese minority of approximately three and a half million has its roots both in colonial experience and in the period of national revolution. It has been sustained because of the influential role which that minority has continued to play in the management of the economy. For its part, the Chinese government has served to vindicate Indonesian suspicions by providing asylum for exiled members of the PKI and by a persistent refusal to

179

renounce party-to-party relations while dealing on a governmental basis with non-communist administrations in South-East Asia. The administration in Indonesia which charged China with complicity in the abortive coup of October 1965 has been ambivalent about resuming diplomatic relations suspended since October 1967. For example, in March 1978, shortly before his re-election by the People's Consultative Assembly for a further five-year term, President Suharto indicated his government's intention to prepare the way for restoring diplomatic relations with China. This announcement drew critical response from the Muslim United Development Party and the initiative was stopped. The following year China's military act of punishment against Vietnam and the continuing exodus of ethnic Chinese refugees from that country served to delay further any serious consideration of the matter. There is no doubt that Indonesia's relationship with China is as much a matter of domestic politics as of foreign policy. However, given the long-term sense of threat associated with China and the perceived absence of tangible advantage likely to accrue from the presence of a Chinese embassy in Jakarta, the issue of restoring diplomatic relations has been recurrently deferred.

Within South-East Asia, Indonesia has sought, without conspicuous success, to prevent its regional environment from becoming an arena of conflict for outside powers. Such an ideal has remained well beyond its grasp. Its limitations were pointed up during the course of the first two Indochina wars in which first France and then the United States sought to determine post-colonial political succession. The outcome of the second of those conflicts has had a profound influence on the balance of external influences bearing on South-East Asia. At its conclusion, Indonesia and its regional partners were not in a position to seize the opportunity to translate an ideal design for a Zone of Peace, Freedom and Neutrality into an orderly structure of regional relations. Initially, the legacy of that conflict in the form of Vietnamese suspicions of ASEAN was interposed between Indonesia and its regional partners on the one hand, and the revolutionary successor governments in Indochina on the other. And then a revival of pre-colonial antagonisms combined with ideological incompatibility in a manner which served to aggravate already deteriorating Sino-Vietnamese relations perceived in Peking and Moscow as an adjunct of Sino-Soviet relations. One dramatic outcome was Vietnam's invasion of Kampuchea, involving the violation of a principle which Indonesia had sought to make the basis of a system of regional order. Moreover, an attendant competitive engagement of external power interests appeared to return the region virtually full circle to the very condition which the Indonesian government had laboured diplomatically to prevent.

Despite this major setback, Indonesia has retained its regional vision based on an exclusive pattern of relations among resident states. But it is still some distance from assuming the position of a regional power centre able to shape that pattern. Within the Republic, it is regarded as the logical candidate for such a role and current development strategy is related to that end. The gap between aspiration and achievement remains, none the less, and has been sustained because, in certain important respects, quantitative assets such as population and territorial scale remain liabilities – thus ensuring that continuity prevails over change. Indeed, the Achilles heel lies in the economy, which has yet to overcome the burden of a population whose constant growth cancels out achievement. President Suharto's comment in 1969 cited earlier that 'We shall only be able to play an effective role if we ourselves are possessed of a great national vitality' is likely to remain valid for the rest of the twentieth century.

Notes

Chapter 1

1 The most comprehensive account of Indonesia's struggle for independence remains George McT. Kahin, *Nationalism and Revolution in Indonesia*, (Ithaca: Cornell University Press, 1952). A work which supplements Kahin within a more limited period is Benedict R. O'G. Anderson, *Java in a Time of Revolution*, (Ithaca: Cornell University Press, 1972). A shorter general appraisal is Anthony J. S. Reid, *The Indonesian National Revolution*, (Camberwell, Australia: Longman, 1974). Indonesian documents and commentary relating to the period may be found in Osman Raliby, *Documenta Historica: Sedjarah documenter dari pertumbuhan dan perdjuangan negara Republik Indonesia*, (Djarkarta: Bulan Bintang, 1953).

2 Harry J. Benda *et al.*, *Japanese Military Administration in Indonesia: Selected Documents*, (New Haven: Yale University, Southeast Asia Studies, 1965), p. 259.

3 A record of these deliberations is reproduced in Mohammad Yamin, *Naskah-Persiapan Undang-Undang Dasar 1945*, (Djarkarta: Jajasan Prapantja, 1959), Vol. 1. see also Angus McIntyre, 'The Greater Indonesia Idea of Nationalism in Malaya and Indonesia', *Modern Asian Studies*, January 1973.

4 For Indonesian thinking on this issue, see Benedict R. O'G. Anderson, *Some Aspects of Indonesian Politics Under the Japanese Occupation 1944–1945*, (Ithaca: Cornell University, Modern Indonesia Project, 1961), pp. 98–104.

5 See Anderson, *Java in a Time of Revolution* for an exegesis of *pemuda* outlook.

6 ibid. pp. 78–80; H. J. de Graaf, 'The Indonesian Declaration of Independence' in *Bijdragen tot de taal-, land- en volkenkunde*, 1959 and Louis Allen, *The End of the War in Asia*, (London: Hart-Davis MacGibbon, 1976), Chapter 3.

7 A photograph of the original Indonesian text is reproduced in Adam Malik, *In the Service of the Republic*, (Singapore: Gunung Agung, 1980), p. 123.

8 Quoted in Anderson, *Java in a Time of Revolution*, p. 113. In his memoirs, President Sukarno recalls an impromptu speech to *Pemuda* in 1945. He told them 'As you know, the slogan of the Republic's Government is "All is running well". It is the one item with which we can impress the allies so that they'll see we are capable of self rule.' *Sukarno: An Autobiography. As Told to Cindy Adams*, (Hong Kong: Gunung Agung, 1966), p. 233. See also remarks by Hatta quoted in Abu Hanifah, *Tales of a Revolution*, (Sydney: Angus and Robertson, 1972), p. 152.

9 Vice-Admiral the Earl Mountbatten of Burma, *Post Surrender Tasks*, Section E of the Report to the Combined Chiefs of Staff by the Supreme Allied Commander South-East Asia 1943–1945 (London: HMSO, 1969), p. 282.

10 Text in Foreign Office, *Far Eastern* (General) *1945*, (FO 371-46395. F8659/6398/G1). See also H. Achmad Soebardjo Djojoadisuryo, 'The Beginnings of Statehood', *The New Standard*, Jakarta, 5 July 1972 and also *Christian Science Monitor*, 29 September 1945. The Dutch regarded this approach as conferring 'a kind of international recognition which inexorably prejudiced the future'. See the retrospective comment in H. J. Van Mook, *The Stakes of Democracy in South-East Asia*, (London: Allen & Unwin, 1950), pp. 187–8.

11 *The Times*, 4 October 1945 reported such expectations as expressed in the nationalist newsheet, *Indonesian News Bulletin*.

12 See Mountbatten, *Post Surrender Tasks*, p. 290 and also F. S. V. Donnison, *British Military Administration in the Far East 1943–1946*, (London: HMSO 1956), p. 422.

13 Foreign Office, *Far Eastern*, FO371–46394. F8632/6398/61.

14 ibid. FO371-46397. F9462/6398/61.

15 Note the statement by Information Minister, Amir Sjarifuddin, *Daily Telegraph*, 26 October 1945.

16 For accounts of the battle of Surabaya, see David Wehl, *The Birth of Indonesia*, (London: Allen & Unwin, 1948), Chapter 6; Mountbatten, *Post Surrender Tasks*, pp. 292–3; and J. H. B., 'Sailor in Sourabaya', *Blackwood's Magazine*, August 1946. For an Indonesian version, see H. Roeslan Abdulgani, *Heroes Day and the Indonesian Revolution*, (Jakarta, 1964). For a report on the circumstances of the death of Brigadier Mallaby by General Christison see Foreign Office *Far Eastern*, FO371–46397. F9352/6398/61.

17 See Ali Sastroamijoyo, *Milestones on my Journey* (ed. C. L. M. Penders) (St. Lucia: University of Queensland Press, 1979), pp. 112–13.

18 His intellectual testament is to be found in Sutan Sjahrir, *Out of Exile*, (New York: John Day, 1949).

19 Sutan Sjahrir, *Our Struggle* (translated with an introduction by Benedict R. O'G. Anderson) (Ithaca: Cornell University, Modern Indonesia Project, 1968), p. 24.

20 ibid. p. 31.

21 For the text of this speech, see Harold R. Isaacs (ed.), *New Cycle in Asia*, (New York: Macmillan, 1947), pp. 178–81.

22 Raymond Kennedy, 'Dutch Plan for the Indies', *Far Eastern Survey*, 10 April 1946, p. 102.

23 For a representative expression of Tan Malaka's political outlook, see the extract from *Muslihat* (Strategy) in Herbert Feith and Lance Castles (eds.), *Indonesian Political Thinking 1945–1965*, (Ithaca: Cornell University Press, 1970), pp. 444–8. The nature of the divisions within the nationalist movement over negotiations with the Dutch are well identified in Paul Kattenburg, 'Political Alignments in Indonesia', *Far Eastern Survey*, 10 April 1946. See also Ali Sastroamijoyo, *Milestones*, p. 127.

24 Reid, *Indonesian National Revolution*, p. 91.

25 Anderson, *Java in a Time of Revolution*, p. 323 and Kattenburg, 'Political Alignments', p. 293.

26 The most complete account of those negotiations is to be found in Idrus Nasir Djajadiningrat, *The Beginning of the Indonesian-Dutch Negotiations and the Hoge Veluwe Talks*, (Ithaca: Cornell University, Modern Indonesia Project, 1958).

27 Van Mook, *Stakes of Democracy*, p. 220.

28 Dr Subandrio, 'De Facto Status at Linggadjati', *Far Eastern Survey*, 11 February 1948, p. 31.

29 This correspondence is reproduced in Wehl, *Birth of Indonesia*, Appendix A, pp. 180-90.

30 Sukarno, *Autobiography*, p. 240. See also his statement on the Republican goal of a unitary state in January 1947 quoted in Wehl, *Birth of Indonesia*, p. 157.

31 Charles Wolf Jr., *The Indonesian Story: The Birth, Growth and Structure of the Indonesian Republic*, (New York: John Day, 1948), p. 45.

32 Reproduced in Wehl, *Birth of Indonesia*, p. 193.

33 Documents in English and Dutch dealing with Indonesia in the United Nations between January 1946 and December 1949 are reproduced in *Indonesie in de Veiligheidsraad van de Verenigde Naties* Ministerie van Buitlandse Zaken, Nos. 5 (October 1947); 8 (January 1948); 9 (June 1948); 14 (December 1948); 19 (September 1949) and 21 (March 1950). Staatsdrukker. J-En Uitgeverijbedrjf/ 'S-Gravenhage.

34   Kahin, *Nationalism and Revolution*, pp. 215–21.
35   A. M. Taylor, *Indonesian Independence and the United Nations*, (London: Stevens and Sons, 1960), pp. 88–9.
36   Cited in *Foreign Relations of the United States 1948. Volume VI, The Far East and Australasia*, (Washington: US Government Printing Office, 1974), p. 84.
37   Ali Sastroamijoyo, *Milestones*, pp. 146–7.
38   Taylor, *Indonesian Independence and UN*, p. 96.
39   Reid, *Indonesian National Revolution*, p. 101.
40   John Coast, *Recruit to Revolution: Adventure and Politics in Indonesia*, (London: Christophers, 1952), pp. 131–2; also Kahin, *Nationalism and Revolution*, pp. 256–7.
41   The full statement has been published as Mohammad Hatta, *Mendajung Antara Dua Karang* (Rowing Between Two Rocks) (Djarkarta: Department of Information, 1951). See also H. Roeslan Abdulgani, 'The Origins of the Concept "Free and Active" in Indonesian Foreign Policy', *The Indonesian Quarterly*, Jakarta, October 1975. Hatta subsequently reiterated his view in *Dasar Politik Luar Negeri Republik Indonesia*, (Djakarta: Tintamas, 1953).
42   *Foreign Relations of the United States 1948*, pp. 431–2.
43   Kahin, *Nationalism and Revolution*, pp. 417–18. Note also the comment by Abdul Haris Nasution, *Fundamentals of Guerrilla Warfare*, (London: Pall Mall Press, 1965), p. 15.
44   Leslie H. Palmier, *Indonesia and the Dutch*, (London: Oxford University Press, 1962), p. 72.
45   See Charles B. McLane, *Soviet Strategies in Southeast Asia*, (Princeton, N.J.: Princeton University Press, 1966), pp. 410–11, and also Ruth T. McVey, *The Soviet View of the Indonesian Revolution*, (Ithaca: Cornell University, Modern Indonesia Project, 1957).
46   For an account of the unitarian movement, see Kahin, *Nationalism and Revolution*, Chapter 14.
47   Quoted in Coast, *Recruit to Revolution*, p. 293.
48   For a perceptive analysis of this theme and attendant Indonesian attitudes, see Franklin B. Weinstein, *Indonesian Foreign Policy and the Dilemma of Dependence*, (Ithaca: Cornell University Press, 1976).

Chapter 2

1   A contemporary observer commented 'Indonesia's policy of steering a middle course in foreign affairs is a necessary condition of internal reconstruction. Foreign entanglements and definite commitments to major powers would, in the opinion of most Indonesian leaders at present, upset the precarious balance of internal political life and would hinder Indonesia's development as a free nation.' Justus M. Van Der Kroef, 'Indonesia and the West', *Far Eastern Survey*, 21 February 1951.
2   *Summary of Government Statement Delivered by the Prime Minister before Parliament on 21 September, 1950*, (Information Department, Embassy of Republic of Indonesia, London, 1950), p. 42.
3   See Lawrence S. Finkelstein, 'Indonesia's Record in the United Nations', *International Conciliation*, November 1951.
4   Mohammad Hatta, 'Indonesia's Foreign Policy', *Foreign Affairs*, April 1953. A concise survey of Indonesia's foreign policy in the first two years of independence is Justus M. Van Der Kroef, 'Indonesia: Independent in the Cold War', *International Journal*, Autumn 1952.
5   For an account of the dispute as it emerged at the Round Table Conference and

subsequently, see Robert C. Bone, *The Dynamics of the Western New Guinea (Irian Barat) Problem*, (Ithaca: Cornell University, Modern Indonesia Project, 1958).

6   Note the comment in Palmier, *Indonesia and the Dutch*, p. 115 that 'Indonesia's diminished inheritance distinguishes her from the other newly independent nations and makes Indonesians feel that they have been cheated and that their country's standing has been lowered in the world.'

7   ibid., p. 168.

8   See the view expressed by Deputy Under-Secretary of State, Dean Rusk, in *Foreign Relations of the United States 1950. Volume VI. East Asia and the Pacific*, (Washington: US Government Printing Office, 1976), p. 986.

9   See Ide Anak Agung Gde Agung, *Twenty Years Indonesian Foreign Policy 1945–1965*, (The Hague: Mouton, 1973), p. 92. For a consideration of the role of West Irian in domestic politics, see also Herbert Feith, *The Decline of Constitutional Democracy in Indonesia*, (Ithaca: Cornell University Press, 1962), pp. 158–9.

10 See David Mozingo, *Chinese Policy Towards Indonesia 1949–1967*, (Ithaca: Cornell University Press, 1976), pp. 94–101.

11 See the account by Ali Sastroamijoyo, *Milestones*, pp. 238–41 and also by Achmad Subarjo Djoyoadisurjo, *Jakarta Times*, 14 and 15 July 1972.

12 For Subarjo's rationale see *Jakarta Times*, 24 and 25 July 1972.

13 See Feith, *Decline of Constitutional Democracy*, pp. 198–207 for a detailed account of the episode.

14 *Hope and Facts*, (Information Service, Embassy of Indonesia, New Delhi 1952), p. 60.

15 ibid., p. 72.

16 See Bone, *Dynamics of Western New Guinea Problem*, p. 117.

17 McLane, *Soviet Strategies*, pp. 456–7.

18 For a vivid account of the 17 October 1952 affair and its political aftermath, see Feith, *Decline of Constitutional Democracy*, pp. 246–73.

19 For a full account of the fall of the Wilopo cabinet, see ibid. pp. 285–302.

20 Ali Sastroamijoyo has pointed out in his memoirs that 'The Republic of Indonesia did not want to be regarded as of no significance in the world. Our territories were extensive, our inhabitants numbered millions. We had natural resources in abundance and our country was situated very strategically in the Indian and Pacific Oceans.' *Milestones*, p. 255.

21 For an account of this issue and its attendant consequences, see Hans O. Schmitt, 'Foreign Capital and Social Conflict in Indonesia 1952–1958' in Robert I. Rhodes (ed.) *Imperialism and Underdevelopment*, (New York: Monthly Review Press, 1970).

22 Ali Sastroamijoyo, *Milestones*, p. 304. For an eye-witness account of the conference, see George McT. Kahin, *The Asian-African Conference, Bandung, Indonesia, April 1955*, (Ithaca: Cornell University Press, 1956).

23 This treaty and its political context are discussed in Stephen Fitzgerald, *China and the Overseas Chinese*, (Cambridge: Cambridge University Press, 1972); Mary F. Somers Heidhues, *Southeast Asia's Chinese Minorities*, (Hawthorn, Australia: Longman, 1974); and Mozingo, *Chinese Policy*.

24 Ali Sastroamijoyo, *Milestones*, p. 311.

25 Reproduced in Agung, *Twenty Years*, pp. 554–9.

26 Burhanuddin's Foreign Minister has pointed out 'Without a doubt the domestic political conditions in Indonesia had propelled the West Irian problem into a national issue of the first magnitude: no cabinet could afford to fail in finding a solution. President Sukarno had used the issue to rally all radical nationalist elements to his side and enlarge his power base.' ibid., p. 111.

27   See Feith, *Decline of Constitutional Democracy*, p. 456. For a detailed account of the negotiations in Geneva and their aftermath, see Agung, *Twenty Years*, Chapter 4.

28   Ali Sastroamijoyo, *Milestones*, p. 327.

29   See Palmier, *Indonesia and the Dutch*, pp. 85–93. Indonesian allegations are contained in *Subversive Activities in Indonesia: The Jungschlager and Schmidt Affair*, (Djakarta: Ministry of Foreign Affairs, n.d.).

30   For a first hand account of this episode, see Ganis Harsono, *Recollections of an Indonesian Diplomat in the Sukarno Era* (eds. C. L. M. Penders and B. B. Hering) (St. Lucia: University of Queensland Press, 1979), pp. 148–52.

31   Palmier, *Indonesia and the Dutch*, p. 108.

32   Reprinted in Dr Subandrio, *Indonesia on the March, Vol. II*, (Djakarta: Department of Foreign Affairs, 1963), p. 49.

33   For a broader discussion of the archipelago declaration, see Michael Leifer, *Malacca, Singapore and Indonesia (Vol. II. International Straits of the World)*, (Alphen aan den Rijn, Netherlands: Sijthoff & Noordhoff, 1978).

34   United Nations Conference on the Law of the Sea, *Official Records* Vol. III, First Committee, A/Conf. 13/39, p. 44.

35   For accounts of the rebellion and external involvement see James Mossman, *Rebels in Paradise*, (London: Jonathan Cape, 1961); William Stevenson, *Birds Nests in Their Beards*, (London: Hutchinson, 1965); Barbara Harvey, *Permesta – Half a Revolution*, (Ithaca: Cornell University, Modern Indonesia Project, 1977); and Herbert Feith and Daniel S. Lev, 'The End of the Indonesian Revolution', *Pacific Affairs*, Spring 1963.

36   See John M. Allison, *Ambassador from the Prairie*, (Tokyo: Charles E. Tuttle Co.. 1975), pp. 342–3.

37   *New York Times*, 12 February 1958.

38   Howard Palfrey Jones, *Indonesia: The Possible Dream*, (New York: Harcourt Brace, 1971), pp. 133.

39   Sukarno had publicly condemned the participation of pilots from Taiwan and the United States in bombing East Indonesia at the beginning of May 1958 in a lecture to students at Pajajaran University in Bandung.

40   For a discussion of Indonesian-Japanese relations, see Masashi Nishihara, *The Japanese and Sukarno's Indonesia, Tokyo–Jakarta Relations 1951–1966*, (Honolulu: University Press of Hawaii, 1976).

41   *Asian African Conference Bulletin*, (Djakarta, Ministry of Foreign Affairs, No. 3, 18 April 1955), p. 4.

Chapter 3

1   For an extensive discussion of the nature of Guided Democracy, see Herbert Feith, 'Dynamics of Guided Democracy' in Ruth T. McVey (ed.) *Indonesia*, (New Haven: Yale University, Southeast Asia Studies, 1963), Chapter 8. See also his 'Indonesia's Political Symbols and Their Wielders', *World Politics*, October 1963.

2   J. M. Pluvier, *Confrontations*, (Kuala Lumpur: Oxford University Press, 1965) argues persuasively that the government of Sukarno was occupied primarily with defending the political and economic power of Indonesia's ruling elite against any attempt at social change.

3   Feith, 'Dynamics of Guided Democracy', p. 341. The dynamics of the relationship between Sukarno and the PKI are examined in Donald Hindley, 'President Sukarno and the Communists: The Politics of Domestication', *American Political Science Review*, December 1962 and also in *The Communist Party of Indonesia*

1951–63, (Berkeley: University of California Press, 1964).

4　Daniel S. Lev, *The Transition to Guided Democracy: Indonesian Politics 1957–59*, (Ithaca: Cornell University, Modern Indonesia Project, 1966), p. 286.

5　Sukarno, *Autobiography*, p. 293.

6　Note the derisory comments in *Khrushchev Remembers: The Last Testament*, (London: Andre Deutsch, 1974), p. 314.

7　See J. D. Legge, *Sukarno: A Political Biography*, (Harmondsworth: Penguin Books, 1973), pp. 112–14.

8　Sukarno, *Autobiography*, p. 296. For a discussion of motivation in Sukarno's conduct of foreign policy see Frederick P. Bunnell 'Guided Democracy Foreign Policy: 1960–1965, President Sukarno Moves from Non-Alignment to Confrontation', *Indonesia*, October 1960.

9　Allison, *Ambassador from the Prairie*, p. 312.

10　Legge, *Sukarno*, p. 343.

11　Cited in George Modelski (ed.) *The New Emerging Forces. Documents on the Ideology of Indonesian Foreign Policy*, (Canberra: Australian National University, 1963), p. 10.

12　Djakarta: Department of Information, 1961, p. 7.

13　Modelski, *New Emerging Forces*, pp. 123–4. Note also the interpretation that 'The NEFO are the peoples and movements emerging from subjugation who seek to create a new world order of social and economic justice free from the fetters of alien domination and cultural suppression.' Donald Weatherbee, *Ideology in Indonesia: Sukarno's Indonesian Revolution*, (New Haven: Yale University, Southeast Asia Studies, 1966), p. 2.

14　See the argument expounded in George Modelski, *Indonesia and Her Neighbours*, (Princeton, N.J.: Princeton University, Center of International Studies, 1964).

15　Subandrio, *Indonesia on the March*, p. 269.

16　See Arend Lijphart, 'the Indonesian Image of West Irian', *Asian Survey*, July 1961.

17　The most comprehensive account of the West Irian issue is William Henderson, *West New Guinea: The Dispute and its Settlement*, (Seton Hall University Press, 1973).

18　Pluvier, *Confrontations*, p. 46.

19　Australia's attitude to the West Irian issue is well discussed in J. A. C. Mackie, 'Australia and Indonesia 1945–60' in Gordon Greenwood and Norman Harper (eds.) *Australia in World Affairs 1956–60*, (Melbourne: F. W. Cheshire, 1963).

20　See Harsono, *Recollections*.

21　The development of military links between the Soviet Union and Indonesia between 1956–9 is recounted in Uri Ra'anan, *The USSR Arms The Third World*, (Cambridge, Mass; MIT Press, 1969), Chapters 8 and 9.

22　Usha Mahajani, *Soviet and American Aid to Indonesia 1949–68*, (Athens, Ohio: Ohio University, Center for International Studies, 1970), p. 16.

23　Allison, *Ambassador from the Prairie*, p. 304.

24　Jones, *Indonesia: The Impossible Dream*, p. 191. Sukarno's strategy was even echoed by Hatta who maintained 'to permit West Irian to continue indefinitely as a bone of contention between Indonesia and the Netherlands is to afford Communism an opportunity to spread in Indonesia', in 'Indonesia Between the Power Blocs', *Foreign Affairs*, April 1958.

25　Feith, 'Dynamics of Guided Democracy', p. 351.

26　Ulf Sundhaussen, *The Road to Power: Indonesian Military Politics 1945–1965*, (Kuala Lumpur: Oxford University Press, 1982), p. 155.

27　Subandrio, *Indonesia on the March*, p. 261.

28　Note the assessment of President Kennedy's thinking on the matter in Arthur M. Schlesinger, *A Thousand Days*, (Boston: Houghton Mifflin, 1965), p. 533.

29　Jones, *Indonesia: The Possible Dream*, p. 203.

30 The text of Sukarno's letter is reproduced in Harsono, *Recollections*, p. 237.
31 Malik, *In the Service of the Republic*, p. 242.
32 ibid., p. 241.
33 Note Krushchev's sour comment on Sukarno playing-off 'one power against the other'. *Krushchev Remembers*, p. 327.
34 Roger Hilsman, *To Move a Nation*, (New York: Dell Publishing Co., 1967), p. 382.
35 Mozingo, *Chinese Policy*, p. 162.
36 Recounted by George McT. Kahin in 'Malaysia and Indonesia', *Pacific Affairs*, Fall 1964. See also Willard Hanna, *Bung Karno's Indonesia*, (New York: American Universities Field Staff, Inc., 1961) Part XXII: *The Chinese Take a Second Look*.
37 Agung, *Twenty Years*, pp. 515–6.
38 Jones, *Indonesia: The Possible Dream*, p. 81.
39 Mohammad Hatta, 'One Indonesian View of the Malaysia Issue', *Asian Survey*, March 1965.
40 Jones, *Indonesia: The Possible Dream*, pp. 213–4.
41 Modelski, *The New Emerging Forces*, p. 129.

Chapter 4

1 The most complete and authoritative account of Indonesia's confrontation against Malaysia is J. A. C. Mackie, *Konfrontasi: The Indonesia–Malaysia Dispute 1963–1966*, (Kuala Lumpur: Oxford University Press, 1974).
2 *Jakarta Radio*, 19 December 1962, in a speech commemorating the first anniversary of the Triple Command.
3 In an article on Indonesia's foreign policy published in *Le Monde Diplomatique*, May 1964.
4 Franklin B. Weinstein, *Indonesia Abandons Confrontation*, (Ithaca: Cornell University, Modern Indonesia Project, 1969), pp. 3–4.
5 Dr Subandrio had remarked 'It is a matter for the countries concerned to decide for themselves.' *The Straits Times*, 14 June 1961.
6 For an account of this episode, see Anthony Reid, *The Blood of the People*, (Kuala Lumpur: Oxford University Press, 1979).
7 *The Straits Times*, 12 February 1962.
8 *New York Times*, 17 November 1961.
9 See the discussion in Herbert Feith, 'President Sukarno, the Army and the Communists: the Triangle Changes Shape', *Asian Survey*, August 1964 and also Rex Mortimer, *Indonesian Communism under Sukarno*, (Ithaca: Cornell University Press, 1974).
10 Mackie, *Konfrontasi*, pp. 120–1.
11 For an account of the Brunei revolt as well as the military dimension of confrontation, see Harold James and Denis Sheil-Small, *The Undeclared War*, (Singapore: Asia Pacific Press, 1971); and also General Sir Walter Walker, 'How Borneo Was Won', *The Round Table*, January 1969.
12 Modelski, *New Emerging Forces*, pp. 74–5. Note also the theme of encirclement in Subandrio, *Indonesia on the March*, pp. 98–9.
13 See the discussion in Donald Hindley, 'Indonesia's Confrontation with Malaysia: A Search for Motives', *Asian Survey*, June 1954; and also Legge, *Sukarno*, Chapter 14.
14 Note the elucidation of Indonesian attitudes in Kahin, 'Malaysia and Indonesia', p. 261.
15 Indonesia's expansionist motive is discussed by Bernard K. Gordon, 'The Potential

for Indonesian Expansionism', *Pacific Affairs*, Winter 1963/64 and also in *The Dimensions of Conflict in South-East Asia*, (Englewood Cliffs, N.J.: Prentice-Hall, 1966).

16 Reproduced in *The Problem of 'Malaysia'*, Embassy of the Republic of Indonesia, London, 1964, p. 2.

17 See Lela Garner Noble, *Philippine Policy Towards Sabah*, (Tucson: University of Arizona Press, 1977); and Michael Leifer, *The Philippine Claim to Sabah*, (Zug, Switzerland: Interdocumentation Co., 1968).

18 According to Hilsman, *To Move a Nation*, p. 104, Washington's motives were 'designed to support those elements who opposed the growing strength of the Communists and who would have to fight the communists if they attempted to take over control in a coup d'etat and it came to an armed struggle'.

19 *Let Us Transform the World!* Opening address by President Sukarno at the Asian–African Journalists' Conference on 24 April 1963. (Djakarta: Department of Information, 1963), p. 9.

20 Manila Accord reproduced in *The Malaysia Issue: Background and Documents* (Djakarta: Department of Foreign Affairs, 1964), p. 31.

21 ibid., p. 35.

22 Modelski, *New Emerging Forces*, pp. 126–7.

23 *United Nations, Malaysia Mission Report*, (Kuala Lumpur: Department of Information, 1963), p. ii.

24 Sukarno, *Autobiography*, p. 301. Note also Jones, *Indonesia: The Possible Dream*, p. 289. Indonesia's Ambassador in London commented on 'This insolent announcement marking the petulant impertinence of neo-colonialist conspiracy', M. Burhanuddin Diah, 'Asian Solutions for Asian Problems', *The Diplomatist*, May 1964.

25 Modelski, *New Emerging Forces*, p. 80.

26 *The Problem of 'Malaysia'*, p. 12.

27 Hilsman, *To Move a Nation*, pp. 407–9.

28 *Tripartite Ministerial Conference*, Bangkok, 5-10 February 1964. Verbatim record of First Meeting of Political Committee held at Thai Ministry of Foreign Affairs, 7 February 1964.

29 See K. J. Ratnam and R. S. Milne, *The Malayan Parliamentary Election of 1964*, (Singapore: University of Malaya Press, 1967).

30 *Record of the Meeting of Heads of Government held on 20 June 1964* at 9.30 a.m. at the official residence of the Japanese Prime Minister, Tokyo.

31 Guy Pauker, 'Indonesia in 1964: Towards A "People's " Democracy?', *Asian Survey*, February 1965.

32 Jones, *Indonesia: The Possible Dream*, p. 344.

33 Michael Leifer, 'Communal Violence in Singapore', *Asian Survey*, October 1964.

34 Sundhaussen, *The Road to Power*, pp. 187–8.

35 See *Malaysia's Case in the Security Council*. Documents reproduced from the official records of the Security Council proceedings, (Kuala Lumpur: Ministry of Foreign Affairs, 1964), p. 15.

36 See Harsono, *Recollections*, p. 270.

37 See Mozingo, *Chinese Policy*, pp. 211–12 and also J. D. Armstrong, *Revolutionary Diplomacy*, (Berkeley: University of California Press, 1977), p. 131. For an indication of underlying Sino-Indonesian differences, see Harsono, *Recollections*, pp. 293–94.

38 Sundhaussen, *The Road to Power*, p. 181.

39 ibid., p. 189.

40 See *The Sunday Times*, London, 12 September 1965.

41 *Reach to the Stars, A Year of Self-Reliance*, (Djakarta: Department of Information, 1965), p. 16.

42 Diverse accounts of the abortive coup may be found in Nugroho Notosusanto and Ismail Saleh, *The Coup Attempt of the 'September 30 Movement'*, (Djarkarta: P. T. Pembimbing Masa, 1968); Benedict R. Anderson and Ruth T. McVey, *A Preliminary Analysis of the October 1, 1965, Coup in Indonesia*, (Ithaca: Cornell University, Modern Indonesia Project, 1971); Mortimer, *Indonesian Communism*, pp. 413–41; Harold Crouch, *The Army and Politics in Indonesia*, (Ithaca: Cornell University Press, 1978), Chapter 4; Brian May, *The Indonesian Tragedy*, (London: Routledge & Kegan Paul, 1978), Chapter 3; Legge, *Sukarno*, Chapter 15; Leslie Palmier, *Communists in Indonesia*, (London: Weidenfeld & Nicolson, 1973), Chapters 18 and 19 and Sundhaussen, *The Road to Power*, pp.194–206.

43 Weinstein points out 'Thus in the months just after the attempted coup, confrontation served as a justificaiton for the moves against the PKI, as a basis for demonstrating loyalty to Indonesia's revolution and as a much needed shelter offering security at a time of great uncertainty.' *Indonesia Abandons Confrontation*, p. 32.

44 ibid., p. 29.

45 ibid., pp. 83–6 and also Crouch, *The Army and Politics*, p. 332.

46 This thesis is advanced in Jon M. Reinhardt, *Foreign Policy and National Integration: The Case of Indonesia*, (New Haven: Yale University, Southeast Asia Studies, 1971), pp. 126–8.

47 Sudjatmoko, 'Indonesia and the World', *Australian Outlook*, December 1967.

Chapter 5

1 See Peter Polomka, 'Indonesia and the Stability of South-East Asia', *Survival*, May/June 1973, pp. 111–13 and also Weinstein, *Indonesian Foreign Policy*.

2 Speech delivered on 16 August 1969 reprinted in *The Indonesian Review of International Affairs*, July 1970.

3 'National resilience is the ability of a nation to cope with, endure and survive any kind of challenges or threats she meets in the course of her struggle to achieve her national goals.' In *The Function and Role of the Indonesian Armed Forces in the Period of Consolidation and Integration (1969–1973)* (Djakarta: Department of Defence and Security, 1970), p. 3.

4 For an account of Indonesia's economic circumstances and policies in 1966, see *Government's Statement on Economic and Financial Policies*, (Djarkarta: Department of Information, 1966) and also Ingrid Palmer, *The Indonesian Economy since 1965*, (London; Frank Cass, 1978).

5 Nishihara, *Japanese and Sukarno's Indonesia*, pp. 200–2.

6 Statement on Foreign Policy by the Minister of Foreign Affairs Adam Malik on 4 April 1966 in *Indonesia's Foreign Policy as Based on the Pantja Sila Principles*, Djakarta: Department of Information, 1966), pp. 3–5.

7 Government Statement Before the House of Representatives, 5 May 1966. ibid. p. 8.

8 ibid. p. 23. Note also Adam Malik, 'Promise in Indonesia', *Foreign Affairs*, January 1968.

9 For a summary of steps taken to this end, see Mahajani, *Soviet and American Aid*, pp. 31–8.

10 For a discussion of the priorities in that plan, see Martin Rudner, 'The Indonesian Military and Economic Policy', *Modern Asian Studies*, April 1976.

11 Government Report to the People by the Chairman of the Ampera Cabinet Presidium, 31 December 1966 in *Government Report to the People*, (Djakarta: Department of Information, 1967), p. 18.

12 See Bernard K. Gordon, *Towards Disengagement in Asia*, (Englewood Cliffs, N.J.: Prentice-Hall, 1969), p. 111. Note also the comment in *The Times*, 3 June 1966 that 'It has been clear that regional cooperation was the vital background to the talks on ending confrontation'.

13 *Government Statement Before the Gotong-Royong House of Representatives on 16 August, 1966*, (Djakarta: Department of Information, 1966), p. 48.

14 Gordon, *Towards Disengagement*, pp. 114–9.

15 'The ASEAN Declaration' reprinted in *10 Years ASEAN*, (Jakarta: ASEAN Secretariat, 1978), pp. 14–16.

16 Reprinted in *The Association of South-East Asian Nations* (ASEAN), (Djakarta: Department of Information, 1969), p. 5.

17 *The Fifth Plenary Session of the Madjelis Permusjawaratan Rakjat Sementara*, (Djakarta: Department of Information, 1968), p. 42.

18 John M. Allison, 'Indonesia: Year of the Pragmatists', *Asian Survey*, February 1969.

19 See Kathryn E. Young, *The Guam Doctrine: Elements of Implementation. Key State Relations: Australia and Indonesia*, Mclean, Virginia: Research Analysis Corporation, 1970).

20 See Nadia Derkach, 'The Soviet Policy Towards Indonesia in the West Irian and Malaysian Disputes', *Asian Survey*, November 1965.

21 Robert C. Horn, 'Soviet-Indonesian Relations Since 1965', *Survey*, Winter 1971.

22 *Indonesian Review of International Affairs*, July 1970.

23 Mozingo, *Chinese Policy*, pp. 249–63.

24 Crouch, *Army and Politics*, p. 333.

25 Foreign Minister Mochtar Kusumaatmadja has commented concerning Muslim opposition to any restoration of diplomatic relations with China: 'In fact, there are two important sections in Indonesian political life – the Muslims and the armed forces. We cannot ignore that.' *Impact International*, London, 22 May – 11 June, 1981, p. 9.

26 See Justus M. Van Der Kroef, 'West New Guinea: The Uncertain Future', *Asian Survey*, August 1968.

27 For a first-hand account of 'The United Nations Fiasco', see May, *Indonesian Tragedy*, Chapter 4. See also Henderson, *West New Guinea*, Chapter 14.

28 See O. G. Roeder, *The Smiling General*, (Djakarta: Gunung Agung, 1969), pp. 177–8.

29 Crouch, *Army and Politics*, p. 332.

30 Aide-Memoire, 28 April 1970, reprinted in *Conference of Foreign Ministers Djakarta 16/17 May 1970*, (Djakarta: Department of Foreign Affairs, 1970), p. 10.

31 ibid., p. 18.

32 For a discussion of the limited achievement of the Jakarta Conference, see Lau Teik Soon, *Indonesia and Regional Security: The Djakarta Conference on Cambodia*, (Singapore: Institute of South-East Asian Studies, 1972).

33 *Statement by General Suharto, President of the Republic of Indonesia to the Summit Meeting of the Third Conference of the Non-Aligned States, Lusaka. September 8/10, 1970*, (Djakarta: Department of Information, 1970).

34 'Foreign Policy and the Development of Indonesia', *Sinar Harapan*, 22/24 June 1971.

35 Peter Polomka, *Indonesia Since Sukarno*, (Harmondsworth: Penguin Books, 1971) p. 187.

36 *Indonesia Raya*, 18 August 1971.

Chapter 6

1 Adam Malik, 'Indonesia's Foreign Policy', *The Indonesian Quarterly*, October 1972.

2 *The Function and Role of the Indonesian Armed Forces in the Period of Consolidation and Integration (1969–1973)*, p. 4.

3 For a discussion of the issue of the Straits of Malacca and Singapore see Leifer, *Malacca, Singapore and Indonesia*.

4 For the background to and discussion of Malaysia's proposal, see Dick Wilson, *The Neutralisation of Southeast Asia*, (New York: Praeger, 1975).

5 Reprinted in *Far Eastern Economic Review*, 25 September 1971.

6 Reproduced in *10 Years ASEAN*, pp. 240–1.

7 *Address by H. E. President Suharto to the Joint Session of the Philippine Congress*, 14 February 1972, (Jakarta: Department of Information, Republic of Indonesia, 1972).

8 See the proposal for an Asia-Pacific Triangle in Ali Moertopo, *Indonesia in Regional and International Co-operation: Principles of Implementation and Construction*, (Jakarta: Centre for Strategic and International Studies, 1973).

9 Malik, *In the Service of the Republic*.

10 Indonesia's security perceptions are well summarised in Peter Polomka, *Indonesia's Future and South-East Asia*, (London: International Institute for Strategic Studies, Adelphi Papers No. 104, 1974).

11 For accounts of the East Timor episode, see Hamish McDonald, *Suharto's Indonesia*, (Blackburn, Victoria: Fontana/Collins, 1980), Chapter 9 and Jill Jolliffe, *East Timor: Nationalism and Colonialism*, (Brisbane: University of Queensland Press, 1978).

12 BBC *Summary of World Broadcasts*, FE/5078/B11–12.

13 *The Times*, 8 December 1975.

14 *Address of State by His Excellency the President of the Republic of Indonesia General Soeharto. Before the House of People's Representatives on the occasion of the 31st Independence Day August 17th*, (Jakarta: Department of Information 1976), p. 48.

15 ASEAN National Secretariat of Indonesia, 'Indonesian Foreign Policy and ASEAN Regional Co-operation', *Indonesia Magazine* No. 27, Jakarta, September 1974, p. 17.

16 *10 Years ASEAN*, p. 88.

17 ibid., p. 111.

18 ibid., p. 120.

19 BBC *SWB* FE/5298/A2/3.

20 Text of joint statement on 23 September 1978 by President Suharto and Premier Pham Van Dong in BBC *SWB* FE/5925/A3/2-3.

21 See his interview in *Far Eastern Economic Review*, 15 December 1978.

22 See the interview with President Suharto in *The Asian Wall Street Journal*, 21 February 1979.

23 *Government Statement on the Draft State Budget for 1982/3 to the House of People's Representatives*. Delivered by the President of the Republic of Indonesia on 5 January 1982, (Jakarta: Department of Information, 1982).

24 Jakarta Home Service. BBC *SWB* FE/6969/A3/6. See also Juwono Sudarsono, 'Security in Southeast Asia: The Circle of Conflict' in Robert A. Scalapino and Jusuf Wanandi (eds.) *Economic, Political and Security Issues in Southeast Asia in the 1980s*, (Berkeley: University of California, Institute of East Asian Studies, 1982).

25   *The Military Balance 1982–1983*, (London: International Institute for Strategic Studies, 1982), pp. 86–7.
26   Note the interview given by Foreign Minister Mochtar Kusumaatmadja in *Tempo*, 29 March 1980.

Index